CHRIS MCQUILLAN was born in Oldham where he trained as an electrical engineer, and later went on to work in project management several social housing provid

Chris has also worked i charitable sector, fundraising on bei of several non-profit organisations and charities.

At the age of forty-two he decided that the time for his mid-life adventure/crisis was ripe, and so grabbed a tent, rucksack, and his trusted companion Moose, to begin a coastal walk all the way around mainland Britain.

When not walking, Chris resides in Wiltshire.

MOOSE is a four-year-old Mastador (mastiff/Labrador cross) who Chris met at Bath Cats and Dogs Home in 2017.

Very little is known about his past prior to meeting Chris, only that he came from a loving family whose changing circumstances meant that they had to give him up.

Moose is energetic, friendly to most folk, and obsessed with playing ball! He has bags of personality and likes to groan a lot – hence the name Moose!

When not walking, Moose usually resides on the lion's share of Chris's bed.

Part 1
Crisis on the
Coast Path

CHRIS & MOOSE'S
WAGGY WALK

Chris McQuillan

SilverWood

Published in 2021 by SilverWood Books

SilverWood Books Ltd
14 Small Street, Bristol, BS1 1DE, United Kingdom
www.silverwoodbooks.co.uk

ISBN 978-1-80042-057-1 (paperback)
ISBN 978-1-80042-058-8 (ebook)

British Library Cataloguing in Publication Data
A CIP catalogue record for this book is
available from the British Library

Pages designed and typeset according to the author's creative direction

CHRIS & MOOSE'S WAGGY WALK

To Mum. Thank you for everything!

To my friends – Greg, Anya, John and Sue…thanks for all your patience.

To Rosy, Ruth, Hannah and Liam – my army of proofreaders.
Your unabashed honesty and heart-felt criticism are woven throughout this
tome. Without you all, none of what follows would be digestible.
By way of thanks, and at the very least, I owe you all cake.

Karina – Thanks for that final kick up the arse to get this written!

I'd like to believe that I was well prepared for what my future would bring…

Boy, was I in for a shock!

This story is dedicated to all we met on our journey, especially those
who contributed to it, either by intent, sympathy, donations, or
down-right human decency.

Moose and I can never thank you enough.

This story is also dedicated to anyone who feels the compulsion to do
something but can't quite get themselves around to making that first step.

My advice: start by making just one, and then keep it up…
You'll get there eventually!

And finally!

To all those former managers and peers back in the office.

If you ever saw fit to correct grammar, rewrite my reports without asking
permission, or claim credit for my work through some
misplaced sense of ego or position…

It would seem that 'irrelevant content' may be a precursor to creative literacy.

Who knew?

Look at me go!

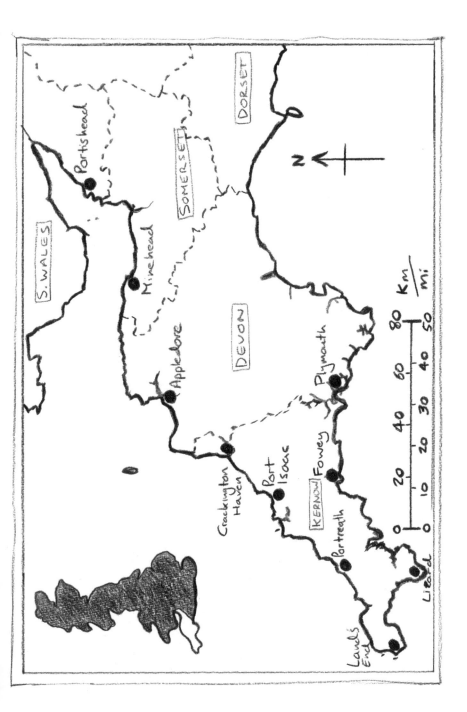

Preface

It's difficult for me to pin down where it all started.

I'm sure there must've been a tipping point somewhere along the way...a place where thoughts and ideas coalesced into a coherent plan. If I'm honest though, this adventure was probably years in the making, even before I knew it was there...festering away in the back of my mind, amid a million other random thoughts.

Those who know me best would probably describe me as being slightly impulsive, which is a generous understatement, to say the least. Even by my own estimation, I'm a *run-off-the-edge-of-a-cliff* kinda guy, and my life's replete with shining examples where, for good or for ill, I've done just that.

The success I've gained through my dubious adventures is somewhat subjective, but suffice it to say that I rarely listen to any advice other than my own – my own largely comprising an optimistic sense of adventure (or stupidity?). I have found that the most interesting characters I've met on any road I've travelled have shown these same two characteristics in glorious complexity.

I seek only to follow their shining example.

I'll not bore you with tedious details regarding the story of my life. After all, I'm trying to ingratiate myself to you as a reader and not render you senseless with boredom after the first couple of paragraphs. With that in mind, I really should attempt to give some kind of detail as to what went on before my coastal escapades, even if only to give a touch of context to what will follow.

Think of it as grease to make the wheels of the story turn that little bit smoother.

Without getting philosophical, I think that as a species we tend to gravitate towards the easiest and most comfortable thing. I'd bet I'm on safe ground in assuming that most of us operate in a similar manner when faced with any sort of challenge, and by that I mean trying to find the simplest way around obstacles, putting in the least amount of effort possible, so as to get a moderately satisfactory result.

Just so long as it's easy, right?

Such has been my mindset throughout most of my life. I'd start by putting in place mental justifications as to why something wouldn't work and then keep those firmly in plain sight, at least until the stupid thing, whatever it happens to have been, goes away. In this way, I could shrug off any difficult tasks or ideas as mere flights of idiocy and then get straight back on with my life.

The problem I have with *that* life philosophy is that it butts horns very nicely with my impulsiveness which, in turn, leads me into making some very dubious decisions – and believe me, walking the entire coast of Britain was definitely one of my more dubious decisions.

So, where did it start?

I think this is the part where I'm supposed to write something like…

"I remember it vividly. It was Saturday at a quarter to three, on the 18th May, and, like a revelation, it hit me…"

12

*

Well, I warn you now that my memory is absolutely shocking and, in addition to that, what I *do* remember is probably jaded with rosy hindsight sprinkled with a decent dosing of imagination and storytelling.

If there was a beginning to be told, then this is probably it (and I should just get right on with the telling of it):

A few years ago, a friend of mine, Greg, had invited me round to his place so we could get merry, watch a few films and chill out on his couch. It was pretty standard fare between us, and something we didn't get much chance to do anymore since he'd left me in Bristol and swanned off for the glitz and glamour of Surrey several years before. We'd both sit down and slowly get drunk while talking over one another, giving film critiques like we were shortlisting on behalf of the Academy. In these situations, we'd usually opt for DVDs with reasonable 'take your brain out' qualities. On this occasion, it was Greg's choice, and he insisted we watch something he'd seen before and had absolutely loved.

By our usual standards, his choice that day was an intensely sober affair, called *The Way*, by Emilio Estevez, which, after watching it, had an incredibly unexpected effect on me.

I'm not going to go into massive detail here; if you're really all that interested, then I'm sure you'll be able to get a copy of it somewhere online or, if you're lucky, there will be one lurking on the dusty shelf of a charity shop. Trust me – it's a good use of a couple of hours of your life, and a heart-warming, charming and inspiring story to boot!

The backdrop to the film is something that I'd lived my life up until then being blissfully unaware of...a long-distance walk called the Camino de Santiago.

You can easily google this but, in a nutshell, the Camino (or the 'Way of St James') is a thousand-year-old pilgrimage trail through Spain to the city of Santiago de Compostela, which sits near the north-west coast of the Atlantic. It is said that the basilica of St James in Santiago is the final resting place of St James the apostle (as in, the actual guy himself!).

Even those of you reading this who aren't religious should be aware of the famous painting of the last supper of Christ. Well, one of those dudes sitting around the table with Jesus was St James. Just to be clear – I'm not religious in the slightest and, in its usual terms, a pilgrimage wouldn't be something I'd gravitate towards. Yet, the concept of this experience captivated me instantly, as it had countless others over the years, and as hard as I tried, I just couldn't stop thinking about it.

The initial barrier to any undertaking like this is the immediate dismissal of the entire thing as being something either too difficult, too daft, or just too expensive to run out and do tomorrow. I mean, I hate walking (even to the shops), and like everybody else, I had bills to pay.

So there it sat, in the back of my mind, just mouldering away... waiting for the right opportunity to present itself. Over time, that little thought ate away at my subconscious to the point where I vowed to myself, at the very least, that I'd walk the Camino in my fortieth year.

With a bit of accidental planning, I'd made sure that 2016 was that year. I'd saved up the annual leave I needed in order to complete my Camino, which I intended to begin over the August bank holiday weekend. It'd be tough, but I supposed I could manage the 800-kilometre trek in the thirty-five days I had set aside and be back in work before anyone noticed I was gone.

I'll give you one guess as to the response from my employers when I glibly asked for the whole of September (and the spare change into the first week of October) off work.

Bang went *that* Camino dream!

It would be a further two years before another opportunity for me to pursue this ambition arose and, as on previous occasions, the catalyst came from something that initially went awry in my life, but that inadvertently pushed me in a direction I never could've have foreseen.

At that time, work was becoming more and more relentless, with events such as London's Grenfell Tower disaster creating a ripple effect across the sector I worked in. Things were always challenging but that one, tragic event affected every social housing provider in the UK – one of which I happened to work for.

Since 2012, I'd been heavily involved in something called 'Landlord Statutory Compliance'. It's an engineering field that looks after things like fire, electrical, gas, and water safety in social housing buildings. As I hope you can appreciate, it was an understandably tense job. The risk of similar occurrences to those in London happening in my line of work were a constant worry. It's one thing to assure yourself that you have all the correct measures in place but when you're managing a property stock numbered in the thousands, there's a niggling feeling in the back of your mind that you just might have missed something. Don't get me wrong, I loved my job and I'd like to think I was bloody good at it too, but oh my word was it full on!

The last project I was working on came to an end in May 2018 and no sooner had I submitted my final report than another bold, shiny project came sliding across my desk.

Suffice it to say that I didn't even bother to open the envelope.

I'd had enough and I needed a break from the intensity of statutory compliance and front-line social housing. It's also worth noting that by way of a 'happy' little twist of coincidence, my relationship with my girlfriend had fallen by the wayside not twenty-four hours before (quite mutually and amicably, I might add). For a bloke in his early forties, I now had a unique paradigm of circumstances not usually afforded to someone my age. I don't have kids; I lived on my own in private rental accommodation. It wasn't lost on me that I now had a juicy 'house deposit' sitting in my bank account, winking away at me...and very few other ties except for Moose, who we'll get to later.

And so, I found myself facing the proverbial crossroads!

The Camino was my first option, and the obvious choice, although I'd never before considered undertaking the journey with a dog in tow. I quickly took to the internet to gauge the complications (if any) of having a dog the size of a small horse with me on an 800-kilometre journey across the coastline of northern Spain.

Next, I began to draw up lists – two of them, in fact!

They looked something like this:

Pros:

- Good company (for who doesn't need a stalwart travelling companion?).

- A chance for a dog to be wild and free, as nature intended (good owner brownie points there).

- The mystique and prestige of walking the Camino with man's best friend.

- A great talking point for meeting strangers. For all his faults, Moose is an absolute beauty and would attract all sorts of attention along the way!

Cons:

- Availability of dog food.

- My Spanish was substandard, to the point of not being able to understand a vet should I need to.

- The burning heat of European summers.

- Limited availability of 'doggy friendly' accommodation.

- Wild bears!

- Wild dogs!!

- Dog thieves!!!

- Rabies!!!!

- Other exotic European doggy diseases!!!!!

- Oh my.

…and so the 'cons' list went on.

Once again, I shelved the Camino dream and began looking for something safer and closer to home.

It's at this point that I think I should properly introduce Moose to you. He is, after all, the other half of this story, and in addition to him being my stalwart companion, there's some detail here that'll make the rest of the story far less confusing.

Moose was one of those happy little accidents that crop up in life from time to time. I'd long since come to the understanding that, as a private renter, I'd never be able to get permission from a landlord to own a dog. Why? I never understood. It's not like they're going to draw crayon all over the paintwork. Anyway, I resigned myself to the fact that I'd never really get the opportunity to have a dog, as long as I was renting privately. With that firmly in mind though, I'd still occasionally rock up to the local shelter to 'window shop' (after all, looking couldn't hurt, could it?).

The story of Moose (or indeed Ryder, as he was known back then) was one of sheer fluke, and it goes something like this:

I'd recently received a promotion at work and, while still reeling from the ramifications of my new position, I was working Saturday overtime in order to combat the latest crisis befalling the department before I took a week's annual leave. I left fairly early but the roads along my usual route home that day were closed for essential works. This meant a trip up and across Combe Down – an area of Bath that just so happened to take me past Bath Cats and Dogs Home.

Who was I to argue with an opportunity for indulgence?

It was three in the afternoon and there was still plenty of time to scout about the home before they closed (and I really had nothing better to do for the rest of the day). No sooner had these thoughts entered my mind than I was parked up and sloping across the car park. As I entered the spacious reception area, I was greeted by one of the many enthusiastic workers.

"Good afternoon," he piped up, bouncing towards me, seemingly elated at beating his other colleagues to the punch.

"Er…hello," I replied, somewhat evasively. I could already feel the prickle of a fine sweat building up on the back of my neck.

"Are you looking for something in particular?" he asked with a smile.

That was it – I was done for! I stood there, the fraud I knew I was, and blurted, "Um… I'd just like to have a look around…y'know…see if there's anything that takes my fancy."

Bloody liar! I thought – I had no intention of taking a dog home. I was here on a purely selfish whim to satisfy my own impulsiveness. But the guilt was already rising, and I could feel the flush of red begin to swell into my face.

The chap I was staring at seemed not to notice and continued smiling. "Well just sign in the book on the desk and let me know if there's anything I can help you with."

I nodded an evasive nod, slightly annoyed by his enthusiastically helpful manner, walked up to the desk and began scribbling away.

"Do you know how to get to the kennels from here?" he called from behind.

Well, of course I know how to get to the bloody kenn—

"No," I lied, "would you mind showing me, please?"

"Just go through the door – take a left and follow the signs."

He nodded politely towards the door before gliding off back towards the office.

I placed the pen back into its 'borrowed' NatWest pen holder and bolted through the double doors and out into the open-air kennels.

And then it hit me – the smell, the noise, and the chaos of all the rest!

To be clear, there's something about the aroma of dogs that you'll either love or hate. For me, the musty air of fresh canine is one that elicits a feeling of family, warmth and love. For some others, it can be a pure dank, doggy stink! The outdoor air was permeated with wafts of unwashed paws and doggy ears, with an underlying grot smell of dog shit, urine and disinfectant. Barks and yaps punctuated the air as I took stock and skipped off to see what temporary friends I could make for the rest of the afternoon.

I'll not dwell on the issue of rescue dogs for too long – just to say two things:

Firstly, dogs aren't for Christmas, they're for a lifetime – and, by that, I mean *yours* and not just the lifespan of your future dog. Don't be an arsehole and adopt without recognising the lifelong commitment not only to the dog, but to yourself as well.

Secondly, if you want a dog, go to a home and rescue one! I'm not even gonna justify *that* point.

… Anyway.

I looked around and, sure enough, huddled in one of the enclosures I spotted an incredible specimen of canine beauty: a huge mastiff by the name of Junior. He was a brown, grand-looking thing with a head the size of a pumpkin and droopy eyes to boot! We sat together, either side of the cage, cooing and slobbering at each other through the bars, debating the sad story that had led us both to be sitting on concrete in doggy limbo, chatting away late on a Saturday afternoon. We gazed into each other's eyes for a good half hour, trying to figure each other out. I was really quite smitten.

Eventually, I said farewell and looked around the rest of the pack, before beginning to plan my exit strategy as best I could. I skirted back through reception and gunned for the exit doors, but no sooner had I taken a dozen or so steps than I was suddenly accosted by another, more senior member of the Bath Cats and Dogs team.

"Did you see anyone you liked?" came a chirpy voice from the office.

Shit! I froze in my tracks, planted on my best face and slowly turned around, to be confronted by another beaming smile.

"Hi! I'm Charlotte – I'm one of the rehomers here." She extended a hand to me, which I took, as I introduced myself somewhat shyly and evasively.

Charlotte was dressed in the same uniform, as blue as her colleague before her, but with a demeanour far more determined and confident. Her stance was one that instantly indicated to me that she had a more hands-on (and, no doubt, paws-on…) role at the home – and was probably adept at dealing with 'tricky' customers such as myself.

"Did you meet anyone you liked?" she asked again.

"Errr – yes…" I responded, as confidently as I could. Clearly, I wasn't going to get out of this one alive. "I met Junior," I blurted.

"Aww, Junior – he's one of our gentle giants." She gently placed her hand against my elbow and began leading me back towards the desk.

I squirmed…

"Would you like to arrange an adoption interview?"

The question blindsided me. *Bollocks!* I thought, as I smiled pathetically and replied, "Um…of course…but only if you have time."

With the efficiency of a train conductor catching a wayward traveller without a ticket, she grabbed a pen, planted me solidly in a chair and began scrawling away at an appointment card. "I can fit you in on Tuesday, if you'd like?" She scribbled, not looking up.

"Um…"

"We also have appointments available at three, half past and ten to five…"

"Umm…"

"Or Thursday, if that's better for you?" she continued.

In an effort to maintain some kind of respectability, I quickly agreed to the time of three on Tuesday, shook Charlotte's hand and left, clutching the appointment slip between my shaking fingers.

Sheepishly I ducked back towards my car, figurative tail between my legs. I shook myself out of the temporary slip of madness I'd fallen into, but as the countryside slid by the window as I sped out of Bath, I could feel a faint glimmer of hope begin to spark in my mind…a spark that would grow as the weekend passed until it began to ignite one simple thought:

What if…?

There were several trains of thought teeming through my mind that weekend. The two most prevalent being *'If you don't ask, you don't get'* and *'Better to beg forgiveness than ask permission'*.

I quickly opted for the former and emailed my landlord about the possibility of getting a dog, who I assured them would be 'no trouble'.

The unexpected reply was:

Yes, although please limit your choice to a small/medium-sized dog.

As I dragged myself up from the floor, hardly believing my luck, I cautiously began the mental preparations of at long last getting a dog!

Pfft…of *course* I wasn't going to actually get a dog, but what an enticing thought it was that I could have one, if I wanted.

I drove across to the home again on Tuesday, this time untethered by the emotional shackles of being an imposter. I was filled, instead, with the demeanour of 'interested optimist' as I made my way over Bath downs and into the university campus, which bordered the shelter.

It became apparent in the first two minutes of my chat with Charlotte that Junior wasn't a suitable match for me or my lifestyle. Then Charlotte, who possibly spent way too much time in the company of dogs, looked at me and did that doggy head-tilt thing.

"I wonder…" she mused. "We have an animal here that's got great personality, but he can be a bit woofy. He's a bit on the big side, too."

…limit your choice to a small/medium-sized dog.

"Sure," I replied, a little more wild-eyed than I intended.

Charlotte smiled as she went on to tell me about this 'boisterous giant', who'd had to be kept separate because of his proclivity to boom at every living thing that came within ten feet of him.

"He really is a gentle thing, though…" she reassured me as she, once again hand on elbow, led me outside.

Across from the main compound, glittering in the sunlight, was a section of fenced-off scrubland that held several decrepit static caravans, all of which had been crudely furnished to resemble Grandma's living room. I was escorted into one of the suffocating cabins and, instantly, the miasma of dog hit me as I crossed the threshold. The place had been slowly baking in the sun the entire morning and I immediately broke into a sweat.

"Whew… I'll just crack open a few windows," said Charlotte, before scurrying off again, leaving me to while away my time in the heat and stench of this strange and abstract living room.

I dusted off one of the more respectable-looking chairs and sat down to wait. The place held all the hallmarks of doggy use, with claw and teeth marks adorning most of the interior. Here and there, I could see the bulging of swollen wood panelling where each subsequent entrant had overridden the previous markings by cocking a leg, giving the entire room a slightly shop-soiled feel.

BOOM!

I instantly started, and turned towards the door, which had been flung almost off its hinges by the bulk of what could only be described as a small brown horse as it bolted into the room!

Ryder grandly strode in, tail wagging furiously and nose twitching, as he dragged Charlotte somewhat raggedly behind. He stopped, lifted

22

his head to me and fixed me with an intense stare from his two huge brown eyes, if only for a second or two. His nose twitched again, before he lost interest, wandered off to the couch in the middle of the room, cocked a leg and grandly laid claim to a coffee table like a mountaineer proudly planting a flag.

By now, Charlotte had managed to detangle herself from this juggernaut, who had neatly wrapped the lead right around her hand. "What do you think?" She grinned.

I was floored.

He was big, brown and smelly, and had paws the size of a bear's. Quite simply, he was absolutely magnificent!

I smiled back and tried my luck.

"Ryder!"

He ignored me while continuing his exploration of the room.

"Ryder!" I called once again, but with slightly more assertiveness to my voice.

He continued to ignore me, far more interested in the room and its cacophony of canine aromas than some random human sitting in a corner. I got the impression that he'd get to me in his own sweet time.

"He's lovely," I said casually, "although a tad bigger than I expected…"

"He's such a gentle soul…" Charlotte trailed off, as we both glanced back across to the other side of the room. Ryder had stopped his sniffing exploration and was now stood stock-still, facing directly towards us, feet planted, and tail raised. For the first time it would seem, we were worthy of this goliath's attention. He fixed me with an intense, curious gaze.

… And then it came.

First was the noise, followed quickly by the intense stench of doggy breath. The windows of the caravan shook as he unleashed a torrent of abuse at me, accentuating each "Woof" with a slight jump of his front quarters as if to give further emphasis to his dialogue.

Daymn – that boy could sing!

Charlotte looked at me worriedly. "This is about as far as we usually get with him, but I assure you his bark is far worse than it sounds."

I barely heard her.

I was already on my feet, enticed and drawn to this show of doggy strength and bravado. As I cautiously approached, a curious thing happened. Ryder, who I assume was as much perplexed by my reaction as others were with his tirade, suddenly stopped his vocal outpour, sat on his haunches and cocked his head to one side as if to say: "That's not usually the reaction I get – what's wrong with you, human?"

He stood…

I stopped in my tracks.

He stared…

I stared right back.

… And then it happened. Ryder, for all his bravado, lowered his gaze, drifted towards me and sat down, tail wagging slightly, before offering me one of his huge paws.

I melted inside…took hold of his giant appendage and shook hands with this hulking creature who was, in time, to become my best friend.

As terse as the initial meeting was, I was hooked. I spent the rest of my week off making trips back and forth to the home, so I could take him out for walks along the downs. Within the first few days of meeting him, I'd hear barks of excitement as I approached, even before we were within view of each other. I'll give him this – he has a damned good sense of smell.

Ten days and several adoptive processes later, we both ended up back at my house, sitting on the edge of my bed, looking somewhat bemusedly at each other, contemplating the whirlwind of sudden events that had brought us together. I'd yet to blag away how Ryder constituted a 'small/ medium-sized dog' to my landlord and, further still, excuse away the time

I'd now be spending with him to my employer instead of slaving away in the office until all hours.

But who cared about that – my priorities were now reset!

In every sense of the word, we rescued each other that day.

It would be a further two weeks before 'Ryder' became Moose, and later still until nicknames like 'Mooch', 'Mr Moose', 'Moo', 'Dickhead' and 'Oii!' would be added as further terms of endearment, all of which he'd learn to ignore depending on his convenience.

Whatever…

As long as there was love, cuddles, morsels of food, and comfort, he wasn't fussed what I called him either way.

Chapter 1

Moose

Trowbridge

The sun beamed in through the patio doors, blinding me in one eye.

Impatiently, I dragged one of the curtains back across the gap to block out the light, before turning back to the map I'd laid out on the living room floor. Kneeling down once again, I began running my hands over the creases to smooth the thing out, looking at the contours as I grinned at the enormity of the British Isles presented before me in glorious colour.

I looked up and caught Moose's eye. "So what do you think?"

Silence.

"Oi, idiot – I'm talking to you!"

I continued to peer at the heaving lump, half asleep on the sofa, hoping for some kind of response. "C'mon, lad…" I goaded. "It'll be fun!"

His eyes inched open as he gave me a slovenly stare. *"Well…"* he started, stretching out a slow yawn. *"It doesn't sound all that fun to me."*

I bit my tongue and took a breath. "It's nature as intended, buddy! Rolling hillsides, gorgeous scenery…" I looked back and caught a flicker of annoyance on his face at my eagerness. I got to my feet and planted myself firmly in his line of sight, and once again tried to spark a bit of enthusiasm. "This is the great outdoors, pal!"

He looked up from the couch and then, slowly and deliberately, began gnawing away at an unoffending toenail. *"... And you want us to go the entire way around, do you?"* he said, with half a paw hanging out of the side of his mouth.

"Of course!" I grinned.

"Nope!" he snorted, closing his eyes once again, as he rested his huge head back onto his soggy appendage.

I gritted my teeth and tried another tack. "You're the one forever moaning that you're bored," I fumed. "'Let's go out...'" I mocked, beginning to pace room, "'Trowbridge is rubbish!'"

Stopping mid-pace I turned, catching him square in the eye.

His eyelids flickered for a moment before he slowly opened them just wide enough to pin me with a cold, hard stare. Snorting, he deliberately cast his eyes away and restarted his DIY pedicure. *"Well, I didn't mean doing something as idiotic as this,"* he spat, sending a fingernail spinning across the room.

My eyebrows creased, ignoring the projectile as it landed on the laminate a few inches from the corner of the map. "You *do* remember who buys the food, don't you?" I snarked, getting irritated by his indifference to the entire thing.

He yawned, stretched out his paws, and lazily slid off the couch before ambling towards me, stopping short of the door. *"Are we taking the sofa with us?"* he asked rather bluntly.

Wrong-footed, I gaped at the stupidity of the question.

"Well, of *course* we're n—" I stopped mid-sentence, thinking quickly as a lie formed. "... Taking the couch with us...sure!" I continued, nodding emphatically.

He drifted through the door into the garden, sauntered up to the half-dead apple tree in the middle of the gravel and threw a line of wee against it. I groaned and rolled my eyes. "You really are a disgusting creature. Why people find you irresistible is beyond me."

He grinned back at me through droopy eyes. "*Part of my charm!*" came the glib reply. He shook a leg and, sauntering back through the door, lumbered himself back on to the couch.

I turned, pulling the door to. "You still haven't answered my question."

He looked at me through rapidly lowering eyelids as I stood there, hand still on the doorknob.

"*OK – fine!*"

I raised an eyebrow.

"*We'll do your stupid walk, then.*"

"Well that's gracious of you," I quipped, looking up only to find him snoring away once more. Glancing back down at the map, now complete with Moose's literal, muddy pawprint stamp of approval, I locked the door, strode into the room and knelt down to assess the damage on my once pristine map.

"Bloody dogs…" I muttered, smug in the begrudging approval I'd just received.

Chapter 2

Day One

Portishead to Clevedon

Our walk began several months later.

Before setting off, I'd tried to spark a bit of enthusiasm by contacting a few local newspapers and radio stations. I thought that if I could raise our profile by way of a bit of publicity, then we might find some benefit somewhere on the way around.

What was the harm in that (especially where the charities are concerned)?

I'd conceded early on that, if we were going to embark on this madcap adventure, we might as well raise some money for good causes as we went.

I ended up choosing three:

- Shelter – A UK housing and homelessness charity
- The Thistle Foundation – Enabling independent living in Scotland
- Bras Not Bombs – a small community interest company which supports refugees

I'd spent my nights on the run-up to 'walk day' compiling a slew of snivelling emails, each foretelling the magnificence of this grand adventure of man and dog like I was the first idiot to ever think of it. I imagined myself as a somewhat more skint and northern version of Sir Ranulph Fiennes, sitting there in front of my desk...charting the expedition of a lifetime, expecting the masses to come banging on my door so they could immerse themselves in the inspirational vibe of it all.

I heard very little back.

If I'm being honest with myself, the story of some random forty-two-year-old bloke and his dog going for a long walk isn't particularly newsworthy. And yet, even though we hadn't even walked a mile yet, I still felt slightly disappointed that the *National Geographic* wasn't banging down my door.

The sole piece of media attention we did achieve was with Somerset Live, a local online outlet.

A young reporter called Max rang me up and asked if he could pop round for a cuppa and a chat. On the day in question, Moose happened to be trying on his waterproof leggings – and so, when I let Max in, he quickly became the focus of our discussions. Adorned in the latest canine hiking get-up, Moose was far more worthy of press attention than some human's misguided attempt at a mid-life crisis! A four-year-old mastiff/Labrador cross in yellow waders was far more click-worthy – and this did give me a bit of reassurance that my choice to slap Moose's face on the cover of *Waggy Walk* was one of my wiser ones.

Credit to Max: it was a great article. Unfortunately for us, no one actually turned up in Portishead, and what other unseen benefit it gave us beyond satisfying curiosity, I'm not entirely sure about.

We finally made it to June 28th 2018: start day.

A friend of mine had kindly offered to run us down to our Portishead starting point in his car.

Well…we'll have the fanfare of at least one *person to cheer us on…* I thought. That was until Tim told me he'd double-booked himself and had to be back in Bristol within the hour.

So much for an entourage!

Tim quickly dropped us off near the local Tesco, leaving us both stranded in Portishead town centre as I fumbled with my outrageously large pack as he sped off. We stumbled our way down towards the lido and sat on a grass verge for ten minutes while I readjusted my rucksack straps, which were already beginning to dig in. Across the way, I could see revellers bathing and splashing away in the pool. They looked like they were enjoying the day far more than we were, so I thought, *Sod it!* I muscled on the pack, grabbed the Moose and set off down the road that ran alongside the shoreline. I left Portishead with a slightly pompous air, full of self-congratulation for the intrepid explorers we had both clearly now become. Moose, meanwhile, sniffed at some leftover wee, such was his interest in the grander scheme.

Ten minutes later, we had our first encounter!

I seem to remember that I was staggering along, desperately trying to get the straps of my behemoth of a pack to settle into a bearable weight. The UK had just entered a particularly glorious patch of summer and the sun was cheerily beating down on us with the vigorous intensity of an overexcited heat lamp. Looking up to wipe the beads of sweat from my brow, I saw a woman wearing council garb, working away at some of the hedgerows. She looked at us curiously, as if to ask just what the bloody hell we were up to, trekking around in this heat, with what could only be described as a house strapped to my back.

"Walking the coastline of Britain!" I proudly announced, beaming ear to ear.

"Oh," she replied, somewhat unimpressed. "Have you come far?"

My ego imploded.

"Er… Portishead Lido."

She leant to her left slightly and peered over my shoulder at the lido glittering away in the sun, less than half a mile back down the track.

"Huh!" she remarked, sounding a tad underwhelmed by the achievement.

I flushed.

"Well, best of luck with that," she said politely, as she carried on past.

Damn! I was going to have to work on that – even *I* felt disappointed just saying it.

Moose drifted around in front, sniffing away at the freshly cut grass with a smirk on his face. *"I'm sure Columbus had similar issues convincing the peasants..."*

I cast down an evil look.

He sniggered before sauntering off to sniff some more wee.

Soon after, we began our trek from Portishead and out on the path to Clevedon – a pretty trail flanked predominantly with trees, coarse undergrowth and bracken. We walked under low canopies of wiry branches, while the trail itself was clear-cut into the ground, about a metre wide. The air was close and there was a constant mist of bugs around us. Moose was in his element, happily snapping away at the flies as he skipped along behind me. Here and there, I caught glimpses of the Severn Estuary glimmering through the hedgerow, and I finally felt the euphoria of just being here, after so many months of planning.

"Here we are, Moose," I chirped, "living the dream!"

Moose picked his head up, long strands of grass hanging out of his gob.

"Wnns Innrr..."

"Not with your mouth full."

He spat out a chewed-up mush of greens and slobber and looked back up at me.

"I said – when's dinner?"

I rolled my eyes. "You're bloody obsessed!" It wasn't even three o'clock yet.

Not missing a beat he flicked his tail somewhat pompously and looked back up at me: *"First order of survival, mate – food!"*

If anything was going to bring down my mood, it was going to be my rucksack – well, that and the accompanying constant beat of the sun. My pack was so heavy that in order to get it on, I needed to sit on my arse, strap it to my back and then roll to my feet. I looked and felt like a bloody turned-up tortoise throughout the entire procedure. I was grossly overloaded but, of course, refused to accept that. In my view, I was just unfit and needed time for my body to adjust to carrying around this huge lump. After all, I was only carrying the bare essentials! The sun, on the other hand, was a different matter – it was something we'd both just have to put up with.

After a couple of hours, we stopped for a break next to a slightly underwhelming steel lighthouse. We guzzled water and set off back under the shade of the bushes. Several hours later, we finally arrived at Ladye Bay – an open beach on the edge of Clevedon.

I kinda liked that: 'Ladye Bay'. It had an alluring quality to it, like some long-lost lover waiting patiently on the shores of home.

That was one of many preconceptions to be shattered by reality before the day was through.

Far from being virgin white sands, Ladye Bay was a mottled pebble beach, teeming with people, dogs and children, all of which sat at the bottom of a thirty-foot staircase. I was worn, tired and aching and, by the time we got to the last step, I felt like collapsing! I mustered what strength I had left and clambered to the far end of the beach before falling into a heap beneath the shade of several huge, rounded rocks.

I doubt I'd have felt worse if I'd have been thrown down those stairs. Moose, on the other hand, grabbed the opportunity as golden.

He scurried under one of the overhangs and plonked himself down into the shade with a satisfied groan. The sun roared on, even though it was now early evening. We lay there catching our breath and drained the last of the water we had. I looked up, knowing that the only way forwards was back up that godawful staircase and, hopefully, to a shady camping spot…somewhere up there.

I posted a quick self-congratulatory video on Facebook before passing out in the shade. It was probably getting on for about eight before we both stirred, each feeling the impending dread of having to clamber back up those stairs. Mooch trailed behind now, obviously tired of the day's excitement and keen to get back to the house, couch and blankets – which I'd shamelessly taken to the charity shop the previous day.

First task: water!

I'd been assured that there were plenty of places I could ask for a quick refill. We inched our way back up and out on to the road, trudging past rows of Georgian houses to find anywhere half-respectable to camp for the night. As desperate as I was for a top-up, I just couldn't quite bring myself to start banging on some random person's door, begging for a refill. Instead, we continued along Bay Road until I could see the glimmer of a hotel in the distance.

That'll do! I thought, crossing the road.

We marched through the car park and into the entrance of this rather elegant building, and I peered around the door, half expecting to be instantly thrown out, dog and all.

I glared intently at Moose. "Behave!"

I pasted on my best face and peered into the foyer.

"Err… Hi!"

I looked across at the ornate desk, which sat twenty yards or so at the opposite end of the grand foyer; there was no response.

"Hello?" I barked again, somewhat louder than I'd anticipated.

The receptionist raised her head and looked around, slightly startled, until she caught a glimpse of my sweaty head peering in from around the side of the doorway.

"Are you dog-friendly?" I asked, considerably more desperately than I'd intended.

"Of course!"

Relief.

I flung open the door and Moose, ignoring my earlier warning, flew into the opulent space and began sniffing away at the fine furnishings with a view to establishing a doggy smallholding. I quickly dragged him back and walked over to the massive oak desk.

"I hope you don't mind but could you fill up my water bottles?"

The receptionist smiled as I planted two water bottles on the desk. "Will tap water do?"

Quite frankly, I'd have settled for sewer water.

"That'd be great," I replied wearily.

She took my containers and disappeared.

I was left to ponder my next move in the luxurious surroundings of this grand, empty space. Limping to a seating area, I began to massage my toes through my trainers. I ached everywhere and could already feel tell-tale hotspots on my feet, indicating unpleasant surprises for when I eventually took my socks off.

The receptionist quickly returned and handed over the water. I said thanks, turned and left as quickly as my aching feet would let me. The heat practically punched me in the face as I walked outside and I instantly broke out into a sweat again. Retracing our steps along the road, we emerged at a small common flanked by a small woodland that we'd passed on our way up. I found a spot along a line of trees that was reasonably level and secluded, threw down my kit, and pitched the tent.

Moose tugged on the lead, eager to be loose; I unclipped the hasp and off he flew, across the field. Where the hell did he get the energy from? I was absolutely knackered!

"Don't drift off!" I shouted.

Completely ignoring me, he bolted into the distance.

Damn! I thought, too tired to even attempt a chase.

I delved into my pack and began littering our camping spot with masses of kit until I finally found my stove. I'd chosen it because of the battery bolted to the side that charged using the heat generated by a steady fuel of pinecones and wood. In addition to cooking dinner, it'd also charge my phone. I'd seen it online and thought it ideal for our adventure...but, unfortunately, the thing (like most of my trek gear) weighed a ton.

After scavenging for dry twigs, I lit the damned thing and began cooking up an uninspired evening meal of couscous and tinned fish. Moose, having eventually drifted back, took one sniff, wolfed down the fish, and unceremoniously tipped the rest of the bowl out on to the grass.

"*What's that rubbish?*" he asked.

"Oii..." I started, scrabbling to get what remained back on to a plate. "That *was* dinner!"

He took another sniff at the steaming mess as I tried desperately to scoop it up.

"*Seriously?*" He smirked as he sat there, tongue lolling out the side of his mouth. "*Wot's* really *for dinner?*"

I frowned.

He cocked his head to one side.

"You just tossed it, bud!" I exclaimed, pointing to the mess on the plate I held.

He closed his mouth and fixed me with a hard stare.

"Fine..." I muttered, delving into the bag for the reserves of Pedigree Chum.

I laid down his dogfood before salvaging what was left of my own meal from the grass, adding more fish to give it some degree of excitement, while Moose dived straight into his food. I sat there in our peaceful little spot, watching the sun settle down behind the trees, and slowly chewed, pausing every once in a while to pull a strand of foliage from my teeth.

No sooner was the last gulp down than Moose raced off deep into the woods, leaving me to digest by the side of the tent.

I washed up with a wet tissue and left it all out to dry on the grass. Leaning back, I watched the stars as they began peeking out across the sky, my head spinning from the day's events. We'd walked less than ten miles over what could only be considered gentle terrain, and while I ached all over and felt the mild sting of sunburn on my face, I couldn't help but smile. There was still the stark realisation that my daily toil was an indicator of what my new lifestyle would now look like for the future. It still felt a bit like a camping holiday, and the reality of doing this day in, day out gnawed at my thoughts but still hadn't quite sunk in yet.

Eventually, Moose tired of his antics and trotted over to curl up by my feet. The heat had finally begun to dissipate and we relaxed together under the darkening sky.

Later that evening, in the tent, I pulled off my shoes and socks and stared down at the horror show that had once been my feet. After grabbing my first aid kit, I closed one eye and began cleaning, snipping and plastering away. Moose, his priorities bang on as ever, shoved his head through the tent flap and peered up at me with sheer panic...

"*Where's The Couch??*"

"What?" I asked, scissors in hand. "What couch?"

"*Y'know – Couch*, The *Couch* – My *Couch!!*"

"Ah. About that..."

Language was no barrier at all as I laid out certain realities to him: there was no 'sofa-at-the-end-of-the-rainbow'. Moose gave a disgruntled huff and, resigned to his disappointment, collapsed on the sleeping bag – farting loudly on my inflatable pillow before falling asleep. Too tired to care, I shrugged, inched inside the somewhat occupied sleeping bag, batted the rancid aroma out of my pillow, and tried for some sleep. My bruised body complained as I struggled to get comfortable.

A night spent on a quarter-inch-thick sponge mattress with a dog who had a proclivity to kick me with his gangly legs every ten minutes was to teach me yet further lessons in adaptability.

I remember that night's sleep very well, if for no reason other than I got very little of it.

I woke the following morning to a mass of paws, doggy breath and dribble inches from my face. I shoved him off, which produced more disapproving grunts punctuated moments later with a further noxious release from beneath his tail. Holding my breath, I fingered at the zip for some much-needed fresh air.

Tents are not renowned for their shading quality when under direct sunlight. Stupidly, I'd not considered this when pitching the night before, and so it was that as soon as the sun rose, so did we. I peered at my watch – it was just after 6am!

I looked out from the gap in the tent door to take in wet grass stretching out across the peaceful little common. Moose, obviously still not over the couch debacle, muscled past me so he could take a pee along the hedge line. Despite having had very little sleep, I was actually feeling a lot better. I followed Moose out for a stretch and began walking along the edges of the common, gripping my toes in the cool, dewy grass. It's remarkable, the recovery mechanism we all have – even when given an only half-decent night's sleep on a slightly smelly pillow. I felt totally rejuvenated, and began setting about the business of breakfast.

I looked over at Moose the Mooch. "Still in a piss about the couch?"

He narrowed his eyes and threw a string of expletives at me.

"Kiss your mother with that mouth, do you?"

He snorted, shook his head and carried on pacing. I knew I hadn't heard the last of this, but damned if I was going to pander.

"Do you want sausages or not?"

He stopped mid-stride… *"Where the hell did you get sausages?"*

I threw down his bowl as he nosied up. "Ha!"

Biscuits and Chum.

With Mooch fed, I began striking camp. It occurred to me that I needed to refine this business of packing up. It's a bit like when you first move in somewhere and have all your stuff strewn everywhere, and my technique to stowing kit was still on a first in, first out basis. Eventually, I'd have this down to a fine art, but today – there was nothing artistic about it! I just rammed it all in until everything fit. What I *had* learned was not to hang things on the back of my rucksack: I'd set off with some really handy illuminated bands that would've been great for night-time and could only assume they now adorned the path somewhere back along the way to Portishead. A good find for whoever followed in our wake!

The entire thing took me well over an hour to get done, by which time Moose was twitching to get going again. After completing my little turtle-roll with the pack, I groaned to my feet, clipped on Moose's lead and grabbed my walking pole. As we reached the bottom of the field, I looked back to our camp spot and felt a slight pang…the fine grass that had acted as our bed for the night was already beginning to unflatten and blend back into the indistinguishable mass of Clevedon Common.

I looked down at Moose, whose nose was already twitching in the morning air. "You good?"

He gave an approving tail-flick, excited to be going somewhere again. We turned and headed off back down towards the path. The sun hadn't quite hit our backs yet as we plunged forth, deeper into Somerset.

My thoughts drifted over our first day, the road ahead, the ache in my feet…and the searing heat I knew would soon return to punish us. I set a foot on the path once more with renewed optimism in my heart, leaving the memory of our first night in the open to fade away behind us, into the distance.

Chapter 3

South Into Somerset

Clevedon to Cannington

In the days that followed, my mindset began to shift. The worries of my previous life – paying rent, preparing for meetings or getting narked off with traffic jams – were slowly being replaced with different concerns like eating, drinking and finding shelter. Out there it was a different kind of survival, and as the miles passed, my attention to weekly routine faded as I lost track of both time and distance.

It was a liberating and yet frightening experience!

We were still in familiar territory, though – it's just that *I* was used to getting there by car and not on foot. I was still getting used to the footpaths, too. Unlike with roads, you'd be merrily walking along and then the thing would just stop dead in the middle of nowhere.

Please try again...

It was incredibly annoying!

A few miles beyond the town limits of Clevedon, we hit such a trail. As it turns out, there *is* no coastal path between Clevedon and Weston-super-Mare – only a gate marked with the stark words:

PRIVATE – NO ENTRY!

So much for an easy coastal route! Moose, not one to be deterred by such things, tried squeezing through the bars of the gate anyway.

"Sorry, Mooch, we'll have to turn around."

"*What for???*"

"It's private land."

"*Woozy-wot-wot now?*"

I shrugged. Try explaining the complexities of land deeds and title to a dog. "It means we go back."

I was honestly expecting an argument but, instead, he just turned and happily trotted back the way we'd come.

We'd wasted hours on our little mystery tour and by now the sun was once again burning our scalps off. I grabbed my phone and started checking maps for a way around. In short, there wasn't one. We'd have to go miles inland to a place called Yatton and then back out again to hit the road to the coast. This detour would end up costing us another day's travel on foot. I threw a few choice words around before trudging on. After a couple more hours, we passed a campsite and I decided to call it quits for the day. Unsurprisingly, Moose didn't argue! We spent the rest of the day lounging and snoring in the shade.

Just before dawn the next day we were up once again, packed and gone before morning had kicked in. As we walked, marching further inland, the traffic became busier. At Yatton, I consulted the map again… Weston was ten miles away and we'd already walked three this morning! I was truly knackered and ached from head to foot.

Sod it, I thought, dragging Moose to the train station. Twenty minutes later, we were racing our way back to the coast in comfort. To be honest, it wasn't a decision I took lightly, but the way I saw it, Yatton to Weston is hardly coastal walking!

We got to Weston-super-Mare and weaved our way in and out of traffic until we were on the promenade. Even though we'd cheated outrageously (especially considering that today had been a relatively short walk), we were back within sight of the sea.

That said, I was absolutely broken!

The pack was becoming a serious issue, making the entire experience thoroughly dreary. Here we were, surrounded by hordes of seaside day-trippers soaking in the rays and enjoying the waves – and yet, all I could think about was getting rid of this solid lump, and sleeping for the rest of the day in a comfy bed! We needed a place to lick our wounds, shed some weight and regroup.

Fortunately, Weston is one of those places filled with dog-friendly hotels. Soon, Moose and I were perched on the edge of a bed with the prospect of a decent meal and a good night's sleep in front of us.

We'd only been on the road for four days.

We needed a strategy.

More importantly, I needed a shower. I absolutely hummed!

I stripped down to my bones and, in what can only be described as the best shower of my life, began to feel my sorrows soaking away. I remember groaning in relief as the water massaged life back into my aching shoulders. There and then, I decided that changes needed to be made regarding the insurmountable hulk of equipment I'd been lugging around all week. I stumbled out and braced myself at the sink, where I wiped off the condensation to take a good look.

What I saw staring back at me was barely recognisable.

My face was a violent red, and my blistered nose glowed angrily out in front of it. I glanced down at my torso and noticed two alarmingly large bruise lines, each mirroring the other, starting at my shoulders, as they contused thick purplish yellow tracks that eventually disappeared under my arms, shadowing lines of where the pack had once clung to my shoulders.

Great, I thought... *Moob bruises!*

I limped into the bedroom, where Moose peered up from the bed with a grin on his face.

"Looking good, Ace!"

I absently threw up two fingers by way of reply, clambered on to the mattress, gathered what sheets I could and fell soundly asleep.

I woke a few hours later in darkness. A faint ruddy glow of amber light shone in from the window, hitting the wall above the bed, smearing the room with an ambient flicker of streetlight. I had no idea what time it was – only that it was getting chilly and that the sun had long gone. Moose snored gently by my side as I reached over to grab my watch from the bedside table. I groaned as I tried to focus on the dimly lit hand shining out from beneath the glass.

It was still only 10pm.

My earlier attempt at covering up had been somewhat half-arsed. I turned awkwardly, hugging a tiny corner of the sheet. Moose took up the rest.

"Oii, Doggo!" I moaned.

He continued to snore.

"Hey!" I shouted.

Further snoring.

With aching limbs, I reached out and gave him a shove.

"... *Sleeping*..." He groaned, and slowly dragged himself off the bed.

No sooner had paws touched the carpet than his entire bulk collapsed down with a disgruntled huff. I pulled the covers clear, rolled on my side and did the same.

"Morning!"

My eyes fluttered.

"Are you getting up or what?"

My eyelids peeled back to a soggy nose not two inches from my face.

"In a minute…" I groaned, barely even able to heave my head off the pillow. I glanced over at the clock hanging on the far wall. "What you waking me up for?"

"*You were snoring!*"

That's rich… I thought, and promptly dozed back off again.

Somewhat later, dim light struck my eyes again, although this time I was wrapped in the comforting envelope of a duvet. It was still early – and only the stillness from the streetlight betrayed the hour. I stretched and immediately felt the aches return.

Inching my way to the bathroom, I peered into the mirror again.

Damn – I really did look awful!

I grabbed my toothbrush in an effort to at least take some of the staleness from my mouth.

Right! I thought. *Today's a day of changes.*

I got dressed and began rummaging through my pack.

Three tubular bandages…

Nope!

A full pack of wet wipes…

Nope!

… And so it went, as I combed through every last inch of kit. After about an hour of this, a neat little pile began to form on the bed until I had about two kilograms of gear heaped up. At this point I still considered the travel guitar I had clipped to the side of the rucksack as essential survival equipment.

I tried on the pack and, for the first time since setting off, I could hoist it up across my shoulders while standing! Bye-bye turtle manoeuvre!

We grabbed something to eat and then set off back across the sands, re-energised and with *almost* a spring in my step. The pack was still way too heavy but, in the context of the last few days, it was freedom itself to just continue walking without buckling under the sheer weight of the damned thing.

Moose was also now carrying his fair share, proudly sporting his panniers for the first time on the trip.

Brean Down was our goal for the evening – specifically, the Napoleonic fort that stood on the edge of the headland, overlooking the Severn. We'd need to brave a fairly open piece of country in order to get there – a wide stone cycle track that had been recently constructed to give easier access between the two towns for those deciding not to go by car.

A few miles outside of town, we cradled in a shady spot just outside a café to top up our water and ready ourselves to begin our three-hour trek in the day's baking sun. At the entrance to a cycleway was a locked gate with a sign announcing that RADAR keys could be bought from the shop we'd just passed. I dumped the pack and raced back to grab what would turn out to be one of the most useful pieces of kit I'd take with me – not least of all because it was small, light and extremely portable.

RADAR is, in a nutshell, a system of locks used throughout the UK. This one key would give me access to toilets and gates dotted all across the country. I felt a pang of guilt – these are generally reserved for disabled access only – but have to admit that having it would well and truly go on to save our skins on more than one occasion.

Cycle tracks aren't notorious for running through shaded areas; by the time we got to the Down, we were thoroughly scorched and absolutely drenched in sweat. I'd managed to grab myself a bottle of wine from a pub we'd passed on the way up and had now pinned the acquisition of this humble fortification as one of the 'hurrah' moments of my walk.

I wanted to sit on the edge of the world and watch the sunset, hand in hand with a glass of vino.

In the end, the 'glass' was more of a tin cup – but the experience was still worth waiting for.

The fort itself is a series of brick-built billets, canteens, store rooms, circled by several decaying concrete lookout points looking out to the River Severn. Beneath one of the more formidable structures, I pitched up, cooked a fish and noodle stew, and perched in our silent surroundings as the sun dipped slowly out of the sky. This was what coastal camping was all about…and I made a mental note to do this more often as we ventured further south.

The next day we headed south across the miles of Brean Sands into Burnham-on-Sea. There we camped in the dunes edging the town, spending most of the evening baking in the shade of the tent, which I'd tentatively pitched in the sand, tying guy lines on to whatever sharp foliage had managed to take root there. Our stay was brief and somewhat hastened by the promise of another B&B stay I'd managed to book just outside a place called Cannington.

Only one thing separating us from that: the huge estuaries surrounding the River Parrett.

The mouth of the River Parrett isn't exactly what I'd describe as pretty. Even Moose skulked behind as we trudged our way along the raised, grass seawall that meandered along the length of the riverbank. To the right was a steep slope of mud that clung to the side of the tributary, while the rest of our surroundings was just acres of farmland, chasing off to the left and into the distance. Bridgwater was our earliest crossing opportunity and that was still miles away, deeper inland.

It was much cooler that morning and, as we arrived at the inlet, a shadow of cloud ushered in the pitter-patter of light rain. Before us was an immense barrier blocking our way, with a huge metal kissing gate to one side.

```
┌─────────────────────────────────────────────┐
│                                               │
│        - Warning – Free-Roaming Cattle -      │
│                                               │
│              Keep dogs on a lead!             │
│                                               │
│    In the event that cattle approach, unleash your dog │
│       and then make your way to the nearest gate       │
│                                               │
└─────────────────────────────────────────────┘
```

Well. *That* put a damper on things.

I sat down with Moose, grabbed his waterproofs out of his panniers and put them on.

"You have to stay close to me now, bud."

"If you say so."

"I'm not kidding…stay away from the animals!"

"But…"

"No '*buts*', pal. Stay close."

He shuffled but could tell from my tone that I wasn't in the mood to be argued with.

We breached the first gate into a vast field filled with herds of Friesian cows. They meandered placidly in the distance to the left of the path we walked – lulling us into a false sense of security. No sooner had we passed the kissing gate than they appeared to organise themselves into a well-formed bovine army with one mission: stop all those who dare to pass.

We hastened our pace…

When we were about halfway to the next gate, they began to storm across the fields en masse, corralling Moose and me into a swift and hasty tromp down a road we couldn't divert from. Luckily, we managed to stay ahead of them until several tense minutes later, when we flung ourselves through the next gate. I glanced behind to see row upon row of huge black eyes staring at us from beyond the gate.

Gulping, I moved us quickly onwards.

Now, I can only assume the farmer had designed this particular cluster of gates to be some sort of trial-by-herd. The first led us from a field of cows right into another filled with sheep, and the one after that took us back into bovine territory, and the third returned us to a land of sheep, and so on. This went on for several hours, with each sheep field departure comprising an increasingly intense test of bravery or stupidity, depending on your point of view.

The sheep, for all their bulk and number, ran away at the very sight of us. Where the cows were concerned, though, we were of interest and very much worth the effort of menacing investigation. It went from intimidating to terrifying very quickly and my mind raced, hoping to find respite so we could wait until they'd all buggered off.

Quite simply, though, there was nowhere to go but forwards.

With 'cowgate' well underway, the emergence of each new opening into a bovine field became a dreaded fear. It was as if the previous passing of cows somehow messaged ahead to the next gate to inform their colleagues of our imminent arrival, and how they had 'tested' our resolve in the previous meeting.

In line with the initial instruction, Moose had been off his lead through all of these gates, which might seem foolish, but I simply had no option than to follow the advice posted on that first gate. For all his excitability, Moose kept to the path, calmly racing ahead of the throng. I staggered on behind while he waited in the shelter of the next kissing gate with a worried look on his face.

Me? I was quietly crapping myself the entire way.

And then, just as the path had seemed to hold no respite, there was a subtle change at one of the gates. The appearance of a thin, electrified barrier between the path and the fields surrounding it – including the cows! I nearly wept in gratitude. "You OK, bud?"

Moose just stood there, relief in his eyes as he took a well-earned pee on a nearby stump.

As worried as I was, I realised that I wasn't alone – he hadn't stopped to do that in hours.

It was while walking along this tricky route that I began to recognise the damage that could be caused if I continued to hold the stubborn mindset of reaching fixed goals. By the time we reached this relative safety, our B&B pilgrimage was taking a heavy toll on our emotional wellbeing – we were still several miles away, with many more challenges to come.

By the time we finally made it to Bridgwater, we were both absolutely exhausted and supremely footsore. Any benefit I felt from our stayover in Weston had long since vanished and had been replaced with desperation. It was only through sheer stubbornness that we managed to cross the river and battle through the remaining three miles towards Cannington and the respite it had promised days before. Moose didn't even complain as we wearily slunk into the inn.

It was just after six and we'd been walking straight for nearly eight hours.

"Room booked for Chris," I said, slumping with relief over the edge of the bar.

A seedy-looking guy peered over the bar and glanced scathingly at Moose.

"… I booked it yesterday," I continued.

He sniffed. "Err – we don't let dogs into the room."

I must have misheard. "I booked it with one of your colleagues yester—"

"We don't allow dogs in the rooms!" he interjected.

I looked at Moose and then back at the bloke behind the bar. "But I asked if you were dog-friendly."

"Oh, we are. Just no dogs in the room."

I was beginning to lose my patience. "Look…" I said, "I asked over the phone if you were dog-friendly and the guy said yes…"

He stared at me blankly, refusal written all over his wiry face.

"Why let me book a room if you didn't allow dogs after I'd told you I had one?" I asked incredulously.

"Yeh…" he slurred, "…no dogs in the rooms!"

I stood there, floored.

A regular drifted in behind me and saddled up at the bar.

The barman shifted his attention to more worthy custom. "Al'ight, Nige… Usual?"

The bloke next to me nodded and placed a tenner on the bar.

Seedy guy just drifted off to serve Nige and left me staring into space.

It was still hot outside the pub but had the potential to turn into a beautiful calm summer's evening. The pavements outside were largely silent and clear as calm whispers of wind lifted high above this idyllic little village.

That gentle breeze and, indeed, most of the air in Cannington, began turning blue as I emerged through the bar door and began spewing obscenities into the air. Safe inside, some of the dog-unfriendly inn's punters shifted curtains for a better view, amused by the kerfuffle outside. 'Livid' doesn't even begin to explain it! I was worn and tired, and still suffering shock from our bovine encounter. All I wanted was to get myself and Moose somewhere safe for the night and, instead, here we were, stranded in the middle of nowhere with no plan, no shelter and no food!

I wanted to scream.

For the first time since we'd started the trip, a desperation took hold of me as I started to feel truly lost.

I wandered around the streets desperately trying to figure out what the hell we were going to do. Moose just looked up at me, his tired eyes pleading for me to pull some vestige of comfort out of thin air, although

I knew I had none to give. I phoned my friend Anya in a panic, asking her to call around for an alternative plan.

She called back after a few minutes: there was none.

I staggered back across town to a shop I'd noticed on the way out, where I bought wine and snacks and drifted back up the road, to…who knows where.

The sun hadn't let up either, baking us all the way up a neat road despite the lateness of the hour. The next village was miles away and I had no plan as to what to do next. I looked across the street and there, below the savage evening sun, was a long shadow cast by a huge drystone wall. As a place to think and regroup, that'd do nicely.

I crossed and shoved Moose into the shade, sunk down in a heap and opened the shopping bag. After quickly throwing a bowl of food on the grass for Moose, I began scoffing down the sandwich I'd just bought.

A voice spoke from above. "Are you OK?"

I stopped, mid-swear, lifted my gaze away from the grass and saw a pair of feet about a foot from my face.

I glanced up and gulped. "Oh…fine," I bumbled as politely as I could.

"… Only I heard you as I drove past," he continued.

I groaned. "Yeh…sorry about that – rough day."

Moose hadn't noticed. He was still snorkelling down his food.

An open hand reached down. "I'm Tyronne," the owner said, in a surprisingly friendly tone.

"Chris…" I muttered, reaching up to accept the handshake.

"Is everything OK?" Another voice approached.

Yet more feet appeared…

Moose perked up, abandoned the empty bowl and began to circle the strangers.

"Chill out, Mooch. They're fine…"

Moose wound his way between the slenderest pair of feet and

53

began purring for attention as a woman huddled down and grabbed him in a gracious hug.

"I'm Kim," she said. Moose immediately planted a multitude of kisses all over her.

I'd usually tell him off, but I was too tired – and, besides which, Kim didn't seem to mind. I quickly explained our predicament, assuring them both that we'd be moving on as soon as the sun died down.

"Nonsense," said Kim. "You'll stay with us!"

"But…"

"This is our place," she quickly explained.

"… And you can camp up in our paddock for the night," Tyronne continued.

I looked beyond the wall, my eyes moving upwards towards the house towering above it.

I nearly wept in gratitude.

Beyond the wall was a beautifully restored period farmhouse, complete with stables and a lush garden of soft grass. I gazed around in wonder – I couldn't have wished for a better place to stay the night if I'd planned it. In the first paddock lay an open field of grass while, in the other, a magnificent horse ambled carelessly about in the evening sun.

I began chatting to my hosts, somewhat calmer (and incredibly relieved, I might add) after the unexpected rescue. Our fortunes had turned on their head. This was an idyllic setting.

I had a flashback to when I was a kid and used to go round to my dad's house. Above the door to the kitchen hung a series of plates. I remember one in particular that showed a garish, colourful picture of a boy and girl holding hands with the caption:

There are no strangers here
Only friends we haven't yet me!

I'd always hated that twee little sliver of porcelain – until now! Not to get mushy, but this situation felt exactly like the world as described by Dad's naff little decoration. I stood there gassing away to Tyronne until I felt a strange 'buzzing' in my hand from the retractable lead. Glancing down, I lifted my hand and stared without comprehension at the fluorescent strip whirling around in the holster. There was a suspicious lack of canine.

"*HORSIIIIEEEE...*"

I saw Moose shoot out of my periphery towards the horse in the paddock, with six inches of fluorescent lead flapping from his collar.

He'd only gone and chewed through the bloody thing!

The little...

I panicked. I ran.

"Moooose!"

"Oh, don't worry," Kim called back. "The horse won't be scared – he's used to barky dogs."

Moose pounded to the fence and started woofing away at the horse, who looked back in sheer disdain. "*Making quite the noise, aren't we?*" he boomed down to Moose.

Oh God! I thought, worried about my recent exposure to the sun. *I can hear horses, now, too.*

"Mooch – get away from there..." I urged, with little effect.

Tyronne caught up, laid a hand on my shoulder and said I really needn't worry. They knew someone from the local dogs' home who'd bring round reactive dogs to let them get used to other animals. To be fair, the look on the horse's face spoke volumes, while Moose carried on barking like a petulant child. I relaxed and got back to talking.

We chatted long into the night about our adventure, family, and the fortune that had allowed us to eventually meet.

From memory, I think it was just another Tuesday. In retrospect, it was possibly one of the more eventful ones I'd ever had in my life.

That thought aside, school nights were a long-distant memory for me, and I'd shamelessly kept both my hosts up long into the early hours. We talked about Tyronne's work and Kim's passion for horses while I prattled on about how my stupidity had led me on this madcap adventure. I settled into a feeling of comfort and safety for the first time in a long time, while this wonderful family welcomed us both into their safe haven.

That night, I unclipped the tattered end of the lead from Moose, grabbed the retractable handle and threw both outside in the grass. I'd have to figure out what to do about that in the morning. We snuggled in close together under our little Banshee tent – and I can honestly say that we had the best night's sleep since we'd set off.

The following morning I awoke, unzipped the tent and found the lead. It was lying in the grass – repaired with a series of expert knots and ties.

Tyronne's work, I thought as I clambered out on to the dewy grass.

Moose bolted out of the tent but returned moments later. *"Meh – horse isn't there."*

He muscled past me and slumped straight back into the sleeping bag.

"You're an idiot," I muttered, as he began snoring loudly in reply.

As the morning sunlight started drifting across the grass, Kim came outside holding a plate of beans, sausages and toast. I wolfed it down while Moose sat and looked on, giving me the evil eye.

I was offered the use of the shower and, after, we chatted until Tyronne and Kim had to leave for work. I lifted the pack, swapped embraces and promises to keep in touch, and walked through the gate with Moose. It's amazing what difference a day makes and – more importantly – the unexpected generosity of others. The sky was blue, the sun still low, and an entire wilderness waited for us beyond.

Chapter 4

Finding Our Stride

Cannington to Minehead

There's strange nostalgia when you're about to leave somewhere that's had a significant effect on your life. The best way I can describe it is like coming down to eat breakfast after a wedding and glancing over to the room where the party raged the evening before. Leaving Tyronne and Kim's place was kind of like that – well, it was for me at least. Moose and I left the Mexson home early that morning and crossed the road back up towards the coast. I paused to take one last glance back at the cottage, wondering if I'd ever see it or the occupants again.

Moose noticed the pause and gave me a glance. *"What's up?"*

"Oh, nothing..." I said, shaking off the impending melancholy. "I was just thinking about how nice they all were."

He sniffed. *"That's fine for you to say..."*

I raised an eyebrow.

He grunted before burying his nose deep in a tuft of grass. *"... Well, you ended up with a cooked breakfast, at least!"*

"You weren't starved, mate!" I retorted.

Moose turned and stared back, his big brown eyes fixing on my blue ones. Then, without blinking, he stood rigid, slowly raised his leg and took the longest pee known to man or dog, his eyes still boring into mine.

I stood there waiting patiently, looking back into his huge, glaring eyes. Try as he might, he was not going to beat me at *that* contest.

"Finished?"

Moose just snorted, turned away and hurled a few chunks of grass at me before prancing up the road towards the towpath.

So much for nostalgia, I thought to myself as I readjusted my pack to follow in his wake.

The rest of the morning was steady going.

The road slowly wound its way through small villages, which eventually ushered us back within sight of the River Parrett. By the time we got back to the shoreline, the sun had once again established its relentless beat above our heads – I couldn't believe it was only eleven o'clock in the morning and yet here we were, once again engulfed by an oppressively stifling heat.

Across the estuary, I could see the flat sea wall flanking the northern side of the river – but, today, the cows and sheep were nowhere in sight. On this side of the bank, the terrain had changed substantially and a mass of tall golden grass stretched out endlessly before us. What little wind there was drifted through the tall, thin stems as they swayed slovenly in reply to what was to be another blisteringly hot day!

In the distance, I could see strings of electricity pylons shimmer into view. They dotted the horizon, rising high above the fields sprawling into the distance, seemingly without end. They appeared to dance in the waves of heat, contorting my view to the horizon as they held the arid heat of the day, all the while taunting us in the stifling air, like menacing Titans casting down a threatening gaze.

Moose, for all his early-morning moodiness, had stopped sulking and was now merrily winding his way in and out of the seas of tufted straw, sniffing furiously as he went. Unburdened by a heavy pack or blistered feet, he raced through the stems, careless to the trials of the previous day. Every now and then he'd saunter up and demand water, before once again loping off to explore the wilderness hidden within the swaying straw.

I could feel the isolation of walking beginning to take its toll, playing tricks on me as I gazed upwards at the magnificent, electrified towers looming high above. My mind drifted to H G Wells and the daunting imagery of Tripods invading this stark and wild landscape. I couldn't help but turn up my ear to listen as they buzzed furiously in the early midday heat, their whispered '*Ullas*' a symphony to the sweltering cacophony of fire hitting down from high above.

Damn it was hot! I was going bloody delirious.

As the path turned up ahead, I saw a small wooden bench planted almost in isolation beside a solitary tourist sign.

Rest stop! I thought.

Despite its apparent size from a distance, it cast a blearily weak shadow barely enough to shelter just one of us. I saw an opportunity for us both to take five minutes' rest.

"Mooch!" I called.

A head emerged from the sea of gold several yards ahead. "*Wot?*"

"Don't you '*wot*' me," I shouted. "C'mere and get under the bench."

He stared to his left and right in bewilderment until he caught my gaze.

"*Now!*" I barked.

He sneezed and, in his lazy fashion that drove me crazy, began to saunter up to where I stood – stopping every now and then to take in a few fake sniffs at something he deemed far worthier of his attention than me.

"Are you still sulking?"

His eyes widened into a feigned innocence. *"About what?"*

I rolled my eyes. "Forget it. Go on – under the bench, pal."

Moose obliged and indignantly flopped into the shade before rolling with a groan back across the patch of grass and into the sunlight again.

Moron! I thought, as my eyes rolled even deeper.

"You're not getting it, bud!" I said, kneeling down and gently but firmly shoving his bulky arse back into the scant shade beneath the seat. "*... Under* the bench!"

Once he was settled, I straddled the bench and slumped down. I reached around and released the still-weighty pack from my shoulders, where it rolled freely with a thud to the other side of the ground to accompany Moose. Sitting up as straight as I could, I took off my hat and wiped away the torrent of sweat collecting on my brow before releasing another deep sigh. Beneath me, I could already hear gentle snoring noises from His Majesty. I slowly began working my shoulders in tentative rolls, back and forth against the clamminess of my sweat-soaked T-shirt to try to get some feeling back in my body.

Damn, it's hot, I thought. Again.

I sat for a few minutes, pondering the road ahead and worrying slightly about where we were going to stop for the night. I glanced upwards to my right, at the tourist sign a few metres away. It'd been bleached almost clean thanks to years of exposure to the British weather. I sighed deeply and mustered what strength I could to heave myself on to my feet and wander across to decipher the faded hieroglyphs baked into the laminate. Cocking my head to one side, I could just make out the faded silhouettes of local marshland birds alongside a description that read:

In summer, look out for little egret fishing in the lagoons or at the breach. Avocet, little ringed plover and lapwing have all bred in the first summers at Steart Marshes.

"So much for directions," I muttered.

Gasping in a stale breath, I wiped another bead of sweat from my forehead and glanced back to where Moose was snoring contentedly in the shade. Beyond it, I could see the stone path as it veered sharply inland to follow the line of pylons towards a landscape that gave way to murky pools of marshland and tall reeds. And then I spotted it! There, shimmering away in the distance, was a tall, bold path sign, complete with long directional wooden arrows.

"Sod it..." I shrugged. "A sign usually means something."

I pushed away from the faded inscription on the standing platform and slouched back towards Moose. Picking up my pack and garnering my remaining strength, I started down the path again. Sure enough, about an hour later we'd reached the sanctuary of the Steart Marshes visitor centre and, after a quick ten-minute chat with its staff, trudged a further twenty minutes towards the shoreline and the haven I'd been desperately seeking for the last few days.

This place was perfect! The land flattened out on to an oasis of tranquillity, graciously cooled by a breeze billowing from the Severn Estuary. The path before us stopped abruptly before a World War II pillbox with open sides. All around it lay the restful silence of a million possible camp spots spread across acres of soft, loamy sand and trampled mudflats.

Steart Marshes turned out to be just what Moose and I needed. We ended up staying there for two days before eventually succumbing to boredom – and a dwindling stock of food. We pushed back on to the path and down the shoreline to Hinkley Point power station – a hulking stain on the land if ever I saw one.

Its colossal, grey and uninspired mass squatted smack-bang in the middle of what had once been a gloriously unspoiled stretch of coastline. There it loomed, as a true testament as to how unimaginative industrial architecture can be, as is the case with many such edifices. Sandy beaches gave way to rattling, rusty gates and barriers adorned with twisted, forgotten barbed wire.

There were garish signs plastered everywhere, just to emphasise the foreboding nature of the structure they were intended to protect:

Keep Out!

And...

Trespassers will be prosecuted!

I glared up at the huge bulk that dominated the immediate view as it stared back down from above, a staring contest I had no inclination to participate in.

"Stay close, Mooch," I muttered in spite of myself. The fact that he was clipped and leashed meant he needed no such reassurance, but it was clear that Moose liked this place even less than I did.

As the day passed, we made our way around Hinkley and came upon a series of pretty lanes leading back to villages, all of which were at risk of one day being swallowed up by the ever-expanding mass of towers in the distance. At Stogursey we found a B&B – and the first shower I'd had since leaving the Mexson farmhouse. Moose did his usual thing and gunned straight for the bed, where he quickly collapsed and began snoring his box off.

The gentle soundtrack of doggy snuffling from the other room set the mood as I went about the business of bathing and washing clothes in the tiny en-suite sink. I peeled off my trainers and socks to set about the business of repairing my feet. The older blisters were hardening nicely –

only to be replaced by new ones. I gently massaged my feet in an attempt to ease a growing ache that had developed in both heels. This new, dull ache throbbed continually and made the pain of blisters pale in comparison. I began second-guessing my choice of footwear, conceding that I'd have to invest in some proper walking boots at the next opportunity. I sat back into the soft bedding and closed my eyes. Nothing could compare to the shelter of a real room – *that* very room – the first we'd had since Weston-super-Mare. The air con hummed contentedly as we dozed. Beyond the window, the summer of 2018 was raging on as Moose and I chilled, quite literally, in opulent surroundings.

It was only the 9th of July, just eleven days into our trek, but I was beginning to feel more comfortable with life on the road. The following morning I strapped on my trainers, dragged Moose downstairs and ordered two full breakfasts.

"Sausages this morning, bud!" I said, cheerfully.

Moose wasn't even breathing as he scoffed the entire banquet laid beneath his nose. I began to tuck in myself – until a moment later when a head poked its way up between my knees. *"Any left?"*

"You cheeky bugger – you've just had yours!" I said, chomping eagerly on a hash brown.

"M'ungry..." he said, with pleading eyes and slobbering chops.

"Pfft – who you trying to kid."

"Still 'ungry..." Moose insisted.

"Well...you should learn to savour your food, then, mate." I stared right back and, in the most deliberate manner, stuffed a full rasher of bacon into my mouth before feigning as much enjoyment as possible.

He wound his way beneath my feet with a disgruntled huff. *"Fine – but the next chance I get, I'm calling the RSPCA to dob you in for neglect..."*

I coughed at the comment, nearly showering the table with half chewed bacon.

*

We packed up and left early.

Until now, my idea of coastal walking had been confined to flat sandy beaches. As we headed up towards Watchet, however, the coast began to reward us with new backdrops. The shoreline peeled away from sea level, rising through layers of ancient rock to peak high above us in a lovely array of cliffs and singular waterfalls. Sometimes grey, sometimes a brick red typical to that region of Somerset, the jagged cliff surfaces displayed the sedimented layers of the earth's buried history for all to see.

Moose darted off and indulged in his favourite game of 'Bite the Water', as it streamed down in torrents all along a cliff edge. At one point, the silly bugger tried to scale an immense mudflat and fell, flat as the mud, on his arse – something I found highly amusing. What had escaped me up until then was the fact that Moose had never really encountered the sea… I looked on in amusement as to how he'd take to it.

I expected him to run headlong into it and find his inner mermaid, but, instead, he screeched to a halt inches before the roiling waves and tentatively backed off. I stood there laughing at his timid reaction. "You bloody coward!" I jeered.

Moose glared and instantly tried to reassert his bravery by charging back into the sea. Again, he instantly retreated…

"*It's cold,*" he whined, backing away from the surf as quickly as his paws could take him.

"How would you know?" I said, sauntering past. "You didn't even get your paws wet!"

Moose just stood there and glowered.

We walked further up until the cliffs corralled us into a niche that broke into a magnificent waterfall. On hearing the sound, Moose once again broke off into a run so he could play in the tumbling fall. Nearby, some children saw the antics and decided to join in with Moose's play. Mum and Dad were perched on the rocks not far away and, once again, I was asked what I was doing with such a daft dog while carrying such a massive load. 'Walking the coast' was an easier sell this time, especially with Portishead so far behind, although I didn't have the heart to elaborate on our story too much in this heat. They looked at Moose, who was behaving like a lunatic, gathered up their kids and wandered off, wishing us well as they went.

That afternoon we entered Watchet and quickly found a shaded seat in the middle of the high street belonging to one of the side-street cafés. Tourists bustled here and there between the shamble of seaside shops and stalls. The place wasn't as busy as could be expected on a sunny day like this – so I could only assume it was a weekday. After nearly two weeks on the road, I was already starting to lose track of things like that. I glanced around so as to ask a passer-by what day it was, but quickly dismissed the idea – I didn't really care anyway. Moose was curled up with his head resting on my foot, his chest puffing rapidly in and out as he half-dozed there.

Out of the corner of my eye, I noticed a slender figure weaving his way through the tables towards us.

"Hi," he said, in a slightly bored tone.

I glanced up. A young lad dressed in dreadful shorts and a pinny breathed at me from above. "My name's Mark. Can I get you anything?"

Moose stuck his huge head out from under the table. Mark took two involuntary steps backwards.

"Don't worry." I smiled reassuringly. "He won't eat you."

Mark didn't look convinced.

"A tea, please."

Mark scurried off without even asking if I wanted anything else.

Two minutes later, a tray slid on to my table and I glanced by only to see Mark, in his pale shorts and wrap-around apron, scurry away before Moose had a chance to add anything to the conversation.

"What's his problem?"

"You stink," I said absently, relaxing back into my chair.

The tea was pale and weak. Far too much milk in it to make it worthy of the title 'tea'. I sipped half of it down before paying up and saddling my enormous pack to set off once more.

We marched down the harbour side and emerged on to a grassy verge that held the remnants of an old Saxon fort. The land that lay beyond was sloped and flat – the sort of place that would attract early-morning dogs and their walkers. I looked behind at the kissing gate we'd just entered, noticing a sign that could only be read from the common-side of the entrance.

> ## 'Welcome to Daw's Castle'

I looked deep into the heather opposite where the castle stood and could only make out the random arrangement of a few ancient stones. Floods of Greek myths filled my head while I set about looking for a good spot for the night.

Well, here's as good a place as any... I thought.

Within minutes, the tent was up and a cheap noodle stew was on the boil. I shuffled around inside the rucksack to retrieve whatever version of dog food I had and dutifully served up Moose's dinner. As the sun set over the ridge of bushes that hid us from the shoreline far below, summer insects darted furiously in and out, nibbling on faces and paws until we were both thoroughly irritated. We crawled inside the stuffy confines of the canvas and gave up for the night.

At sometime the morning after, I woke with a start. Moose, deep in some random dream, had kicked me in the ribs before shuffling his way to the bottom of the tent. I groaned, trying to make myself more comfortable.

"It's a two-man tent!" I moaned, half asleep.

"*Snrff-gggr— sn-ff...rrr.*"

I shuffled back and, immediately, my ribs were hit by another sharp dig from a paw as Moose rearranged himself again.

"*Fine!*" I grunted, unzipping my side of the tent so I could let some air in.

Sticking my head out, I gasped at the cool air drifting through the dawn mists.

The heels of my feet still ached despite the scant night's rest I'd had. I decided that a walk in the dewy grass might do them some good. Pacing back and forth and squeezing my toes as I walked, I managed to slowly begin to dissipate the ache – although the thought of putting on those godawful trainers again filled me with dread. Sleeping, I'd realised, had tremendous regenerative effects when it came to the aches in my shoulders and legs. *This* thing buried deep in the heels of my feet, though, wasn't going anywhere.

I dismissed the thought and set about the task of getting breakfast ready, packing up and leaving town. A '*rosy-fingered dawn*' hadn't yet threatened the day, so we scurried off before we gave her the opportunity to roast our scalps off. Before long, we were buried deep in woodland, where the absence of sun gave way to flurries of insects making the air before us sing with their buzzing. I looked behind at Moose, who began chomping on the droning mist as if gifted with helpings of a second breakfast. I sighed and wrapped my snood tightly around my mouth before panting onwards through the trees.

To be honest, after spending so long on exposed, sandy beaches, it was nice to be somewhere sheltered. There was a slight breeze coming in through the hedge and I could see that the woods were thinning out. Moose and I vaulted a stile and the ground broke way on to pavement that graded downwards to the village of Blue Anchor. The place was deserted save for a camper van parked in a layby next to the public toilets. As we walked by, I nodded to a rather dishevelled-looking chap who was trawling water from the bib tap back up the slope to his van.

"Morning!" I chirped, cheerfully.

He glanced up slightly, nodded and toiled on about his business.

Ten minutes later, the road fell away to our right and Blue Anchor became just another lost town fading into the distance.

There was one important aspect I'd planned for this trip that we'd not had the nerve or opportunity to try out: foraging.

As we hit the sand dunes on the run-up to Minehead, I glanced down and saw my first opportunity. Some late-night revellers had been sitting in a sandy nook and had no doubt been either too tired, preoccupied or drunk to move their stash of goodies…and so there it lay! Almost as though just waiting for intrepid adventurers such as Moose and me to come along and harvest the bounty. Moose rushed ahead and beat me to it, shoving his nose deep into the bag before dumping about a half-litre of urine all over it.

"Ah – ya little shite-bag!" I exclaimed.

He glanced up, looking somewhat bewildered. *"Uh…"*

"There might've been something good in that!"

Moose looked back down at the sopping mess. *"Oops…you might be able to shake it off."* He shrugged.

I shuddered at the thought, glancing around to see if there was a bin nearby that I could drop the entire thing in. So much for living off the land.

Once I'd disposed of the soggy bag, I clambered back up the dunes. Just short of the summit, my foot caught a tuft of weed – I stumbled arse-first, tripped on a rock and was dragged down the incline by the weight of the pack. Scrambling desperately, I dimly remember a savage tearing noise as I gracelessly descended the dune in an increasingly wild knot of arms, legs and straps. On landing, I untangled the pack and was immediately standing bolt upright searching for ruptured spleens and broken bones.

Phew! I thought.

Moose sauntered past on all fours. *"Enjoy your trip?"*

"Ha-ha! Very funny." I muttered, patting the sand off my clothes.

He stopped and looked back as if noticing something I hadn't. *"So, I have to ask…"*

Still shaking the sand from my clothes, I narrowed my eyes.

"…is the new hole in your trousers there for ventilation?"

I patted around my backside and came across the offending tear: a tremendous rip down the inside leg of my combats.

"Perfect!" I swore. It wasn't even ten o'clock and today was shaping up nicely.

Those had been my last pair.

We set off across a golf course that led to the bustling heart of Minehead. Unlike others we'd passed, Minehead was home to Butlins – a thriving holiday destination. Even this early, the place was teeming with families and kids on school trips. I sheepishly grabbed the 'flap' of my trouser leg as closely to my arse cheek as I could and shuffled off to the nearest clothes shop.

There's a logistical issue when you're lugging a twenty-five-kilo pack and a mastiff cross around. Walking into a bigger store is something akin to shopping on the moon. It may as well be that far away for all the chance I have of going there. Fortunately, there was a twee little shop on the front that had shorts hung outside on a rail. I grabbed one pair and tried them on in the time-honoured fashion of men the world over: by holding the elasticated band across my waist.

"They'll do," I muttered.

I shouted in through the open door, got the attention of the owner and managed to pay with what little cash I had left on me. Continuing the little butt-clench-shuffle until reaching the public loos, I quickly changed into my new electric blue nylon holiday shorts. I came back out to Moose, who sat with his tail swishing and an amused grin plastered across his face.

"Not one bloody word!" I warned.

He sniggered and skipped off to hide his laughter around the back of a nearby tree.

At the end of Minehead promenade, there's a grand metal sculpture of an unfolding map that marks the start of England's longest coastal route, the South West Coast Path. The path stretches 630 miles from where we were in Minehead all around the Cornish peninsula and across the south coast to Poole in Dorset. I felt a skip inside…this was the first real challenge we'd encounter, and it was one that would take us to all the places I'd really been looking forward to on this trip.

"Ready, Mooch?"

He looked up at me…then at the sculpture…then back at me…

You can guess the rest.

Chapter 5

The South West Coast Path

Minehead to Watermouth (Exmoor National Park)

We left Moose's trademark trickle behind and headed out of the bustle. It was getting hotter and busier; I felt ever more ridiculous in my electric blue 'dad' shorts. On the outskirts of town, I found a nice secluded spot and threw up the tent even though it was still only early afternoon. No one would notice, let alone care, about some random bloke and his dog. The new shorts dug in high around my inner thighs... I'd also begun to notice a persistent thudding in the heels of my feet. I de-trainered and stretched out with Moose for a snooze in the shade of a nearby bush.

"What do you fancy for dinner?" I yawned.

"Pedigree Chum and that other godawful crap you bought the other day!" came the sarcastic reply. I couldn't argue. Our diet was becoming boring – even I was beginning to tire of noodles and tinned fish. I began to feel guilty about the steady diet of dry-mix and cheap dog food he was being exposed to every mealtime.

"I promise, mate," I said, tussling behind his ears, "something better tomorrow!"

*

On my dad-shorts-jaunt, I'd also managed to pick up a couple of charging packs for my phone. Until now I'd been lucky in that I usually found a café or pub that'd been kind enough to let me plug in and charge up without much fuss or bribery. The only snag was that we'd have to hang around for a few hours while my phone charged up.

I sat there on the grass unwrapping my new toys, trying to figure out how they worked – and, indeed, if they'd be any good. I was carrying far too much weight anyway; what difference would a couple of extra chargers make? I delved into the instructions until a 'slap' of tail caught me squarely in the face.

"*C'mon, dude... I'm bored!*"

I rubbed my cheek. "That hurt!"

I began to massage away at my stinging skin and unclipped his panniers off the back of my pack. He started prancing away enthusiastically on the grass. "*Play!!!*"

"Na-ah," I said. "It's way too hot and I'm way too tired." In an effort to placate his mood, I fished out a handful of gravy bones and threw them into the grass before packing away the chargers, perching my hat on my face and nodding off once again.

The day after, we encountered our first hill. And, by 'hill', I mean 'horrifying mountain of death'. I trudged up the little steps cut into the grade, panting under the weight of my pack. Glancing up towards the top, which was hidden by the ridge of the tier above us, I sunk inside, wondering just how many others were above it.

We continued our climb until it eventually plateaued into a rolling plain of moorland, filled with stubborn spiny gorse and glittering with an array of red, yellow and purple flowers. Worn tracks weaved among the flowers and, every now and then, up popped ankle-high way-markers, each adorned with the simple sigil of an acorn. I was absolutely exhausted…so much so that the vibrant display of colour hurt my eyes. In a clearing, I muscled off the pack, grabbed a mouthful of water and fell into a heap on the ground. As I lay there staring at the clear blue above, a tangle of legs and fur pounced across me as Moose raced off to my left, frantically trying to catch a wasp.

"You'll regret that…" I groaned, barely able to lift my head.

He ignored me and continued vaulting between the bushes after the buzzing insect.

Sitting up, legs out in front, I planted my hands in the ground behind me. To my right lay the path from which we'd just come and beyond that was a sharp drop down to the sea. At this point, I couldn't see much ahead except for the spotting of wildflowers, although I knew that North Devon waited beyond. I stood and found a vantage point by which I could see the immense stretch of headlands over which we'd already traversed. In the misty distance, I could just make out Brean Down and, somewhat closer, Hinkley. After today, these landmarks and all they represented for us would be forever lost behind – as would the county of Somerset.

"Ah, ya soft sod…" I muttered to myself, dismissing the pang of melancholy before it rose.

"*What you looking at?*"

I glanced down at Moose, his tail slicing back and forth through the air.

"Oh, nothing…" I muttered. "Did you get the wasp?"

"*Nope – but I will next time!*" he chirped, tongue lolling to one side.

"You're in for a nasty shock," I promised.

"*Meh – yellow things usually taste nice.*" And with that he turned, slapping me in the leg with his tail, before bouncing back up the path.

Ah, the vigour of youth (and four legs)!

*

An hour or so later, we crested the last rise.

We were met by one of the most stunning sights I have ever seen.

North Devon lay in glorious splendour before us. A mass of lushly forested peaks flowed to the horizon while, off to the right, the coastline tore away and raced into the distance. Large and languorous hillsides boasting vast swathes of green rolled across the landscape, stopping abruptly at rugged cliff edges to meet the sea as it glittered gently in the searing sun.

Quite simply, it took my breath away.

Even Moose seemed to appreciate the sheer vastness of Exmoor National Park, tearing past me and delving deep into the brush that lined both sides of the path. The toil of the morning was absolutely worth the effort as we both marched onwards into this incredible place.

And then, as surely as it went up...the path took a steep dive along the hillside. The uneven ground and killing weight of the pack took their toll on my knees with each step. I was almost tempted to just unsling the damned thing, chuck it down the steep verge and accept my losses to whatever damage might be caused. Then I remembered the stove and my tent poles and decided better of it. As with the trek up, once we finally got to the bottom, I was absolutely exhausted.

In the valley close to the woods, we noticed things getting busier, with the odd hiker passing us on the track. We forded a small brook and entered a little National Trust place called Bossington. The car park was lined with brick-built barbeques and a little toilet block nestled under some trees near the entrance. Off to one side lay a neat picnic area set out on a field of finely manicured grass complete with wooden bench-tables.

"Are we staying here tonight?" Moose ventured.

I threw my pack off into the grass. "You bet your arse we are."

I'd learned to take certain liberties where my backpack was concerned, especially in places like this. I'd noticed signs to a town on the way in but didn't fancy traipsing there and back carrying that thing around. I tethered the weighty lump to a tree and tied my charity flag to it, hoping that would be enough to ward off any potential opportunists. Why anyone would want a bag filled with dirty laundry, smelly waterproofs and dog food was beyond me. Besides which, best of luck to them if they could cart the dammed thing off!

I realised that I was taking a bit of a punt going into town. I didn't even know if there'd be a shop there, but it was still early enough to take the risk. Sure enough, tucked away between a terrace of quaint, crooked buildings was a nice little local shop. I nipped in, grabbed some goodies and headed back to Bossington.

The place was deserted when we returned and, thankfully, my bag was still tied securely to the tree. I unclipped Moose and he skipped off, nose twitching as he charged head-first into a cluster of nettles. True to my word, I'd decided to give us both a rest from the cardboard that usually constituted dinner and, instead, served up generous helpings of sausages, beans and mash. Moose drank water, I had wine and there we both sat for the remainder of the evening, soaking up the beauty of this lovely place.

That night, I tossed restlessly in my sleep. I dreamt of climbing endless flights of crooked steps while carrying an elephant on my back. I could hear Moose's voice taunting me as I heaved while, all around, the air was filled with violent buzzes from wasps the size of small birds.

My nose twitched and I woke instantly, sat bolt upright, scraping my head on the nylon roof of the tent, as a noxious poison flooded the tiny space where we slept.

I gagged!

Moose shuffled slightly, snoring gently in the stillness.

And then it came again…a gentle '*wheezing*' noise as he polluted the confined air once more. I tore at the zip and lunged out of the tent, gasping for fresh air.

"*Close the door.*" Moose groaned.

I sat trying to catch my breath as a thin green vapour drifted out of the door flap.

"What the hell have you been eating?"

A sleepy head popped out, licked its lips and yawned. "*...Beans were nice tonight.*"

He let out another wheeze.

"Not *in* the tent!" I cried.

He stood and pulled himself halfway out, dragging the sleeping bag with him on to the dewy grass. He shook and trotted off in the darkness to wee against some unoffending bush. I opened the tent flaps, held my breath and began trying to shake out the toxic stench.

"Are you going to be doing that all night?" I called after him.

"*Nope – think I'm done now.*"

I raised an eyebrow.

"*Honest!*" he said, clambering back into the tent.

I tentatively followed suit, snuggled up and began dozing off into my weird world of sparrow-sized wasps and elephants...

'*Wheeze!*'

I woke once again to a painful ache shooting up the lengths of my heels. Rolling over and crawling out on to the grass, I could see that it was just getting light.

The sheer beauty of this place caught me again.

I got to my feet gently and began limping across the field, trying to work the stiffness out of my limbs. Back in the tent, I could hear Moose roaring in his sleep – boy, could that lad snore! Fortunately, we'd polished off the last of the beans the night before and were back on our standard fare of cardboard food for breakfast.

I packed, he peed and we left before the sun could obliterate the shadows littering the valley.

It took us about half an hour to get back to the coast. We marched past two huge lime kilns – relics from a bygone time when Porlock Weir still had a thriving industry. The coast here was flat and vast pools of water collected here and there, giving it a marsh-like quality. Weaving in and out, we turned towards a strait and, up ahead, a gathering of people were busy loading boxes and rolls of tarpaulin on to a trailer. I clipped Moose on to my waist and approached, expecting to be turned away – it had *that* kind of official feel about it.

In the forefront, a woman noticed our approach and stopped what she was doing.

"Hi," she greeted us.

I paused and gathered Moose in close. For all his friendly demeanour, he could get a bit 'woofy' when encountering strangers. The woman marched boldly forwards.

"Hi…" I returned. "… Are we allowed to come through?"

"Oh sure – we're just packing up filming."

Well, *that* piqued my interest. "Oh," I said casually, "filming what?"

"A drama for Sky Atlantic."

PleasebeGameofThronespleasebeGameofThronespleasebeGameof Thrones.

"… It's called *Britannia* – ever watched it?"

My heart sank slightly. I'd never heard of it. "Sorry." I shrugged. "I don't watch much TV."

"Oh, well," she said, "we're just pulling down the location set."

Moose was tugging furiously at his short lead, excited for the attention to be back on him. She looked down, remarkably unshaken by his show of excitement. I gave her a pleading look of apology.

"Oh don't mind, you can let him off." She smiled. "I have mastiffs at home."

Fair enough, I thought and unclipped the lead. Moose shot away, tail raging furiously as he ran and dived at the woman. To her credit, she hunkered to her knees and began patting her legs.

"Here, boy…aren't you beautiful!"

This was the first woman we'd come across in days and Moose was stealing all the attention!

After a brief greeting, we stood there chatting about the various things we were up to. Moose larked around, pulling out every last 'cute dog' trick, desperate for more attention.

She looked over at the guys carrying boxes and called out: "Mike?"

A head turned.

"… Would you mind taking a couple of photos of us?"

Mike dumped the two heavy boxes on the ground and walked over. "Sure!"

We huddled together near a fence, trying desperately to smile together while getting Moose to sit with us.

"Sit still, you little bugger," I said, as he barked at the camera. "Sorry…he gets a bit giddy."

Mike stood still, snapping away until he was satisfied we had a good shot.

Once done, we said our farewells and I dragged Moose past the crew, following the line of the fence until they were all out of sight. Ahead, we entered fields dotted with hundreds of props. I have to say the entire set-up was very convincing. Stands of faux-dried-skins and straw huts lined our way, giving the place a truly medieval feel. Minutes later, we were back on the path and winding our way upwards into Exmoor.

As welcoming as the view had been, walking through it was something else entirely.

Immediately, we hit sharp inclines that seemed to go on forever. Each time we emerged, panting, atop a peak, the path twisted and dived right back down into similarly severe descents. Sharp stones buried deep in the path dug through the soles of my trainers and into all the soft spots of my feet.

I'd known today would be tough but *this* was something else. Across my back, between my shoulders and deep, deep into my knees and feet, thudding aches began to develop.

Up and down, up and down, up and down. This went on relentlessly, seemingly going nowhere. I began grimacing with every step. The palms of my hands were raw from bracing falls, trips and stumbles as I clawed my way onwards through forest and brush.

It was by far the longest and hardest stretch we'd traipsed so far. Leaning heavily on my walking pole, I despaired more with every stony step. The pounding of my feet against the rocks sent shocks racing to my core, yet I had no choice but to clamber on. No longer conscious of any destination, I staggered towards a goal I no longer thought, or even cared, about.

It was twilight before we reached a high plateau where below us in the distance lay the twin villages of Lynmouth and Lynton. They were miles away and I was almost in tears from the pain and frustration of it all. God, I needed to rest!

Moose looked up, his eyes creased with concern. *"Are you OK?"*

I threw him a pitiful glance.

"C'mon," he urged, *"not far, now!"*

Lynmouth, which was the lower of the two towns, lay in a deep recess next to the sea. That would be our stop but I'd no idea as to how we were going to manage to reach it tonight.

"I can't make it, bud," I whimpered, pain throbbing everywhere.

"I'll help!" he said excitedly, skipping away in front.

I couldn't help but smile. Moose halted high above the next ridge and began barking furiously: *"I found it – I found it – I found it!"*

I inched my way up, step by tentative step and, sure enough, there to the side of the road at the top of the hill was an inn. I fell to my knees, released the pack and grabbed him in a bear hug. "Cheers, mate," I whispered as he gently licked my ear.

It was only a breath away. I just needed to make it there…

*

The Blue Ball Inn edged the tiny village of Countisbury, which sits on a high peak, about a mile or two preceding the descent into Lynmouth. We crawled through the churchyard and into the car park out front. I dumped the pack on a bench and limped to the reception desk.

"Please tell me you're dog-friendly?" I whimpered.

"Of course we are!" came the bright reply from the woman behind reception.

"Do you have any rooms for tonight?"

She shuffled behind the counter, grabbed the guest book and began leafing through. "I'm sorry but we're full…" she started.

I almost collapsed on the floor in despair.

"…but I'll see if there are any places in town that are free," she continued quickly.

I must've looked a pathetic sight. "Would you?"

Five minutes later, she was back at the desk, proudly announcing that the Bath Hotel in Lynmouth had rooms and was dog-friendly. 'Thanks' wasn't a strong enough word for it. I dragged my arse from the waiting area and out the door, ready to leave.

"Would you like me to run you down there?" she called from behind.

Barely conscious of my luck, I just nodded limply.

Ten minutes later, we were racing down the road to Lynmouth. Outside the hotel, I collapsed out of the car. I blubbered my thanks, grabbed my pack, walking pole and dog, and staggered inside. After a quick faff in reception, we were ushered into a room where I collapsed hard on to the bed, grabbed Moose tight against me and then slowly, and literally, cried myself to sleep.

'Plantar fasciitis' was a term I'd not learn until much later on. Writing this now, I can unabashedly state that it's pain unlike any other.

Only, I didn't know this at the time. We'd have made it all the way to Dorset before I figured out that little quandary, so a world of pain awaited between here and there. I awoke in the darkness, peeled off my shoes and clothes, and quickly wrapped myself up in the cool cotton sheets. I fell back into a restless sleep.

We'd paid 120 quid for the room but I'd barely even noticed. In the morning, we emerged slowly into consciousness and I gently tested my ruined feet against the plush carpet.

"Sorry about last night..." I said, scratching Moose behind his sleepy ears.

"S'alright..." He yawned. "M'ungry though."

I braced myself and, rather guiltily, got up to limp across the room and feed him a meal of stale biscuits and chum. I staggered back into the bedroom after my morning ablutions, crawled on the bed and collapsed back into an unconscious heap.

Lynton is connected to lower Lynmouth by a water tram that regularly runs up and down a cliff line separating the twin villages. The alternative was to scramble up a steep stairway comprising hundreds of steps cut deep into the hillside.

After yesterday, no way I was doing that! I opted for the tram.

Moose was in fine form that morning and quickly won over the affection of the tram engineers, swinging us free passage to the top. I thanked them on my way out, quickly ushering Moose past the café and down into the town itself.

This place was gorgeous, I had to say. Even in my state, I could appreciate the rustic array of crooked buildings and shops that had sprung up in this picturesque setting. Nestled in among all of this was an outdoors store – and, by that, I mean a real bona fide hiking shop. I leant inside and asked if they had any decent boots for sale.

"Oh don't worry – you can bring in the dog."

Christmas! I thought.

We muscled our way inside and, after several minutes of boot talk, I emerged with £280's worth of the highest-quality footwear available.

This'll do the trick, I thought as we limped back down towards Lynmouth and the green at the mouth of the harbour. I decided against cardboard and treated us both to proper seaside fish and chips.

The next morning, we set off again – I simply couldn't justify another expensive night in a hotel. As the day passed, I alternated between trainer and boot, depending on how each fared with the terrain. It's worth bearing in mind that I still didn't know what the bloody hell was going on with my feet but this method saw me through for the foreseeable.

The path was steady and flat, albeit cut precariously into the side of a narrow edge across the side of the hilltop. Accompanied by stunning views out to sea, we walked along the severe path. Eventually, as it did the day before, the terrain began to punish us with the harsh peaks and troughs of Exmoor. After miles of coast, we were eventually ejected on to the side of a road. We sheltered under a bus stop for a while, taking in water and a moment of rest before continuing.

The stop did us little good for no sooner had we begun tramping our way upwards than we were once more met by sharp descents along pavements flanked with streaming traffic. The sun burned all day as we made our way up and down, hugging trees and bushes for shade as we moved.

I hurled expletives at every pitch and grade; clearly, I was beginning to resent Devon's famous contours. Moose paused for water frequently and I could tell that even his spirit was beginning to be affected by the coarse and tough monotony of the warm, smooth tarmac. It was a little past two and I was done! I looked at Moose and knew he felt it, too. He grumbled continually but I reassured him that rest lay waiting just around the next corner.

Panting, we eventually breached a clearing – to be met by a scene right out of a brochure.

From high above, we looked down on to Broadside Beach. The bay comprised sharp cliffs and pools interspersed with rocky outcroppings and a wide beach of golden yellow sands sweeping around in a tight arc. It was an exquisite sight.

I looked along to a makeshift sign that was perched on the side of a fence:

Passing Trekker – £8
Ask at Reception for details.

"Thank God for that..." I sighed.

Moose perked up instantly and began tugging on his lead. *"Can we, can we, can we?"*

We most certainly could! I thought, trying to get sight of the office.

We plunged down through the tiered site and out into a mass of caravans, motorhomes and canvas. Upon our arrival, I explained what we were doing and we were immediately offered bacon sandwiches and the promise of free camping wherever we wanted. I graciously accepted and stuffed a meaty roll in my mouth while the owner taunted Moose with other juicy morsels from the barbeque. Once paws and kisses were exchanged, we drifted off and I began looking for a good out-of-the-way pitch for the night.

And a shower!

Watermouth Valley Camp Site was a perfect retreat. Its idyllic setting not only provided us with rest but also a place to chat with other campers. As we settled down and cooked supper on the stove, a couple who were camped opposite came over and introduced themselves. We began chatting and shared beer and stories, the evening wearing on in the summer heat. As the sun set, we said our goodbyes and settled down for the night. Moose, contented with his lot, fell fast asleep – with me not far behind.

We woke the following morning and poked our heads out of the tent just in time to catch waving hands driving off the pitch where we'd all sat the night before, the couple and their VW camper trundling off the site and into the distance.

I looked down at Moose. "Well… I suppose we'd better get cracking!"

Chapter 6

The First Interview...
and Back Again!

Watermouth to Appledore

North Devon was proving to be tricky; I'd somehow underestimated this place.

It was only a couple of days after coming through Exmoor that we bumped into a local who mentioned in passing that we'd just walked the highest cliff peaks in England.

I felt that – or, at least, my feet did!

I'd been sporting my electric blue shorts the entire time since Minehead's little trouser mishap. Keen to be rid of them, I'd called Anya again and asked her to grab me some shorts and lightweights and send them on to a post office in Ilfracombe. I was looking forward to today.

I shoved my driving licence under the partition at Ilfracombe Post Office. "I have a 'care of' package waiting for me."

A rather peevish-looking woman glared back at me through the glass. "You're not allowed to do that..."

The comment caught me off guard. "Do what?" I asked, somewhat confused.

"… Send things to the Post Office."

I shuffled, unsure how to respond. "Err – is it here, then?"

She pulled her glasses off slowly and began cleaning the lenses with her blouse. "It is. But it's against Post Office policy."

I took a breath. "Sorry about that," I muttered, "…could I still have it, though?"

She huffed, planted the frames back on her face and slovenly got up to retrieve my parcel. Another voice emerged from out of view behind the counter and asked, "Is this the guy?"

"Yes – and I've told him he's not allowed to do that."

I was beginning to lose patience.

A lady in her fifties came out and began instructing me at length on Post Office policy.

"I'm sorry," I began, "but it really is an emergency."

That plus the fact that the people at the other post office didn't mention this wasn't allowed when the package was dropped in for delivery! I thought.

She threw a slip of paper at me from under the glass. "Sign here!"

I scribbled, grabbed my package and quickly left.

Moose was waiting patiently by the door. *"What was all that about?"*

I didn't reply as I stormed off in a huff. The entire encounter had put a dampener on Ilfracombe, and I wanted out of that place as quickly as I could so I could shed my dad-shorts and get into something more comfortable.

Out on the headland, I found a nice little nook to get changed. Knowing my luck, a troupe of school kids could bounce around the corner at any moment! A grubby bloke in his forties, half-naked in the scorching sun, with dog and camping gear in tow was a situation that I felt altogether too uncomfortable having to explain to the local police.

I stashed the rest of my little care package and continued onwards.

*

86

The terrain was still rolling but nowhere near as bad as it had been. Looking up, I whispered a prayer of small thanks and strode on.

We began to relax into a steady pace as the sea glistened off to our right and an impressive vista of valleys and bold crags fell away into the openness before us. We cleared the lighthouse at Bull Point, where I unclipped Moose and he gleefully bounded off into the distance, rolling among the ferns and heather casually gracing the sides of the valley.

Bloody lunatic, I thought, my spirits beginning to lift as we wandered on through the beauty of North Devon.

At Lee, we were given one last taste of just how unrelenting Devon could be; the path gave way to a single-track road and possibly the longest and steepest incline we'd encountered so far. The village lay at the bottom of a narrow valley next to the sea. After perhaps 500 yards of town, we were presented with a winding narrow stretch of black tarmac…back up what could only be described as a cliff face!

I was pouring with sweat and tears as this winding little road heaved ever upwards. At one point, feeling pretty close to passing out, I paused to grab some water. A lovely older woman popped her head out from one of the houses flanking the road.

"Ooo – it's a bit of hill, isn't it?" she commented lightly.

I could barely focus.

"… But that's Devon for you!" she chirped on.

I grunted as politely as I could, fighting for breath in the heat.

Moose stood panting and threw an evil look her way. *"She kidding, right? I'm bloody knackered!"*

"Be polite," I muttered. I turned, now facing the lady as she stood there in a brightly coloured woven beret.

"It's really taking its toll…" I replied. "These hills are a bit hard to climb."

Moose raised an eyebrow and slumped to the floor. *"A BIT???"*

I tried to focus on her thin frame. "I never thought it would be this bad, to be honest."

"Well, if you choose to walk Devon…" she started.

Moose looked up. *"Do you want to bite her or should I?"*

Thankfully, things settled down a bit after that. For the most part, we were now walking coastal trails in earnest. It was challenging terrain but nothing too extreme. In a small village, we stocked up on food and water and I met a fellow dog walker where we exchanged pleasantries while Moose and 'the Fluff' tried to kill each other from the ends of their respective leads.

Not only were we now on ground similar to what I'd imagined before setting off, but the air wasn't sucking every last inch of breath out of our lungs. We met other walkers for a quick chat along the way, before continuing on down the coast. Overhead, the sun finally began to relent, and for the first time I could remember since starting, a cool breeze accompanied us as we walked through gentle up-and-downs of an idyllic coastal path.

This was bliss!

As walking became less exertive, I began to wander about this new lifestyle I found myself living in with Moose. There was an incredible sense of freedom tempered only by the slightest streak of loneliness. That said, and as strange as it seemed to me, word was beginning to spread about our little 'Waggy Walk' and I'd begun accumulating a grand little following on our Facebook page. As solitary as I sometimes felt, we frequently encountered people who had come out to see us after they'd stumbled across our social media pages. It floored me that people were *actually* interested in what Moose and I were up to – as misguided an attempt to hike the coast of Britain as our adventure was. One such person – a person I'd never met – got in touch with me with an offer of respite when we got to Appledore. Her name was Sian.

PING

I looked down at the message on my phone.

> North Devon gazette wants to chat with you. Can I give your
> number so you can sort timings etc? What is your number if
> you're ok with my having it 😊

Butterflies! I quickly tapped out a message back with my number.

> That'd be awesome.

PING

> Grand! I'll call my contact from the gazette now. Also a local
> reporter... 😊

I'd never even met this woman and here she was, setting us up for a bit
of local stardom. I slumped down on the grass and re-read the messages,
hardly believing my luck. Once again, the kindness of strangers raised its
unexpected but cheerful head!

The next morning I decided that it might be worth planning
out our route around the upcoming tangle of inlets that made up the
Torridge estuary. The map revealed that there was quite a way to go before
Appledore. Our immediate challenge was getting around the triple fork
tributaries around Barnstaple and then back out again. It was frustrating!
I could see Appledore from our vantage point on the headlands of the
dune field and, all told, it was probably about half a mile away as the crow
flies. The map, on the other hand, told a very different story – it would be
a couple of days before we'd eventually get there.

I began shovelling the night's camp into my bag, when a random bit of
wind caught hold of my rolled-up mattress and casually chucked it out to sea.

"Bollocks." I swore, knowing instantly that my nights were just about to get a lot more uncomfortable.

Moose just stood there, grinning.

"Well, at least I can pick up another when we get to Applefor— errr… Apple…worth…?"

"*Appledore, you moron!*" he interjected, swishing his tail as he sauntered past me up the path.

I picked up what remained of my kit and followed, wondering why the hell I ever thought bringing a dog along was a good idea.

I finally spoke to Sian later that morning as we were coming up to a golf course. The shoreline was at our backs, now, and we were heading inland. She told me I could expect a call from someone called Sarah regarding a local article about our trip. Sure enough, about half an hour later, in came the call.

"Just a minute…" I faffed, trying to grab Moose, keep my phone to my ear, put down the pack and hold about ten things in my hands all at the same time. After some shuffling, I got myself sorted.

"Hi," I said again.

The voice on the other end of the line introduced herself and started chatting about an article: "We think our readers would be really interested in your adventure."

I instantly thought about the horrors of my feet and the dull ache in my heels that hadn't yet dissipated.

"We do have some fun tales to tell…" I said, wiping sweat off my forehead with a grubby hand.

"Could we meet tomorrow in a café to take an interview?"

My heart skipped.

"Of course," I said calmly. "What time?"

"Is nine OK?"

Anytime would've been OK – I really had nothing better to do.

"Nine it is!"

She told me that she'd text the details and see us both in the morning.

I gathered up my stuff then carried on across to the path and down to the cycle track that flanked the immense triple estuary. At Wrafton, we stopped for a bite to eat before heading on inland where the trail muscled up into a flood defence barrier with a path on top. Halfway down, we were approached by a group of teens holding maps, obviously on some orienteering school expedition.

"Excuse me, sir…"

Sir? – I looked like a bag of spanners!

"What can I help you with?" I asked, as the girls in the group fussed and giggled with Moose in the grass.

"We're trying to get to Velator…"

I looked over my shoulder at the village behind us. "Just keep going and you'll be fine," I assured them. I marched past, leaving a gaggle of young lads poring over the map with bewildered expressions. Moose was lolling around, belly-up on the ground, very much enjoying strokes and attention from the schoolgirls.

"Mooch!" I called.

He reluctantly flipped to his feet and sped off down the path to catch me up.

We were now past the first river fork and were heading into Barnstaple itself. The rugged path had gone and we were now stood on the solid footing of a tarmac cycleway. Glistening away in the distance was the bridge over the next river.

I did a little video for the Facebook page as we walked, with absolutely no idea as to where we'd stop that night. Usually, I'd avoid big towns like the plague but I was meeting the reporter the next morning, which meant we'd need to town-camp – something I was already beginning to get anxious about. We crossed the road bridge later that evening and wandered into a big Asda shop that sat on the other side of the crossing.

Sod it, I thought. *If you don't ask, you don't get!*

I scurried up to the wide opening of the store and began waving my arms like a madman to try to get the attention of the guys on the security desk.

"You OK?" a burly chap in a uniform asked.

"Err – fine…" I responded. "Could I have a chat with the store manager?"

He nodded and stomped inside. Five minutes later, a finely tailored suit appeared at the door. "Can I help you?"

"Are you the manager?"

"Deputy…"

"Oh…good!"

I started explaining about our little trek and then glibly asked if I could camp in the brush surrounding the store – completely expecting to be told to sod off.

"Sure. That'd be fine."

I stood there, stunned, as he continued, "I'll just let the staff and security know as well."

He asked me to wait as he vanished inside. I looked around the car park trying to scout an ideal spot between where I was standing and the petrol station. The deputy manager returned moments later with a handful of sandwiches, drinks and doggy treats!

"Courtesy of Asda!" He beamed.

I gabbled some words of thanks, grabbed the goodies and tromped off to find a decent, out-of-the-way place to camp for the night. I cannot tell you the relief I felt at having this secure luxury for the evening! Here we both were, in a town centre – irrespective of exactly where we were, we could attract unwanted attention.

I relaxed in the safe surroundings of lights, cameras and our very own personal security detail to guard us as we slept, ready for our interview in the morning. I pitched the tent in a thin loam of gravel and rocks. God,

I missed the mattress! After elbowing my way around the rubble trying to get a comfortable spot, I settled in for the night.

Later that evening, I heard a rustling outside.

"Er...hello?" called out a voice.

Moose erupted as I peered out, looked up and saw two pairs of feet – atop of which were two bright Asda uniforms.

"We thought you might like something warm." A hot cup of coffee and some chocolate muffins promptly appeared on the ground.

I looked at the darkening sky and glanced at my watch.

"We finished our shift and heard from our manager what you were doing..." said the first.

"... Can we meet Moose?" the other interrupted.

Moose shot out. He barked, sniffed and was quickly enveloped in a flurry of cuddles.

"He's adorable!"

Not when he's farting all the tent oxygen away... I thought.

"Ah, he has that effect on people," I said, before thanking them for the unexpected supper.

Sarah arrived a few minutes before nine to find Moose and I perched on a low wall surrounding a plaza filled with bars and restaurants. We quickly found a café and Sarah went inside to buy tea while I manhandled Moose into position under our table. We spoke for about twenty minutes about the walk, some of the people we'd met along the way, and my reasons for doing the whole thing in the first place. You can hear some bad things about reporters, so I was a little nervous about what to expect at first but Sarah was lovely. She took a few photos of me and the Moose before wishing us well and heading off to her next assignment.

It was starting to get busy in town as we headed back past Asda and out along the other side of the river. The sun was getting high and there was only the faintest breeze to keep us company. Today was going to be another scorcher!

All along the side of the path were idyllic little cottages overlooking the river. It seemed a very nice place to eventually settle down one day. We frequently passed other walkers on the path, some of whom congregated in the occasional shadows cast by the huge trees dotting the hedgerows here and there.

"You alright, Mooch?"

He looked up, his huge tongue lolling out. *"Bit of shade and water wouldn't go amiss."*

He was right: we were really exposed and being slowly barbequed in the heat. We found a big tree, collapsed under its shade and both dozed off for a bit.

At Instow, the estuary opened up before us. To our right, about a quarter of a mile across the water, was the golf course we'd passed yesterday. To the left, about the same distance again (over yet more water I might add), was Appledore. We had one more crossing to do but my maps assured me this would only take another couple of hours. I called Sian to let her know we'd be arriving just after six.

On this final stretch, we were blessed with a lush overhanging canopy of trees and hedges, which kept most of the sun off. Moose perked up and started chasing after flies and wasps again.

"I'm not kidding, bud – one of these days you're gonna regret doing that."

"Na-a…" He snapped as a yellow and black bug flashed by.

I shrugged and left him to his own devices.

I'm not his mother, after all.

Our final crossing can only be described as hair-raising.

It was a busy road bridge over which the A39 stretched, carrying with it a cacophony of speeding traffic. For the most part, it's pavemented

– albeit scarcely-used and covered in discarded car-seat litter. Dotted all down the path were remnants of glass bottles, shredded cans and a whole host of other assorted rubbish that careless drivers had seen fit to just chuck out of their windows.

I had Moose in close as I tried to manoeuvre us along the grass banks hugging the road, sighing a final breath of relief when we eventually made it to the footpath on the other side. An hour later we were turning a hill and descending into the harbour at Appledore.

I glanced down at Moose and noticed he'd developed a mild twitch in his back leg.

"Hold up, bud," I said, kneeling down to inspect his paw. Sure enough, there on the edge of the big pad on his right foot was a long, neat cut about a quarter of an inch long.

"Why the hell didn't you tell me about that?" I asked, raising my voice a little higher than I intended.

"*About what?*" He sniffed, indifferently.

"The ruddy great big cut on your paw."

His face dropped in instant panic. "*What cut on my paw?!*"

He began racing around in tight circles, trying to assess the damage.

"*Where... Where?? Is it bad???*"

"No, it's—"

"*WILL WE HAVE TO AMPUTATE?!*"

"Calm down, you bloody drama queen."

He squealed, collapsing into the grass.

"Oh for God's sake!" I said, taking his head in my hands and stroking his ears. "You'll be fine."

He looked at me, big brown eyes welling up.

I gave him a little reassuring kiss on his nose. "Trust me – it's nothing."

He instantly perked up. "*Oh, good*," he said, getting back to his feet and continuing his sniffing, as if his little near-death experience had never happened.

I rolled my eyes. "Bloody dogs!"

I got to my feet, grabbed my gear and carried on down the road as Moose leapt about the hedges like a lunatic in the afternoon sun.

Not long after, we were admiring Appledore harbour when Sian joined us. It was getting late, so we grabbed a quick pint, had a chat and began hiking back up a mini-mountain to her house, which sat at the top of the hill overlooking the harbour. In her driveway was a cosy little VW camper, which was to be our home for the next few nights.

I set about feeding Moose while Sian whipped up a veggie salad in her kitchen. She'd enquired with the local vet about getting Moose in for a check-up and, as she handed over my dinner plate, she told me we'd be seen first thing in the morning. That night, I lay next to Moose, hardly believing our luck, as we both nodded off with elbow-room to spare in our cosy surroundings.

The next morning, we awoke to a sharp knock on the van. I slid open the door only to see Sian's face drop as she was hit with a miasma of feet, sweat, dog and dog-fart. I mumbled an apology as Moose dived headlong at her for early-morning cuddles.

She let out a laugh, despite the aroma. "Boys will be boys…" She shrugged.

Moose and I grinned boyishly.

"Tea?" she asked.

"That'd be perfect!" I nodded.

We arrived at the vet just as they were opening but I stayed outside with Moose; the last thing I wanted was an incident with another dog – believe me, there's no talking him down where other mutts are concerned. The vet came out, gave a quick inspection and immediately told me not to worry.

"It's superficial and should heal over in a few days."

I sighed in relief and grabbed my wallet to pay.

"Nonsense!" he said, himself shoving twenty quid into my hand to put in our charity pot.

I just stood there, jaw flapping, as he gave Moose a quick tussle behind the ears and turned back into the surgery. I glanced across at the sign: Witten Park Vets. I'd have to remember that.

We had a busy day planned, so we clambered back into Sian's camper and headed off down the coast to meet up with a guy called Wayne and his dog Koda, who were also walking the coast of Britain for charity. Wayne's mission was a bit different to ours in that he was litter-picking as he went. So far, he'd been walking for two years and had covered over 3,000 miles.

By comparison, Moose and I were just bumbling amateurs.

I couldn't wait to meet this guy! Sian knew him from the year before when he and Koda had stayed in the same camper in which we were all now sitting. He was staying with friends in Bude before picking up his trail again in South Devon. This was one of those rare chances for us all to meet up and compare notes. What Koda and Moose would make of each other was something else altogether... I guessed we'd find out.

Now it's not entirely true to say that Wayne and I didn't know each other. When prepping for the walk, I'd talked to several people who were, or had been, doing something similar with dogs. Wayne was one of those people and we'd chatted a couple of times since over the phone. Like me, he's a Lancashire lad and – as is the case with most walkers – thin as a reed with a touch of 'scruff' thrown in for good measure. He has a nice, casual way about him and is a strong advocate of the environment, particularly where littering is concerned.

When we got to Bude, I jumped out of the camper and left Moose with Sian while I had a quick chat with Wayne about how to manage the dog thing. I looked across at Koda, a magnificent-looking Northern

Inuit Husky, who sat calmly waiting on Wayne's instruction while Moose bellowed like a lunatic from inside the van. We decided between us to take a stroll around the estate with a pair on each pavement, either side of the road, to see how it went.

Eventually Koda grew impatient with the tirade of abuse coming from Moose, and it wasn't long before they were both hurling obscenities at the other from opposite sides of the tarmac. As we walked, and Wayne and I got chatting, things seemed to settle down between the two.

"*But he'll eat you!*" Moose protested.

"No, he won't. We're friends."

Moose looked hurt. "*I thought* I *was your friend!*"

"I'm allowed more than one friend, you know."

Moose narrowed his eyes and glared, assuring me that that was not the case.

"Just try to get along."

"*Fine. But if he eats you, I'll gnaw his ears off.*"

I raised an eyebrow and looked at the majestic Arctic wolf walking next to Wayne on the other side of the road. I wasn't convinced about Moose's chances.

"I'm sure it won't come to that, bud."

At the house, we took turns going through the gate and into the back garden. Fortunately, the lawn was big enough for us to sit on with enough distance between us to talk while the dogs just lay there glaring at each other. We began discussing all things 'Walk' while Sian chatted to our host on the porch. I won't go into detail but it was mostly geek-gassing about kit, weight, the places we'd been to and the people we'd met – and the complications of having a dog with us 24/7.

Meeting Wayne and Koda that afternoon taught me some valuable lessons and, as we waved each other off, I knew we'd meet these wizened travellers again somewhere further along the coast.

Chapter 7

Friends and Angel Wings

Appledore to Widemouth Bay

The next morning was Regatta Day. I'll be honest: I had no idea what one of those was, but played along politely as Sian excitedly ushered us both down to the harbour front.

A spectacle awaited!

Stalls lined the sea wall while music blasted out from a DJ booth. All around, throngs of people buzzed and bustled while long, wooden row-boats filled with athletic competitors bobbed in the water just beyond the slipway. At first, they reminded me of those narrow racing boats you'd see in the rivers around university towns. These 'gig' boats, though, were on another, far more substantial and brutal level. Sian told me that each gig weighed a ton (literally) and that teams of five would hurl themselves in a mad dash far out to the estuary and then back again in a bid to be first across the line. Each group of rowers was accompanied by a cox, yelling out timings and encouragement while precariously perched at the prow. Considering the weight I'd been throwing around recently, I couldn't help but look at the sheer effort involved in all this and shudder.

The crowd erupted.

The music was replaced by a distorted commentary as massive wooden oars began tugging at the waves amid a cacophony of yells, grunts and applause.

They were off! Five or six local teams, hurtling into the distance in a flurry of determination and skill. I can honestly say that I'd never witnessed anything quite like it in my life. The atmosphere was electric, as race after race took place from beneath where Moose and I sat watching on the edge of a huge steel anchor that decorated the head of the harbour wall. Sian, who would usually compete in one of these races, sat with us for the day and guided us with commentary of who was who as each gig crossed the finish. I couldn't believe our luck at arriving here in time to witness such a vibrant local event.

That evening, I was still buzzing as we settled down to sleep on what would be our final night's stay in Appledore.

Saying goodbye to Sian was a surreal experience. A few days earlier, I'd never even heard of her and yet here we were, hugging our farewells like old friends. We walked along the flats and warrens that took us out of town and onward, towards Westward Ho! Our sights were solidly set on Bude – and on Cornwall, beyond.

Over the next couple of days, we walked in relative isolation. The cliff rocks had turned a Martian red colour and Moose raced out around the empty sands, keeping a cautious distance away from the wave-front. At Clovelly, the path turned as it skitted outward towards the peak at Hartland Point. That afternoon, we encountered an ancient wooden sculpture called The Angels Wings – it was little more than an ornate seating pagoda that had been restored decades before and stood hidden in the bush overlooking the sea. It was as good a place as any to spend the night, so I pitched the tent in a tiny patch of grass that lay in the angel's shadow.

As we finished up dinner, another hiker came along and asked to share the spot. She introduced herself as Tammy and we sat chatting, sharing stories, wine and biscuits until dark, under the protection of the beautiful wooden structure. Moose gleaned every last cuddle he could from her until she eventually retired inside her own tiny tent for the night.

Morning came and, as I stuck my head out of the Banshee, I noticed that Tammy had already struck camp and was heading off. Quickly eating, I packed up and followed suit about an hour later.

The air was heavy that day; by lunchtime, we were walking in a torrent of rain. The aches in my feet had returned and we were both sodden to our cores.

"*This is not fun.*" Moose grumbled.

I shrugged. "I never said it would be fun all the time."

"*I'm frozen!*"

"… Says the one wearing the fur coat."

"*It's not my fault you're bald.*"

Moose stopped and looked up with a raised eyebrow. "*… I've always wanted to ask – why* are *you bald, anyway?*"

"Genetic superiority!" I replied haughtily.

Moose snorted. "*I don't see what's so superior about walking around like a shaved monkey.*"

"Well, at least I don't drag my tongue along the floor every time the sun peeks out."

… And so on and so on. Our bickering continued as we trudged along together in the mud and rain.

It was mid-afternoon by the time the sun came back – and it came back with a vengeance!

Moose and I began to steam as the heat dried our clothes and fur, respectively. Devon was going through one of its 'undulating' moods again and, by dinner time, we were heaving, sweaty messes from the heat and exertion. We passed a campsite at a little place called Stoke, where we decided that enough was enough and stopped for the day. I ushered us both into a quieter field to pitch up and, as we walked past one of the other tents, we were greeted with Tammy's familiar face.

"I promise I'm not stalking you…" I blurted.

Moose cast me a sideways glance. "*Smooth!*"

I could barely see as I fumbled with the catches on my pack and dumped it on to the grass. I wiped away the torrents of sweat from my forehead and blinked. Moose looked over his shoulder, gave me a slow wink and casually sauntered over to where Tammy sat. He playfully threw her his best puppy-dog look and then firmly planted a kiss on her cheek as she giggled and rubbed his tummy.

He looked back and gave me another quick wink.

"Bloody dogs," I muttered.

In an effort to re-affirm my earlier 'stalking' statement, I decided to camp at the other side of the small field. Tammy probably wondered what on earth she'd done to offend us but, being unaware of wild camping etiquette, I decided to err on the side of caution and not cramp her style. In the site shop, I treated me and the pooch to a meal of champions that didn't involve beans this time.

After dinner, I carried out some more foot-repair – blisters had taken hold through my wet socks – while Moose snored in the shade.

Camping on a site always took away those niggling worries you'd get when sleeping in the middle of nowhere – being mauled by rabid zombie badgers wasn't high on my bucket list – so we slept soundly that night.

In the morning, I popped my head out of the tent and Tammy was nowhere to be seen.

*

PING

Great article in the gazette... 😊

It was Sian.

I quickly opened up the *Gazette* website and tapped in the first keyword that came to mind...

M-O-O-S-E

Sure enough, a picture of both our mugs greeted me from the article header. I read through the story, delighted with the 'hard work' vibe of the piece – and the flattery laced throughout the entire thing.

I looked down at Moose, half asleep under the sleeping bag, and messaged back:

Well impressed – Thanks! 😊

I decided to loiter around for most of the day before heading out again. Yesterday's rain was a long-distant memory, as blue skies and heat reasserted themselves with gusto. That morning, another camper, wearing a bandana and well-worn kit, turned up. He pitched his tent in expert fashion and had his lunch bubbling away on a neat little stove in a matter of minutes. It turns out that he'd written guidebooks for this stretch of the SWCP and was just walking the trail to update his latest edition.

He listened to our story, took one look at my stuff and calmly suggested that I was carrying too much gear. I'd already convinced myself that I was down to the bare minimum and began justifying my need for a carrying not only things like a camping kettle and other bits and pieces, but primary essentials like my travel guitar as well. He thought better of arguing and, instead, offered to mosey down to the Wreckers Retreat – a pub that sat at the bottom of a series of cliff edges – and buy me a pint.

As we walked, we continued talking. His story was fascinating; he went on to explain that he'd written about these trails years before and had built up an impressive series of guides and introspectives about the local topography.

One pint turned into several.

By the time Moose and I set off back on the path, it was well past 7pm and we were looking at taking our first night walk. I wobbled back up the stairs cut into the cliff and was greeted by a small sign indicating an even smaller place: Hawkers Hut. A shed, no more than a couple of metres long, built directly into the side of the cliff face, overlooking the sea.

If you google it, you'll read about the ingenuity and historic significance of it all. In reality, it was a place where the then vicar of Morwenstow would hook up with his mates Tennyson and Dickens to chat existential nonsense all night while gazing out into the ocean, and smoking opium until the sun set and their brains dribbled out to sea. I guess Tennyson and Dickens got the better of the deal because I'd never heard of the vicar of Morwenstow until I got there.

The shack itself held a treasure trove of signatories that'd been scratched into the wood over the generations. Moose and I sheltered out of the sun with this amazing view as I gleaned over the names and stories carved into the ageing wood:

Steve & Sonya – FOREVER!

Looking at this inscription, I couldn't help but wonder whether Steve and Sonya were old and married and surrounded by their 2,000 grandchildren…or had broken up six months after they'd scrawled their names there. Such are the mysteries of life!

We carried on walking until we reached another steep staircase descending before us. By now, I could barely see in the fading light and so decided not to risk it. I pitched up the tent as best as I could in the darkness, threw in the Moose and quickly fell asleep.

Pitching 'as best as I could' meant that I'd spent the night fighting with tufts of grass that seemed to dig in no matter where I lay. As per usual, Moose was no help at all, with his constant tangle of legs and tail.

I was up before the sun was and scoping out the land in the pre-dawn light. The staircase I'd thought better of the night before lay a couple of hundred yards from where we'd pitched. I decided to move on and grab something to eat somewhere a bit more suitable than the exposed spot in which we were currently perched. As we started our descent, I quietly congratulated myself on the decision not to do this in the dark – I'd have tripped and broken my bloody neck for sure!

About halfway down, a brick-built hut sprang out of the side of the path, clinging to the edge of the cliff face. I tried the door and found it was unlocked, so we both clambered inside.

On every wall were photos and dedications to Ronald Duncan – a local playwright, philanthropist and, from what I could gather, playboy.

The wall on the opposite side of the door was occupied by two windows, beyond which were the most stunning views out to sea. Centred beneath the windows was a plain wooden table, complete with guestbook. I'd found our spot for breakfast!

We spent about an hour there, soaking in the atmosphere and reading all about Mr Duncan and his exploits. I signed the book and closed the door to continue our descent to the bottom of the valley.

And then I saw it...

In the valley basin was a small wooden bridge over which, on the other side, was a tiny wooden plaque nailed to the cliff face.

It read, very simply:

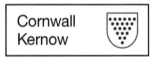

Cornwall
Kernow

I nearly collapsed with the emotion of it all: we'd made it! Portishead to Cornwall!

I grabbed Moose in a giant bear hug.

"*Gerroff!*" He shrugged.

"We made it, buddy!" I beamed enthusiastically.

"*What you on about?*"

"We're in Cornwall, pal!"

He tilted his head to one side, eyes showing instant interest. "*Is that like corned beef?*"

"No, you stupid sod – it's a place."

His face fell. "*Oh...well, I prefer corned beef.*"

I shook my head despairingly. "Maybe I can pick you up a pasty in the next village."

His ears pricked up. "*I like pasties.*"

"Don't I know it," I muttered, marching past the sign and on to our first steps in a new county.

Just after midday, we reached the village of Morwenstow. We stayed in the shade just outside of Rectory Farm where, for lack of anything better to do, I sat playing my guitar for the local passers-by, much to the pleasure/annoyance of the folks enjoying afternoon tea in a nearby café.

Today was one of the hottest we'd had so far, which meant we'd not knocked too much off our mileage since crossing the border. I fed Moose by the side of the road as he whined about not getting his pasty for dinner.

It wasn't until seven that evening when the heat had finally diminished enough for us to continue. Out on the headland, we weren't so much coastal walking as we were cliff climbing. At some points, the signage pointed almost guiltily at a trail that just disappeared off a sheer cliff face, with the implication that we'd just have to manage to scale upwards as best as we could before we hit solid path again. Moose bounded over rocks and disappeared, his head appearing a few seconds later, several metres above mine.

"You coming or wot?"

I threw a look of daggers but could barely even catch my breath let alone give a telling-off.

Eventually, we encountered a concrete World War II lookout post that, despite spending seventy-odd years exposed to the elements, still stood with walls and roof intact. I collapsed inside and stared, panting at the ceiling until a slobbering dog-tongue brought me sloppily back to reality.

"Arrwwr – ya bloody…" I muttered, wiping the drool off my face.

"Mmmm – salty!" Moose grinned, as he sat there panting happily in the shade.

I rolled to my knees and began weighing up whether or not we should spend the night there. Could I make the place a little more homely? Grabbing a few random fronds of bramble from outside, I began brushing the floor of the concrete hut to make it more habitable. Embedded in the wall was the remnants of a thick wooden shelf, which I filled with cooking apparel, and I began rolling out our sleeping bags on the floor, ready for a night's kip. Moose snuggled in close and we both abruptly passed out in the heat.

We woke a couple of hours later to the beaming light of a full moon tinged with the afterglow of a deep red sunset. I moved on to my elbow and immediately felt the bite of the concrete floor dig in.

"It's not very comfortable…" Moose complained.

I couldn't help but agree – I was already beginning to ache in the strangest of places and we'd not been here that long.

"Do you fancy moving on?" I asked, hoping he'd had enough of the stone floor.

Moose jumped up, bounced outside the hut and stared around keenly, wagging his tail – until he stopped short, his eyes glued to my forehead in concern. *"What's that?"*

The question caught me off guard. "What's what?"

"That! On your face!"

I involuntarily started groping around my clammy forehead.

"You've sprouted a lump…" he said.

I grabbed my phone, turned the camera around and began a detailed inspection of my brow.

It didn't take long. There sat an enormous zit with apparently Everest-like ambition.

"Crap!"

"Looks kinda funky!"

I threw a couple of swear words his way and quickly smooshed out the problem.

"Better?"

He grinned at the angry red lump forming just above my eyebrow. *"Much…"* he sniggered, before skipping off to take a pee in the bushes.

In the last dregs of sunlight, we reached the top of the cliff line and found that the path began winding inland. Eventually, we were ejected on to a single-track road that seemed to be there only as a form of farmers' access, and beyond it, open fields stretching as far as the eye could see.

Huge round bales of hay covered in white plastic reflected the eerie glow of the diminishing sun and blue pulse of the moon. We were alone and, combined with the stillness of the night, this odd mix of light gave an eerie atmosphere to the entire place.

We crested a rise – and were hit with an incredible sight.

There, sprawled along the horizon, stood a magnificent array of massive radio telescopes. The road we followed took us closer to the behemoth structures until the path split and we had to choose: were we coastal path walkers or were we authorised GCHQ Bude personnel? Opting for the more likely choice, I steered us back towards the sea.

Glancing back, I could see the red glow of the fading sun hit the dishes while the moon covered the wilderness in a shimmer of blue. It brought to mind the surreal dimensions of old sci-fi novels, each contrasting colour clashing to create an indescribable ambience, like walking along the surface of some forgotten mystical world.

I couldn't help but hold my breath as we walked. There was a surreal stillness in the air and I can honestly say that it felt as though we were walking through the ruins of some long-lost civilisation, the last two beings on the surface of an abandoned world.

Eventually, we hit a rise that threw us sharply down into the bay at Combe. Nestled in the wilderness of the valley was a long car park with a toilet block. The light was still strong enough for us to make our way down to a mass of campers already set up for the night and waiting for the morning surf to arrive.

That morning, we were woken by a gentle rustling outside. Moose went into his usual berserker mode, barking for all he was worth inside our little tent.

"Err – hello?" I asked.

"Would you like a cuppa?" came a voice from beyond the canvas.

I couldn't believe my luck. Moose continued gobbing off as I kindly accepted. "Tea with just milk would be lovely..."

Two minutes later and there was another rustling, followed by more barking, and a polite reply: "It's there on the grass for you."

I secured Mooch and stepped outside to grab my cuppa. "What the hell are you barking for?"

"I thought that was my job?" came the flustered reply.

I ruffled his head, leant down to give him a peck on the ear and whispered, "Not at people who bring tea, bud!" I grabbed the cup, clipped Moose on to his lead and took him for a stomp around the car park before he could object.

As the sun rose, wetsuit-clad families erupted from their campers, carrying all manner of surfing apparel, and headed for the beach.

"That's our cue," I muttered, packing our stuff.

We set off over the next rise. Hill followed hill until, foaming like rabid dogs, we finally descended into a bay that, thankfully, had a shop well-stocked with water and walking poles.

During my stay with Sian, we'd discussed the virtue of walking poles. To some, they were just a clitter-clatter of noise as they'd meander along gentle trails, swinging wildly like unofficial members of the Ministry of Silly Walks. To travellers like me, though, a sturdy pole was akin to carrying a mobile bannister rail that I could use to tug myself up the steep steps and inclines that challenged our every step. I'd only set off with the one pole and Sian had strongly advocated the use of two – especially for someone carrying the kind of weight I was. The constant ache in my feet and the toll the pack was taking on my torso pushed me to give a two-pole approach a try.

Just like the kit-cull I'd done in Somerset, I never looked back: this was a two-pole journey from here on!

I couldn't believe the difference it made. I practically vaulted up and down the remaining contours with renewed vigour until, given the choice between clifftop or beach, we decided to walk the flat sands for the remainder of the way into Bude.

The beach route turned out to be a great choice. From the settled sands, I peered up at the clifftop and could just make out the ridgeline of the path on top of it – we'd have been puffing and heaving the entire way.

As it happened, the sands on the beach flattened out into a wide boulevard with plenty of space for Mooch and me to roam. It was just a matter of finding that sweet spot between the dry sand and the sea that offered a firm footing. Too close to the water and we'd sink, too far into the dry sand and we'd get mired down in sandy dust.

I began to make out the remains of some long-lost mechanical edifice jarring out of the sand in the distance. As we approached, I could see that the engineering skill and precision put into its creation had been dulled and smoothed away by the steady wearing of the salt water. As impressive as it was, the sea would continue to do its work until eventually there'd be nothing left but beach, rust and sand. I could just see the bay at Bude as we weaved in and out of huge boulders and crags that were covered in mussels.

I stared. And then I had an idea.

Mussels for dinner!

I tossed the pack, grabbed my kettle and began foraging away until my kettle was full to the brim. Bude turned out to be way too busy to stop in, anyway – this would do us grand! On his lead, Moose was chirping at every dog in eyeshot and began dragging me left, right and centre along the sand.

Across from the beach, on the other side of the inlet, the bay lifted to form a set of small cliffs that curved around the headland. We climbed up until we reached a plateau of grasslands and fields and continued on to the small town of Widemouth.

After crossing the bay, we found a nice little camp spot tucked away about half a mile into the heather adorning the foreshore. I set about the task of scraping the mussels of their barnacles with my knife and washing them in clean water. There was a little shop in Widemouth where I'd managed to pick up a little bottle of white wine and some garlic. I got all this on the boil and then dumped in the harvest…here went nothing!

I've cooked mussels before – and, by 'mussels', I mean the fresh ones you get from the fishmonger – and have happily lived to tell the tale every time. This time, however…it was different. I opened the lid tentatively, half expecting some alien face-hugger to come leaping out at me.

Moose kept a safe distance as I held the first one to my nose. "*I'm not convinced.*"

I had to admit – neither was I.

I lifted it tentatively to my lips and took the plunge.

Moose grimaced. "*You're gonna die, you lunatic.*"

"Will you shut up!" I snapped while nibbling away.

It *tasted* fine…whether I'd wake up in the morning was another matter.

Actually, it tasted fairly good…

"Sod it!" I said, shovelling the lot down.

I offered one to Mooch. "*Na-a…*" he said, wrinkling his nose. "*They're all yours, mate.*"

I shrugged, too hungry and too tired to care. I polished off the lot.

Chapter 8

Slammed!

Widemouth Bay to Crackington Haven

I survived dinner!

Later that night, the air turned angry and we found ourselves bombarded with a torrent of lightning and thunderstorms. It was one of the things I'd been most worried about, especially where Moose was concerned. I, for one, was never bothered by storms – I remember sitting at home as a kid, perching myself by the edge of the window every time a decent lightning storm passed, soaking in the splendour. To me, this was one of the greatest shows on earth. For pooch, on the other hand... I wondered how he'd take to it when huddled in a tent in the middle of nowhere.

I underestimated Mooch – he wasn't fazed at all! The flashes and bangs only served to distract me from his groaning as he tossed and turned beside me. I keenly felt the light kick of doggy paws as he made himself more comfortable amid a barrage of snores and farts.

Ignoring his toxic snoozing, I lay there fascinated by the random and quick-lived illumination of the fabric as the spectacle played out in the air above, counting down the seconds until the tell-tale rumbling followed. I felt the excitement as the storm grew closer. In my mind, I was ten years old again, camping in the back yard of my mum's house in Manchester, giddy with the excitement of it all!

Eventually, it passed by and we were once again surrounded by the peaceful silence of a still night.

Moose snored on as the entire event passed him by.

The morning after, I peeked outside to find the world in a state of recovery from the storm. It was incredibly relieving to breathe fresh cool air for once, after so many weeks of oppressive heat.

Our journey that morning was one of stops and starts. It was quite bright setting off but, after a while, we started getting passes of rain, as random squalls came in from the sea every twenty minutes or so. No sooner had we gone through the palaver of putting layers of waterproofs on than the sun would peek out and start cooking us alive in them, and so off they came, again!

And this went on for hours, until I finally settled for keeping waterproofs donned, contented with sweltering our way through the dry patches without the need to stop and change every twenty minutes.

We came off the coastline and on to a head of stretching farmland edged by a single-track road. Further down, a narrow stairwell peeked out from the hedgerow and we were soon back on the coast path, overlooking breathtaking views of Cornish cliffs and rugged shorelines. In a bid (I assume) to compete with its neighbouring county, Cornwall began to throw steep inclines our way. Instead of heading away from the cliff edges and keeping the path level, it cruelly cut down and then back up the jagged lines of each headland as we encountered them. The effort it took completing all this was quite simply exhausting!

The wind had also begun to pick up, and out to sea we could see the weather fronts moving in, line by line. The horizon was dotted with patches of angry-looking sky and a tell-tale mist of rainfall beneath them. Pitter-patters became torrents within a matter of minutes, only for them to be quickly pushed inland as the sun came out to bake us again. I'd started to time these as they came in and would find a shaded spot to lay low until it was safe to move again.

Through one unusually long sunny patch, we cleared the shelter of some overhanging bushes on a high headland, which revealed a particularly sharp and nasty descent point. Far below, I could see the base of the narrow valley and a severe cut of steps on the other side heading back up to the top of the cliffs opposite us. In the distance, I could see a mass of bubbling black cloud churning the waves as it raced to shore. If we were quick, we could miss it. I grabbed the pooch and started working my way down the steep stair as quickly as I could.

And then…it hit us!

At first, it felt like someone had pushed me hard from behind. I turned and saw, for the first time, not the squall ahead in the distance but another, which had crept up from the side, obscured by the treeline we'd passed five minutes earlier. I felt another push – but this one came directly from the sea and brought fistfuls of sharp rain with it.

Dropping to my knees and clinging to the stairs as the wind tore at me, I glanced back at the top of the staircase and saw that we were barely a third of the way down. I had a decision to make.

Knowing there was no shelter to be had back at the top, I decided to head down as fast as we could – a choice that the wind seemed to acknowledge by responding in kind.

Racing air grabbed hold of my rucksack and almost twisted me into the brush. I glanced at the drop a good couple of hundred metres below and staggered back upright. The rain was coming in so hard now that I could barely see as it battered into my right side. Its impact hurt as much as a barrage of hailstones.

I unclipped Moose and screamed at him to get to the bottom. All around, the air roared an incomprehensible din of confusion as I staggered along in Moose's trail. I looked on, envious of his agility and low centre of gravity as the gale threatened to twist me off my feet.

That's it! I thought. I decided to dump the pack.

I unclipped the straps and hurled the thing down the remaining 100 or so metres to the valley floor, where it bounced between the heather. The rain was coming in horizontally now and the wind tore at my jacket, threatening to hurl me back inland. Inching my way down, I staggered with each step. My muscles screamed in protest as I fought to stay on the staircase.

Eventually, I staggered to the valley floor and fell to my knees. I was soaked to the core and could barely see through the sheets of rain as they coursed obliviously past us. In panic, I cast around for shelter…but there was none to be had.

I could make out Moose as he lay shivering in a sodden mess not far from the track; he peered at me through sheets of slanting rain with pleading eyes. I retrieved my pack, grabbed my tent and threw the damned thing up as fast as I could. We both crawled in, a muddy, sopping, heaving mess, and shivered in silence as the wind wrestled angrily at the fabric, as if desperate to follow us inside.

I lay there catching my breath, wondering what the hell that was and how stupid I'd been to get blindsided like that. We'd been on the stairs no more than three or four minutes, although it felt like the ordeal had lasted an hour.

We remained in the tent for the next couple of hours, with me slowly working through the process of peeling away wet clothes and waterproofs and sifting through our saturated kit to find something dry. I towelled Moose down, wrapped us both up in my sleeping bag (which, thankfully, had remained dry) and spooned for body heat until we were both warm.

About an hour later, the heat of the sun began to seep into the tent and I began to repack – something of a challenge, in a two-man tent. I chanced a look outside and the sun was back in the sky, with the storm nowhere to be found. I gazed upwards at the climb we had ahead of us and gulped – Crackington Haven was only a few miles away but the thought of a repeat of the last few hours filled me with terror. The only thing I knew for sure was that staying here would be idiotic; this was no place to weather out a storm. I looked out to sea and saw another dark gale racing towards us in our narrow valley.

No sooner had we got our first foot on the stairs than the weather hit again. I glanced back and could see two other walkers staggering down the descent from which we'd just come. I decided to wait and get a second opinion. As they got closer, I could see they were experiencing the same level of panic as me.

We introduced ourselves; they'd done this walk before and assured me that this was usually a pleasant stretch. We set out together and stayed within eyeshot of each other as the rolling path continued its challenging course along cliff lines and stairs. The rain had eased somewhat, leaving only a tearing wind that froze my skin as my soaking clothes clung to it. We took each step one at a time until, a few hours later, we crested a ridge and headed down into the cove at Crackington Haven.

At the bottom of the path lay a beautiful white building with the words 'The Coombe Barton Inn' stencilled elegantly on the huge gable end.

I needed no invitation! I crawled inside, bidding goodbye and leaving the couple we'd met to their own devices.

Thankfully, they were dog-friendly (I honestly believe I'd have cried if they weren't). Windswept and freezing, I found a table snuggled in the corner of the taproom, ordered a burger each for me and the Moose, and took stock of the day.

About an hour or so later, the couple returned to come and sit with us. We chatted about our brush with death over a couple of pints and began regaling each other of our experiences on the road. As we talked, they asked how long we'd been walking for… I glanced at the date on my watch and blinked.

To the day, we'd been on the road exactly one month.

Chapter 9

Minnie Driver's Scones and the Quest for Aunty Histamine

Crackington Haven to Tintagel

I can't remember what time it was when we eventually emerged from the pub and fell back into the cold chill of Crackington Haven. I'd been told by the locals that there was a campsite set back from the road a few hundred yards, somewhere up beyond the public toilets in the centre of the village. I scouted around in the dark for about twenty minutes before giving up and staggering back to the centre of town. I'll admit that my slightly inebriated state didn't help, and the constant nagging from Moose to get pitched up forced me to make an off-the-cuff decision to find a convenient spot (devil may care!). We ended up settling for a patch of grass beneath the little road bridge in the centre of the village.

As I lay there in the dark, Moose's head on my chest, I began checking our messages from the last few days as I tried to figure out our next steps. Our encounter on the cliffs outside of town had torn through our kit, leaving most of it sodden and unusable – and, with little or no hope of a campsite or B&B in which to dry out, I began looking for other options to regroup.

I'd been in contact with a couple called Phil and Kinnon, who'd been following our walk on Facebook for a few weeks now. I knew they lived locally – although, for their sins, they were both originally from Yorkshire! I bit the bullet and sent a quick text letting them know where we were, along with a cheeky request to use their tumble dryer.

It was far too late to expect a response; nevertheless, a few minutes later, one came in:

> We know where you are – nice to know you're safe…sit tight and see you in the morning! ☺

That'd do for me. I snuggled down against a snoring Moose and fell away into a deep and relieved sleep.

We awoke the following morning to voices from above us on the road, doubtless wondering who the random stranger was, camped out beneath the recesses of the bridge. We were fortunate that it had been a dry night in Crackington, although most of our kit was still sodden. I'll leave it to your imagination – suffice to say that drying off using a dog instead of a towel creates a special aroma all of its own.

I crawled out of the tent, bleary eyes blinking in the morning sun as I looked around at our surroundings. Crackington Haven was typical of a small Cornish village – a couple of tourist shops selling all manner of beach apparel flanked by two busy cafés. A single-track road ran from town border to town border. No sooner had we risen than I found the enquiring face of a woman with long greying hair stood above us on the bridge, peering down to our camp.

"Chris, I presume?" she asked.

"Kinnon?"

She smiled and nodded.

I looked down at Moose, who was still dozing in the tent. I reached in and scratched his ear.

"C'mon, bud! Our rescue party's arrived."

I could barely even remember what a bed looked like, let alone how it felt to sleep in one. Yet here we both were, sliding side to side in the back seat of a VW camper, hurtling towards our first night of luxury since entering Cornwall.

Kinnon and Phil have a palpable affinity for one another and are the sort of couple that you instantly gel with. From the back, I could see Phil's bald head bobbing behind the wheel as he raced through the Cornish lanes like he was late for Le Mans. Kinnon sat, casually half-turned in the passenger seat, chatting as we tore up lane after country lane. Moose snored away in the cushions with his head on my lap the entire way. She told me that we were headed inland to a place just outside of Launceston and, as we darted through a series of covered country roads, a stray thought of *My God – they could be leading us into the middle of a field to slaughter us both!* crossed my mind once or twice. The sensible and smooth banter between us snapped me back to reality – I knew we were in safe hands!

We screeched to a halt beside a stunning little barn conversion and all piled out of the back. Phil ushered me to the garage and helped me begin to untangle the sopping mess that was my kit, throwing some in the washing machine while hanging out the rest to dry. Kinnon played with Moose on the patio until, out of the corner of his eye, he spied gold...

"COUCH!"

Kinnon looked down.

"*Can I – can I – can I?*"

She slid open the door as he raced by and unceremoniously hurled his gigantic self on to the squishy cushions and throws.

I peered around from the patio. "Found the couch then, bud!"

He was already soundly snoring.

I looked at Kinnon. "Do you want me to kick him off?"

She laughed and shook her head. "He's fine."

That night, I settled down on a comfy sofa surrounded by conversation, great food and, eventually, Phil's homebrew. For all his gusto, Moose had decided that enough was enough and had sauntered upstairs to bed just after 9pm.

Kinnon's jaw dropped. "Did he just…?"

"Put himself to bed?" I smiled and nodded. "Yeah – he does that."

They both laughed.

We talked long into the night. It was easy to see the affection these two wild misfits had for each other and my mind drifted to my own bizarre companion, who was, no doubt, snoring his head off on the bed upstairs. Eventually, tiredness caught up with me and I decided to get some sleep myself. I entered the bedroom to find Moose stretched out across the full length of the bed.

"Oii – shift!" I ordered, manhandling him to one side of the mattress while he grunted, and squeezed my way under the covers. Once I was settled, he snorted and gave me a firm kick to the ribs. I grunted, turned over and fell asleep.

So much for *our* affinity.

The next morning, a fresh breakfast was laid out ready for us both. Mooch scoffed down his before I even had the chance to sit at the table to eat mine. The familiar sight of a head poking up between my knees greeted me as I tucked in…

"No chance, pal!" I grunted, mouth full of scrambled egg.

Nonetheless, he gazed back with hopeful puppy-dog eyes.

Kinnon began distracting him with morsels from her own plate. Phil cast a look but then started to do the same. I ignored all three and wolfed down every last bit before getting up to gather my gear, ready for our trip back to Crackington.

Once the van pulled up in the car park, we exchanged thanks for hugs while His Majesty searched among the other parked cars for a perfect peeing spot. I was too busy saying goodbye to Kinnon and Phil to take notice of which vehicle he ended up defiling...but, in the long run, who cared? That stuff washed off in the rain anyway.

We headed out of the car park and walked back up to the centre of the village. I heard the loud beep of a horn and stopped to wave goodbye as the campervan sped past on its way out of town. We crossed the bridge that was perched at the quiet intersection of the two narrow roads that led in and out of town. Looking down at our previous camp spot, for the first time, I noticed a café there; outside was a sign that boldly read:

> ## "BEST SCONES EVER..."
>
> *– Minnie Driver 2018 –*

I laughed in spite of myself. I never knew Minnie Driver had such bold assertions regarding scone quality in deepest, darkest Cornwall! Nevertheless, I took a leap of faith and stopped for a cream tea before hitching our gear and carrying on again, down the coast towards Tintagel.

The jury was still out on the scone front – while they were very good, I thought it only prudent to try as many as I could along the way before agreeing with Minnie completely. After all – it's hard to argue with the scientific method!

We walked on with renewed vigour. I was showered, Moose was fresh, our clothes were clean and the rucksack was dry. Unfortunately, that didn't last very long! We were once again hit with bouts of rain and sunshine, although nothing as severe as the day before. The coast path continued along a trajectory akin to mountain climbing and abseiling – which, even after a decent breakfast and with two poles, was way beyond what I considered to be hard work. That said, I had it in my mind to reach Tintagel before day-end. As the crow flies, it wasn't that far.

… Or so I thought.

We marched through the pretty bay at Boscastle – a haven for Wiccans, quaint coffee shops and tourists. We sat in the sheltered lea of a pub on the far side of the bay and caught our breath while I had a cup of tea under the shade of a huge outdoor umbrella. I could see the path ahead cut deep into the side of the cliff face and up beyond. Impatient to leave, I quickly drained the last of the cup, shouldered the pack and headed back out with Moose following behind, sniffing furiously at every post and stump he could find. Eventually, we started picking up signs, which, unlike the ones at Minehead, included the helpful addition of mile-markers.

If there's anyone from the South West Coast Path Association reading this, please let me assure you: whoever was responsible for these mile-markers was either wildly optimistic or had been issued a very dodgy tape measure by the bloke in facilities. Five miles turned out to be more like eight, and then ten…although it definitely felt more like fifteen! My battered feet begrudged every extra step as I befouled the idyllic Cornish countryside air with a string of expletives each time we rounded another hill, or encountered one of the mile-markers telling blatant porkies.

During one of our exhausted, drop-to-the-floor-and-gasp-for-air rest stops, we encountered a couple cheerfully hiking the other way.

Moose looked over to them in despair.

"Are we anywhere near to Tintagel?" he asked.

"They don't understand you, mate." I gasped.

I caught my breath and repeated Moose's question to them.

"Just a few more miles to go." The lady smiled. "You're nearly there!"

I looked up somewhat doubtfully. I was sure I'd just read that on a signpost somewhere.

The chap accompanying her must have noticed the dubious expression on both our faces. "It's just around the next couple of valleys and you'll have it in sight – maybe an hour or so."

It was the '...*or so*' bit that filled me with dread!

They asked what we were up to and I duly obliged them with my, by now, very well-rehearsed response. Both were clearly impressed – to the point that I felt guilty at the blasé tone I'd adopted without realising. I stood up, threw on a more enthusiastic attitude, ditched the pack in the grass and introduced us properly.

Alan and his wife (whose name completely escapes me...but let's call her Julie for the sake of continuity) were holidaying here and told me they ran the local Rotary Club back home. Alan was incredibly interested in my anecdotes about the trip, while Julie was interested in Moose's antics – he circled her legs, scrounging for any titbits of affection. We chatted for a good ten minutes or so before exchanging farewells.

True(ish) to their word (almost two hours later), we crawled around the final crag to find the legendary castle at Tintagel shimmering away in the distance.

Tintagel is one of several key sites that sit along a major ley line. If you look at a map, the castle ruin aligns precisely with other mystical sites such as Glastonbury Tor and Stonehenge, connecting them all on a sacred journey through the ancient kingdom of Wessex. I'd been here before and had it in my mind to camp in the castle grounds and watch the sun set, surrounded by the ghosts of King Arthur, Lady Guinevere and the Knights of the Round Table. The site manager, however, had other ideas and was less than impressed at the suggestion!

"This is a grade one listed structure!" she said, in an outraged tone.

I'll admit, I was a bit taken aback by her attitude; it's not like we'd just offered to give the thing a paint job.

I plastered on my best smile and tried again. "I understand that but we'll just pitch up on one of the grassy bits," I said, applying as much charm as I could, "and then be gone before you open up for the tourists tomorrow."

She looked at me like I'd just vomited on her shoes.

"I can't allow you to go around banging tent pegs into a national heritage site!"

My jaw dropped at the logic. This thing had been battered by the Cornish elements since the thirteenth century and here she was, worried about a few four-inch aluminium pegs being hammered into the soft grass.

"But I… I…"

I…looked at the expression on her face, lost interest and gave up arguing. We turned on our heels and marched out of the grounds up to where we'd spotted some National Trust scrubland on the way in. I threw down the pack in a huff and pitched up there for the night instead. It'd have to do!

Along the way, I nipped into the shop and picked up a bottle of authentic Cornish mead, just to get me in the spirit of things… authenticity and all that! I set about making my usual feast of noodles and tinned fish, digging in the bag for Mooch's goodies.

Moose wrinkled his nose up at the simmering broth on the stove. *"Do I get proper food tonight?"*

I tentatively sniffed at his bowl of Butcher's tripe and gagged. "Don't worry, bud – it's that stinky horrible stuff you like!"

He grinned as I threw the bowl down on the grass and he set about demolishing the entire gross mess in a couple of wild chomps! While Moose snuffled in his bowl and my noodles simmered away, I stood by the wall overlooking the castle and watched the sun begin to disappear behind the sea. I opened my bottle of ancient mead and took a sip. How to describe the taste? Honey-flavoured watery syrup, with a 15% kick for good measure! I shrugged, grabbed my dinner and polished off the bottle, despite the taste, before staggering to bed.

That night, my dreams were haunted by gallant knights wielding huge tent pegs, like the lances of old. The leader of the group, who, from what I could see beneath the visor, looked suspiciously like the site manager, chased at me and Moose with piercing shrieks of *"World Heritage Site!"* while flailing a bottle of mead above her head.

I woke the next morning with a mildly sickening taste of honey in my mouth and guzzled the rest of my water reserves in a bid to prevent my throat from shrivelling up.

The village of Tintagel is set back about a mile inland from the ruins, atop another godawful hill. It was still early and the shops weren't yet open, although a few optimistic tourists ambled about the place looking for a café to grab an early-morning cream tea. Outside one of the pubs, I saw a bib tap, so quickly rushed across and replenished our stores of water. I left it running for a minute so Moose could have his fill and play at 'biting the water' while I looked up warily at the clear morning sky: today was set to be another scorcher!

Back at the tent, I began the steady routine of striking camp. As I knelt there stuffing the sleeping bag away, I looked across at Moose who'd been bouncing around in the grasses catching flies.

"You OK?"

"I'm fline." He nodded, tongue lolling out of the side of his mouth.

I looked closer and noticed a swelling above his eye, which was getting bigger by the second. I panicked and ran over to him, holding his chops in both my hands.

"You are not fine, Moose!" I said, eyes bulging almost as much as his.

"*Slereously – I'm flinnne,*" he blubbered out, his lips now swollen to twice their usual size.

"What the hell did you just do?"

"*Wellow bwug!*"

My jaw dropped! "Did you just eat a wasp?!!"

He grinned back. "*Yurp – wassssn vlerry tasty.*"

By now his face was swollen like a balloon.

"You fucking idiot!" I yelled.

Half in annoyance, half in panic, I shoved a finger in his mouth and started fishing around. Sure enough, two twitching halves of a nearly dead wasp fell out on the grass.

I quickly perched myself on the end of a jagged rock, grabbed my phone and called the local vet while Moose dribbled to himself in the corner of the verge. With the phone crooked against my ear, I spoke in a panicked voice to the vet, frantically scribbling notes on the tatters of a shop receipt.

"A-ha…"

Scribble…

"Yup…"

Scribble – scribble…

"Are you sure?"

Relief!

I hung up the phone and looked at the scrawl on the scrap of paper.

'*Look for the source of penetration…*'

I glanced down at the decapitated wasp that had, by now, stopped twitching on the floor.

Check!

'*Next – find a chemist and buy Piriton – 3 tablets, twice daily!*'

I didn't remember seeing any of that when I bought the mead at the castle shop… I looked back up at the village perched on the hill and looked down at Moose and his ever-growing face. "C'mon, you, we need to get some antihistamines."

"*Ooo's Anthy Histhdamine?*" he asked, with a tilt to his head.

"Not who." I frowned. "What. They're tablets to make you well." He gave his shoulders a shake as I looked up towards the town.

"Damn!" I muttered to myself – that was going to be one hell of a climb.

Thankfully, I had no need to cart all of our kit up the hill and left it safely zipped up in the tent. We were firmly stranded in Tintagel for at least another night – Moose and his stupidity had seen to that!

Tintagel, it turns out, has three chemists. By the time we got to the first, the town was teeming with tourists, all clamouring over one another to grab a piece of whatever Arthurian legend they could to stick on their respective mantlepieces when they got back home. We weaved in and out of bus tour groups, arguing parents and excited kids until we reached the first pharmacy.

What the hell to do with Moose?

I settled for standing in the doorway waving my arms like an idiot, with Moose slumped on the floor looking like some reject from a Jim Henson movie. Finally, I caught the eye of the pharmacist, who tentatively approached.

"Do you have any Piriton?"

"I'll go and check," he said, keeping a minimum safe distance.

He came back moments later. "We have Piriteze," he said, apologetically.

The vet was very specific; I said my thanks and moved on.

I repeated the same procedure at the next chemist, where the attendant took one look at us both and eagerly shooed us away, without even bothering to ask what we wanted.

"*Howw rood!*" Moose blubbered from between his swollen chops.

I looked down, still slightly annoyed by the entire escapade, and threw him a hard glance.

At Boots, I decided to try a different tack and asked one of the in-going shoppers to ask for us. Minutes later, a woman in her thirties came bounding out, grabbed Mooch in a bear hug and began cooing.

"Awww – poorly puppy!"

Moose rolled on his back and took full advantage.

"… Wasp sting?" she asked.

I nodded.

"Piriton's the only thing for dogs; three tablets—" she began.

"… Twice a day!" we said in unison.

She laughed and ruffled Mooch's head while he dribbled all over her white apron.

"He'll be fine in two or three days. Antihistamines take a bit longer to work with dogs, so he needs rest."

I thanked her and shoved some money in her hand as Moose sprang to his feet. We weaved our way back through the throngs of tourists in the heaving streets, retreating to where we were still camped up.

I muttered as we walked while, the whole way back to camp, Moose snapped happily at flies, bugs and wasps with his swollen maw.

By far the smartest, yet dumbest, dog I've ever known.

We stayed on our spot in Tintagel for two days while Moose's face slowly deflated. Occasionally, I braved the climb up to the village – if for no reason other than to pop into the local dog-friendly pub to charge stuff up and indulge in a cooked meal.

The swelling had slowly begun to recede and Moose carried on as though the entire episode had never happened in the first place. On the morning of the third day, I restocked our food and water supplies early on before heading out again. All mystique of King Arthur and his knights had long since dissipated, replaced by our own more medicinal quest.

Suffice it to say, I won't remember Tintagel for any reason other than Moose's silly, swollen face.

On the way over the headland, we walked past a church surrounded by a warren of wild grass and intersecting pathways. We headed past a YHA hostel, which was bustling with the excited clamour of young adventurers ready to start the day. I glanced down at Moose, who'd regained his full vigour, and, knowing full well his proclivity for hijinks, ushered us past the place before more crowds emerged.

Before long, we found ourselves back on cliff tops and looking out over magnificent wild views. The sun was back in full force and, down below, the water glistened like glass. As I glanced cautiously over the edge at the grand bays, out to sea I could see magnificent columns of rock that stood immovable. Ahead, the path wound wildly into the bracken. We hugged the drystone walls for our descent until we hit a series of stiles cut into the blockwork.

They must have been four feet high.

"How the hell are we supposed to get over those?"

I looked down at Moose, who gently snorted and then vaulted over the entire thing in a single bound.

I shrugged and followed on. So much for keeping the livestock safe!

Chapter 10

John the Beard

Tintagel to Watergate Bay

We spent the next few days heading over farmland ridges until we reached a vast valley where the twin towns of Port Gaverne and Port Isaac lay. I'd been without phone reception for most of the way since Tintagel but, as I crossed the headland, a familiar set of pings heralded our way back into signal-land. I found a decent patch of shade, crashed to the floor, mopped my brow and began listening to the first of the messages.

"*Hello. Message for Chris and Moose: this is Gemma calling from BBC Radio Bristol...*"

I pulled the phone away from my ear and blinked.

"*...we'd like to feature you on our Breakfast Show...*" the message continued, as the signal drifted in and out while I held my breath, straining to catch each word.

"*...please give* [static] *me a call on 012*[static]*5*[static]*23*[static]*5...*"

"Damn!" I muttered, grabbing my notepad as I cursed my network provider, desperately trying to re-play the message. Eventually, I managed to get most of it written down.

Moose looked up. *"What are you swearing about?"*

"You wouldn't understand," I spat, irritably.

His eyes widened. *"Ooo – now who's being pissy!"*

I chose to ignore the comment, peering down dubiously at the number I'd just scrawled across the pad. "This might mean a bit of publicity, mate."

His head tilted slightly. *"Wot's that?"*

"Maybe a couch..." I threw out absently, just to shut him up.

He began dancing around on the parched grass, excitement brimming in his eyes.

I rolled mine in response. "Pack it in!"

He stood there, drool gathering on the corner of his chops. *"But – couch!"*

"Not if you don't stop arsing about and let me talk on the phone, there won't be..."

Moose immediately stopped, settled on to his paws and lay with his head on my lap, looking at me with those bloody infuriating liquid eyes of his. I gently moved his head off my knees and started wandering about, phone aloft, trying to catch enough signal to call Gemma back. I eventually managed a meagre two-bar signal strength by leaning heavily into a gorse bush, several sharp thorns digging into my legs as I called back.

Between all the pops and breaks, we managed to arrange a telephone interview for the following morning at 10am. I'd hoped that we'd be in town by that time, somewhere I assumed my network provider would deign worthy of a mast installation. I couldn't see the interview going all that well if every second word was clouded by phone static.

We marched down the hill and into Port Gaverne to find out. I still had no idea as to where we were going to stay for the night but I guessed that twin towns like this would have accommodation to spare.

I was mistaken on both counts.

As per the usual set-up in Cornish coastal towns, we tromped down a ruddy great incline and around a bend in the road, where a huge pub was nestled solidly by the bay. Late-afternoon drinkers gathered around masses of tables, chairs and benches enjoying the blistering sun and a cool drink. Rather than risk some last-minute Moosey excitement, I decided not to go in. I was way too tired for any of his nonsense and so I skirted around the outside of the pub to a low flat wall, where I felt a good ten-minute perch was well and truly deserved.

I plopped down and checked my signal...no service!

"Typical," I muttered to myself, stuffing my phone back into my pocket.

"Trouble?" asked a steady voice.

I shook myself out of my reverie and glanced to my right at an unassuming gent who was sitting on the other side of the wall nursing a pint of amber liquid. His weathered features sported a neatly trimmed white beard, atop which fading wisps of white hair clung to the sides of his balding head. He had the seasoned look of someone who'd spent his life outdoors, working hard and playing even harder.

"Sorry! Didn't see you there," I said, pulling Moose close, away from the road.

He shrugged and took a long draught of his ale. "Looks like you've been walking a fair ways."

I smiled and nodded while Moose resisted my urgings to heel and, instead, collapsed in front of the old chap's feet.

"Don't mind the dog..." I said. "He won't eat you."

He chuckled, leant over and gave Mooch a scratch behind the ears. "I've had dogs all my life and this one doesn't look to be much trouble."

I wiped my brow. "He...has his moments, trust me!"

An open hand reached out. "John..." he offered.

"Chris," I said, shaking it in return.

He cast a steady, reassuring gaze. "… John the Beard, they call me 'round here."

I grinned, already taking a liking to his casual demeanour.

We looked at each other and nodded as he slowly raised his glass to his lips and took another long sup. Today had been more of the same blazing hot sunshine and he looked just as knackered as I felt. We sat there in silence for the next minute or so and I began wondering about this strange, silent chap who seemed completely unperturbed by the world as it bustled away around us.

"Walked far?" he asked, eyes casting a casual glance at my pack.

I nodded. "Portishead."

"Oh…dunno where *that* is," he stated, shifting his weight on the wall before continuing, "I expect that's back t'ward Devon someplace?"

"Somerset." I smiled, soaking in the simplicity of the conversation. I looked over and noticed he was reaching the bottom of his glass. "Fancy a beer?"

"Nah – I'll finish this one and head home."

Fair enough, I thought, glancing up the hill towards Port Isaac – and, bloody hell, what a hill it was!

"Well…we need to get up there…" I began, reaching around for my things in preparation for the trek.

"There's a little tuk-tuk service that'll take you up to Port Isaac," he said. "The guy who runs this pub owns the one at the top, too."

I looked down at Mooch, imagining him confined to the back of a tiny two-seater taxi, and thought better of it. "Er – we'll give it a miss, I think," I said, shrugging my shoulders. "Besides," I sniffed, "we could both do with the exercise, anyway."

John laughed and drained the last of his beer. "Suit yerself then, my darlin'."

I nodded farewell, strapped on the pack and headed up the road.

*

135

The gradient from Gaverne to Isaac was no stroll in the park. Every time one of those bloody little motorised tuk-tuks hurtled past, I kicked myself for being so wary about trying new things with the dog. He looked up in amusement as I grunted up the steep incline.

"Imagine how much easier it would've been if we'd have taken a cab." He chuckled, prancing around every lamppost, giddily sniffing at each as he passed.

By the time we got to the top of the hill, I was – once again – absolutely exhausted! I roamed around the town for about half an hour trying to find accommodation, only to discover that everywhere was fully booked. We eventually wandered back to the top of the hill to another pub – romantically called the Stargazy Inn. I timidly enquired about room availability, already knowing that they'd be fully booked; my assumption was correct. In my despair, I meandered my way to the furthest bench, sat down and tried to gather my thoughts.

"Made it, then?" blurted a familiar voice.

I looked around at two eyes grinning above a bristling maw. "Fancy a beer?" John the Beard chirped.

I returned the smile. "This one's on me if you don't mind."

He grinned back. "G'on then – so long as you and the big fella keep me company for a bit."

Without asking, I handed over the lead and nipped in to buy a round. On my way past the reception desk, I ran into the owner who introduced himself as Dave. It turned out that he'd read about our escapades in the *North Devon Gazette* and had several walking stories of his own! I mentioned our current predicament – we needed a phone for our radio interview in the morning. He kindly offered us the use of the pub landline.

As we stood there chatting at the bar, he casually invited me to have a free meal in the restaurant, before shoving £100 in my hand: £50 for Moose and me, and £50 for our charities.

I became conscious of poor John, who I could see perched outside with Moose through the window. I knew it was only a matter of time before another dog owner would turn up and all hell would break loose. I quickly thanked Dave, grabbed the beers and hurried back – just in time to hear Moose gobbing off. Moving faster, I arrived at the scene and quickly handed John the glasses while I reined Mooch in.

John sat there, red-faced from the strain. "Strong bugger, ain't he?"

I shrugged an apology and manhandled Moose into a more secluded spot so I could quiet him down.

"I take it another dog walked in?"

John laughed as he set down the beer. "What made you guess?"

I locked Moo in a stare. "I told you to behave!"

"*But...*" he began to protest.

"But nothing!" I cut him off, staring at the terrified King Charles Spaniel who was now sat shaking in the far corner of the garden next to his very red-faced owner.

"*Well, I didn't like the look of* that *one!*" he continued, shuffling down and snuggling at John's feet.

Shooting an apologetic glance to the chap with the King Charles, I decided against arguing and turned back towards John. Conversation soon gravitated towards our walk and what we were doing in Port Isaac, and to John and his life here in Cornwall. Before long, we were nattering away like we'd known each other for decades.

"So where you staying tonight, then?" John asked.

I shrugged. "Dunno yet."

He inclined his head towards the pub. "No room 'ere, I 'spec?"

"Nope," I said. "High season!"

"So what you two gunna do?"

I tried deflecting the issue: "Probably find a shaded spot somewhere and camp up. I'm sure there's a field nearby."

John paused, reached up and scratched a bristly cheek with one finger... "I don't like the sound of that," he mused. "You both best stay with me!"

I was blown away! "You sure?"

"Wouldn't normally but I get a good feelin' about you two."

He guzzled what remained in his glass and planted it firmly back on the table. "C'mon, lad – we're not far."

I drained my pint, grabbed pack and dog, and followed John up the lanes.

John lived in a modern semi, tucked away in an estate at the highest point of town. He'd lived there alone since the passing of his wife and only had a decrepit parrot and beautiful views over the port bay to keep him company. No sooner had John put his key in the door than Moose barged past, exploring the place like it was his second home.

I shouted after him. "Oii, dickhead!"

John put a reassuring hand on my arm. "He's fine – let him explore."

We walked across the threshold and turned straight into a central porchway where I was guided into a neat kitchen/diner. In the far corner, atop the large counter next to the sink, was a huge bird in a cage. It screeched at John as he calmingly poked a finger in between the bars.

"There, there my darling..." he cooed, the bird hopping closer and butting John's stubby digit with his beak.

Moose took notice for the first time and stood rigid on the linoleum.

"Never you mind," I warned as he twitched, unsure of how to react. A low growl began to murmur in the back of this throat.

John turned and cut him off. "Now don't you be gobbin' off at him, sweetheart!" He gave me a slow wink in the process. "Even guests are expected to behave theirselves."

I laughed in spite of myself and glanced down at Moose's puzzled expression. "Well, that told you!"

He simply puffed his cheeks, flicked his tail and slumped to the floor with a grunt.

John took off his jacket and hung it on a hook behind the door before making his way to the fridge. "I got Guinness or Rum."

I opted for Guinness.

He plonked himself down at the table and poured out a generous measure of rum for himself while sliding a tall black can across the table towards me. Our conversation drifted back to the Waggy Walk.

"I'm impressed," he started, "I would've loved to have done something like that when I were younger."

I shrugged and tried to be a bit blasé about the entire thing. "If I didn't do it now, I probably never would have."

John raised his glass. "Well, as mid-life crises go, yours is a whopper – here's to ya, lad!"

I couldn't argue. I cracked open the can, clinked his glass with the rim and took a gulp. "Good health to you, John."

He nodded and took another gargle of rum.

After that, the night steadily slipped into a drunken mess. In an effort to talk about something other than the walk, I asked about what music he liked.

"You wouldn't know it," he sniffed, "I'd imagine it's a bit too old-fashioned for you."

"Try me!"

"Al'right then," he said, staggering from his chair and grabbing an iPad and speaker from a nearby shelf before plonking himself back down on his stool. He fumbled on the screen for a few seconds and then hit 'play'.

'Don't Pay the Ferryman' by Chris de Burgh came blaring out of the speaker.

Well, that was it for me! I've been a huge fan ever since my dad dragged me off to a concert of his when I was a kid. I leant over, unclipped the travel guitar off my pack and started to play along. John's jaw dropped further as I continued to play other stuff I knew, which turned out to be some of his other favourites. As well as the steady stream of banter between us, it seemed we also liked the same kind of music. Outside, it began to get dark and I realised I'd inadvertently stood up the offer of dinner at the Stargazy.

"Ah, Dave's a good egg," John slurred. "He'll understand!"

The Guinness and rum continued to flow as we talked long into the early hours. I couldn't quite work out whether it was John's amenable character or something else, but I felt that we'd known each other for years – such was the ease of conversation that night. He had an easy way of talking that sparked enthusiasm for each subject, despite the years between us, as we skated around every subject from music to long-lost romances. Of all the people I'd met and were yet to meet on this journey, John the Beard was someone with whom I'd found an incredible affinity.

I'm proud to say that we're still friends to this day.

Somewhat worse for wear, I dragged myself to bed later that evening and passed out atop the covers, sleeping as soundly as I ever have. In the morning, the sun burned into my eyelids to spark the mutha of all hangovers! I glanced at my watch as the hands blurred into view and sat bolt upright.

"Shit!" It was half nine.

I dragged my clothes on and bolted for the door. John was stood in the kitchen with a cup of coffee in one hand, calmly feeding the bird with the other. "Mornin'!" He smiled. "How are you?"

"I'm bloody late…" I blurted, harnessing Moose.

"Good night last night!"

I laughed in spite of my panic to make the interview – indeed it was!

I hurried out the door as the world spun with every step and headed back down the hill to meet Dave at the Stargazy.

*

I finally turned towards the steps leading up to the restaurant to find him casually leaning against the door jamb, holding a cup of coffee in one hand.

"Cutting it a bit fine, aren't we?" He smiled as I clambered up the steps.

"Soooo sorry about last night…" I grunted. "I was knackered and had an early night."

Dave smiled politely and waved away the apology.

Early night? Who was I kidding! I must have smelled like I'd slept in a beer keg!

He nodded towards the bar. "Phone's over there, buddy."

I muttered thanks. Five minutes later, it rang.

"This is Emma from BBC Radio Bristol…"

"Heleau…" I said, unintentionally putting on my best phone voice.

"Err…could we speak to Chris, please?" came the reply, in a contrastingly normal tone of voice.

"Pack it in, you knob!" I muttered to myself, making a conscious effort to tone down my voice. "Speaking…" I replied, still trying to catch my breath.

"Oh – hi," came the response. "We'll have you on in a couple of minutes with our morning host, Johnny."

I scribbled that down on a piece of paper in front of me as the voice on the other end of the phone continued, "Just try to relax and be yourself."

I took a deep breath; the room spun in response and we began the live broadcast.

As interviews go, I think I did OK. I tried to block out the fact that half of Bristol was listening as I prattled on about our walk. Twenty minutes felt like five and, before I knew it, we were done and marching back up the street to John's.

I walked into the kitchen to find him poking treats through the cage at a very uninterested parrot.

"How'd it go?" he asked, still focused on the bird.

"You weren't listening?" I said, in a hurt voice.

"Bloody thing wouldn't tune in," he said, indicating the iPad on the table with a tilt of his head.

We sat and talked through what was said while we enjoyed breakfast together. Before long, it was time for us to gather our things and get back on the road. Just as we were leaving, I asked John if I could take a picture of us all together, to which he stubbornly refused. "I don't take good photos," he muttered. "Besides, let's keep it in our hearts."

I was inclined to agree, I thought, as I shook hands with this wonderful chap one last time and headed down the road towards the port.

The streets there were teeming with tourists and, as much as I'd have liked to stop off for a sample of local crab, I thought better of leaving Moose outside with so many people about. We wandered straight out of town and up again on to the headland. I glanced back at this place and to where John's house sat, twinkling in the distance on the side of the hill. I remember feeling that familiar butterfly twinge in my belly; Port Isaac was somewhere I wouldn't ever forget – if for no other reason than the unlikely friendship I'd made there.

Not one for sentiment, Mooch looked up at me impatiently. "*Are we going or wot?*"

I sighed, took one last peek at the town, and followed him up the path.

The rocky terrain and steep steps were now becoming par for the Cornwall course for us. Up ahead was the popular holiday spot of Polzeath and, for me, this was an important stop. It was the first place I ever visited, back in the hazy days when I was seventeen years old, on my first holiday away with my childhood sweetheart.

It was nothing like how I remembered it...it's funny how your mind works that way.

We trekked on through because it was still early enough to reach the estuary of the River Camel. The path had guided us down to an even level of sandy beach. My maps told me that we could cross by ferry directly into Padstow from the port of Rock, saving us several hours of walking to Wadebridge and back. Just before Rock, we encountered a dune field of warrens and grass where I found an out-of-the-way nook and pitched up for the night.

The next morning, we set off just in time to make the first crossing of the day. As we waited, a congregation of people began to form on the top of the slipway, where we all chatted among ourselves. It quickly became apparent that these weren't your usual gaggle of tourists but, rather, workers on the early-morning commute.

Padstow was a bustling place filled with restaurants, attractions and shops. All were serviced by locals, some of whom lived on this side of the estuary. It was a surreal experience, chatting to folks in this idyllic setting, most of whom were just on their way to work.

During the conversation, one of the girls piped up about 'that Friday feeling!' I was flabbergasted.

Friday? I didn't even know what day of the week we were on anymore.

After the crossing, the land began to flatten out.

At Trevose Head, we reached a lighthouse that I'd seen flickering in the distance two weeks before. The coast really opened up to us from this vantage point. Behind, I could see everywhere we'd spent the last fortnight walking, while ahead lay all the treasures Cornwall had yet to offer.

The breathtaking beauty of this entire region of the UK cannot be understated – cliffs and sea opened up before us and, somewhere in the distance, lay the secret places I'd longed to visit. Cornish mining engines, industrial towers, quarries…these hitherto unknown places had sparked my imagination and formed that initial drive to begin walking in the first place. I closed my eyes and could see the likes of Neil Oliver chatting in my ear about the rich history of a place I simply couldn't wait to immerse myself in. For the short term, though, the next big town on my horizon was a place called Watergate Bay, which sits about a mile or two north up the coast from Newquay.

Watergate Bay had long been a hotspot for surfers and was somewhere I'd stayed for a week with a few friends, one of whom was a lost, beloved companion called Fitz, almost a decade before.

Like Moose, Fitz was a rescue. His Staffie heritage, unfortunately, meant that he'd spent the early part of his life in fighting pits with other dogs. He'd already sported several scars including a torn ear when he was first adopted and his colouring was a brown/grey brindle. Most people found Fitz a bit tricky to get on with…he had that look of a dog who'd chew you up and spit you out, which couldn't be further from the truth if you took the time and courage to get to know him a bit.

Fiercely loyal and protective, that dog was a blessing and one that was shared among the entire group of friends I had at the time. Sometimes he'd stay at my house and at other times he'd stay over with my best friend Greg at his. He'd contentedly hop from house to house, with whomever he felt like staying with that night, content to be the ultimate couch-hopper, and a dog of many homes!

When he died, at the grand old age of seventeen, we'd all decided to take him back to the sea at Watergate Bay. Unlike Moose, Fitz had loved the ocean and always used to jump in head-first, trying to take on the fury of Mother Nature's waves, jaws agape. He'd been so happy at Watergate Bay and so it was somewhere we all felt was appropriate to spread his ashes.

Moose could feel my apprehension as we approached the familiar collection of rocks at the far end of the beach.

"*What's up?*" he asked.

"Nothing..." I mused, not willing to entertain *that* kind of conversation with him. "I used to have a friend that loved this place..." I whispered, too quietly for him to hear.

I unclipped Moose's leash and he flew off into the distance while I sat on a nearby rock and allowed memories to flood in: Fitz deserved, at the very least, to be felt and remembered during this journey. I watched the sea breaking on the shore and imagined that feisty bugger barking headlong into the waves as I saw Moose skirt tentatively around them. I'd almost forgotten Fitz's voracious attitude towards life and his fearless mindset against insurmountable odds.

Emotions flooded me as I remembered my long-gone friend and the special times we'd shared. I sat, gently crying on that rock as the sun set, watching his ghost dance among fading waves. I let go of all those forgotten memories, resurfacing now that I was in this hallowed place... his twitching nose as I'd caress his ears, the snapping bark he'd emit when something exciting caught his attention, and the mass of kisses that remain forever etched across my heart.

Fitz was awesome, and he was all mine...for that short time, anyway.

I called back Moose and wiped away my tears as we walked across the sand in the fading light and back up towards the bay.

Chapter 11

The Chaos Beyond

Watergate Bay to Portreath

We hit Newquay just after sunrise.

We charged headlong into a thick pall of mist, which clung to absolutely everything it touched… It was, perhaps, the strangest day Moose and I had encountered so far.

I grew up in Manchester and was used to its cold foggy days. Here, though, the heat of summer seemed to be trapped in the air as in some ethereal steam room, determined to poach us both alive! We walked from path to pavement and eventually found ourselves on wide boulevards shrouded in a humid, white pall, which, every now and then, exposed huge open parks, grand Victorian townhouses and lines of parked cars. It was hard to believe we were descending into one of the most bustling towns of the county, yet here we both were, fighting through a hot muggy sludge and on into the town of Newquay – a Cornish surfing tourism hotspot and a town that never slept.

Like the mist, the crowds grew thicker as the morning drew on and became increasingly difficult to navigate through. We approached the town centre, where busy road traffic made things even more complicated. Car horns blew amid the bustle of people and barking animals as the suburban sprawl of dust, noise and chaos made our progress even more challenging.

I looked at Moose, who, periodically, had been nudging my leg for reassurance.

"Keep calm, pal," I muttered, keeping him close. "We'll march through this lot and then take a rest once we're on the other side of town."

He nudged his head against my thigh with his ears lowered. *"No argument from me."*

I nodded and gave his ears a reassuring scratch. "Let's keep moving, then."

Across parks, lanes and busy roads, I constantly scanned ahead, scouring for unwelcome encounters with other dogs and their owners. We crossed roads frequently to head off any potential frays before they started and, after an hour or so of dodging and weaving, we made it past the outskirts of the main shopping area and down towards a road that turned out on to the dunes overshadowing Fistral Beach. The air was so warm and thick that we were both absolutely drenched in sweat. We paused for a moment to catch our breath and I looked around, barely able to make out the revellers on the beach below. The sea crashed away beyond the seemingly infinite sun-lit gloom that stretched out over the sands.

Our ultimate goal that morning was Pentire and the Fern Pit Café, and ferry crossing below it. The sting of walking on pavement was once again taking its toll on my feet, which burned in their leather bindings. We quickly found a table and rested beneath the scant shade of a parasol, waiting for the heat of the day to ease off.

Moose curled around my feet, looked up and gave me a parched look.

"Fancy a drink?" I asked.

He lolled his tongue out in reply.

I fumbled in my pack for a canister of water and filled his bowl and sat there listening to him gobble up every last drop while sheltering from the blazing sun. A woman sitting on the bench next to ours noticed and struck up a conversation. She introduced herself as Leslie and, for whatever reason, also happened to have dog treats aplenty in her pocket.

At first, this might seem a bit strange – but, as most dog owners will know, it's not unusual to leave the house for the shops and pull out a handful of doggy-bags and Bonios when reaching in for some change. For Moose, this was another shallow excuse at friendship; she sat nearby, issuing a steady trickle of snacks into his waiting maw.

We continued chatting for an hour or so until I suggested that we'd soon have to start making a move down to the ferry so we could cross the River Gannel and carry on to wherever we'd end up staying for the night. Leslie kindly offered to drive us around the estuary and drop us both on the other side. It was an offer neither of us had the disposition to turn down. Minutes later, we were speeding around the roads to the other side of Pentire, regaling each other with tales of travel as we zoomed along.

She dropped us off in a restaurant car park and we soon found ourselves back in the dunes above town. I decided enough was enough, found us a shaded spot to camp up and set about making us both dinner. We were running dangerously low on food and only had a couple of Super Noodles packets left. Like in Minehead, the opportunity to shop in Newquay may as well have been akin to nipping up to the moon and back, for all the chance I had to make it happen safely. Suppressing the urge to gobble the last of my stores, I reminded myself about the prudence of rationing – the next few days were going to be a tough slog. As the sun set, I could see the lights from Newquay glow in the fading light like some kind of surreal fairground. Vast towers of light lit up the coastline in an array of dotted ambers, blues and reds.

I sat down wearily next to Moose and gave him a gentle tap on the head. "Well done, pal – we made it!" He didn't respond, but I took his snoring as silent agreement.

As I tried to sleep that night, I lay awake wondering whether I'd ruined myself for crowded places forever and if this whole escapade was one huge mistake when it came to that day in the future when we'd both have to settle back down into civilised society again.

Our little hideaway was just what we needed after the manic passage through Newquay. I didn't rush to move the next day. Rather, we drifted from town to town as we headed further south. I tried easing my mind back into cheery thoughts but walking on an empty stomach is not easy, especially when covering this kind of mileage every day. I had enough food to last maybe another day. Convenience shops simply were not forthcoming along our route.

At Perranporth, I decided to take it easy and, as we took shelter under one of the RNLI stations, I took off my boots, socks and shirt and set about my usual routine of foot first aid.

A bit of beachy leisure time was just the thing to lift our spirits!

Mooch looked up at me. "*Look at you, sporting a new T-shirt!*" He quipped, as a cheeky grin crept across his face.

"What new shirt?" I asked, completely aware that the filthy rag I'd been wearing the last few days lay crumpled in the sand next to my boots.

"*You could land aircraft with that chest.*" He sniggered and walked off without saying another word.

I glanced at my arms, bronzed from weeks of walking in the open sun, and, scanning my eyes along my upper body, was nearly blinded by the alabaster blaze of pale skin above my elbows and across my chest. I looked down at my torso, reflected by the midday sun, and realised that my tan was far from being even!

"You cheeky little shit!" I shouted, quickly grabbing a handful of sand and throwing it after him as he scurried off. I picked my top up off the ground and grudgingly put it back on in an effort not to blind any unsuspecting passers-by.

I have to take my hat off to the guys at RNLI: every time we stopped near one of these places, we'd introduce ourselves to the lifeguards and ask for a cheeky battery charge, while we waited out the heat in the shadow beneath their huge lookout posts. While we would usually sit out of the sun's glare, today was different, and I fancied enjoying some time as a tourist.

The beach was teeming with people but its sheer scale meant that Moose and I could roam around the sand mostly unimpeded. For one of the first times on this journey, I could leave the mass of kit I carried with me behind while I soaked up to my knees in seawater as Moose barked at the ocean's wake every time the water got too close for comfort.

It was bliss, feeling so freed from the confines of Waggy Walk. I experienced a new sense of admiration for the tour bus driver, who was forever condemned to stay in the confines of the car park while the sea-faring tourists got to wander about, having fun in the sun all day.

Later, I sat in the shade smooshing my toes in the sand while Moose rolled around in the stuff, far more comfortable on land than he was in water. We people-watched for a while until the sun had dropped low enough for us to continue around the coast to find a nice spot to camp on the headland at St Agnes.

That night, I riffled through our dwindling supplies in an attempt to throw dinner together. I had plenty for Moose – albeit Chum and dry-mix – but was running drastically low on things for me. I fished out the last of my noodles and settled down with a touch of panic at what I feared could be my last meal.

*

I awoke to Moose's nose snuffling away at my ear and, as I felt the tip of his tongue attempt a shot in my lughole, immediately shot upright.

"You can pack *that* in, for starters!"

"*It's wakey time,*" he insisted, as the tip of his wagging tail slapped away at the top of the canvas.

I looked at my watch – it was a little past six in the morning. "You're kidding, right?"

He ran his tongue the length of my cheek in reply.

"Fine!" I grumbled, fumbling about for my shoes. "I suppose you want breakfast?" I enquired, rolling out of the tent.

He gave a good, solid bark of approval right in my ear.

I groaned, stretched and massaged my aching feet, and glanced up at the blue sky. The tip of the sun was already blazing away on the horizon. I grimaced. Today was going to be another hot one!

I rummaged around for pet bowls, fed the Moose and reached for my own – remembering at the last minute that I had nothing left. I shrugged inwardly and began getting our things together.

Moose looked up… "*Not eating?*" he asked, tilting his head to one side.

I smiled and shook my head. "I'm not hungry, bud."

He lowered his ears as he caught the lie, knowing better than to argue.

I probably mentioned this earlier, but some of the things I was most looking forward to seeing were the old Cornish mines that dotted the south coast. The closest I'd ever got to them before was watching documentaries about these huge ruins on TV. As we made our way down the open path, I saw one glistening through the morning haze in the distance – our first engine house!

The experience was somewhat dampened by the gnawing ache and listlessness that came from eating too little. I was getting tetchy – even to the point that I was beginning to lose my patience with Moose. On our way down the path, he met a feisty bulldog and decided to start barking. He bristled and charged at the would-be assailant, nearly yanking me off my feet.

I lost my temper and roared at him.

"*But…*" he began.

"*But* nothing!" I cut him off. "You nearly pulled me over, dickhead!"

He bit back: "*Why are you in such a bad mood?!*"

I stopped myself, realising that I was being a tad unfair. "Sorry, bud – but it doesn't help when you pull and I *really* need something to eat."

"*Why didn't you have any breakfast, then?*" he snapped.

"I ran out!" I snapped back.

He snorted and held his ground. "*Well, don't blame me!*"

He scurried up the path and began sniffing away indignantly, deliberately ignoring me as I miserably trudged along behind. At the next corner, we encountered another dog followed by a bewildered owner. The impending encounter gave Moose the excuse to erupt into another raucous of snarls and barks, half in surprise and half just to piss me off.

"Mooch!" I yelled, keeling over in an effort to hold him back. "What the hell are you doing?"

"*None of your business!*" came the snarky reply, as he continued raging at the end of the lead until, eventually, I ended up in a heap on the side of the path.

Well that was it!

Once I'd picked myself back up off the floor, our conversation spiralled downwards into a series of quips and jibes. We argued our way down the rest of the track like an old married couple. I could see walkers catch sight of this bizarre tiff and avoid us as we hurled insult after insult at each other.

At Chapel Porth Beach, things finally came to a head.

I'd spied a café teeming with families at the far end of the car park. I staggered over to it, already footsore, bruised and light-headed due to the heat and lack of sustenance, tied Moose up and began to queue for something to eat. No sooner was I standing in line than he let out yet another bellowing series of barks and growls at three little fluffballs who'd stepped in line just behind us. Confident in their superiority of numbers, they started egging him on with little barks and snaps of their own, which, in turn, set him off with even fiercer vigour. All around, I could see parents gather their children closer with worried looks as this brown 'monster-dog' unleashed a torrent of deep woofs.

A mist of red suddenly descended.

To say that I screamed at Moose was an understatement. If the patrons weren't worried by the devil dog, then his slightly unhinged owner yelling at the top of his voice definitely put them off. It was hard to tell who was more uncouth – him or me – as we stood there hurling obscenities at each other for all the world to see.

I caught some of the stares from the corner of my eye and instantly flushed. I fell to my knees and pleaded with him to stay calm long enough that I could grab a desperately needed sandwich.

I heard movement and a voice from behind. "Please could you stop screaming at each other! You're disturbing the children!"

I looked over and saw an extremely cross young woman sporting a National Trust T-shirt.

"Err, sorry…" I began.

"In fact," she cut me off, "it's probably better if you both leave!"

She turned and marched back into the café while Moose and I stared at each other shamefaced. I was at once completely gutted by the comment and absolutely appalled at myself for getting so het up. I quickly grabbed the pack and grunted at Moose, and heads bowed, we both got the hell out of Dodge.

High on the path, I glanced back at the café, where life was returning to normal. With a gnawing emptiness in my stomach, we continued on to the next town.

*

Porthtowan was our next stop although it was late afternoon before we eventually dragged ourselves into town. Away from the beach was a series of pubs and restaurants that led upwards from the bay along a narrow, crooked road, and further up the hill, about half a mile inwards, was the town itself. All in all, it was somewhat an odd layout for a village.

I dumped the pack against a bench in a stone seating area near the harbour and trekked up through a lovely little wood before encountering a road that was more a vertical climb than a winding country lane. As I trudged up that hill with Moose, I thought back to my rucksack, sitting unattended, wishing anyone with the wherewithal to lift and carry the damned thing off the very best of luck.

Such was my mindset and hunger.

Once at the top, I found a shop and gratefully replenished my supplies – including a few much-needed Cornish pasties. On the way back down and as I wolfed down the last of them, I reflected on the need to keep better stock of my supplies. By now it was getting late, and with some relief, I recovered my pack and headed back along the line of restaurants and bars again.

Outside one of these, I began talking to a group who were happily getting merry. We were quickly offered a pint as one of the guys noticed the guitar on my pack and asked me for a song.

"Are you that desperate for entertainment?" I quipped.

"Go on, lad!" They egged me on. "Give us a tune!"

I smiled. "Fair enough – but this *is* a charity gig…" I said, slyly.

Fivers and tenners began pushing their way into my hands, and in the space of about five minutes, I had twenty-five quid in the pot.

Well, that had me cornered!

I reached over and picked up the guitar, twiddling the tuners until it sounded something like ready. *This had better be bloody good*, I thought, wiping down the strings to begin playing. Within seconds a crowd had gathered and they all started singing and cheering along as I blasted out a few pub favourites.

Moose jumped up at the commotion and started howling to the melody: *"Ooo, singing! I like singing!"*

Together, we set about destroying some REM, Eagles and Paul Simon classics while people stopped in the street to join in. I'd forgotten how much I enjoyed playing to an audience as we belted out song after song. Before long, I wrapped up and, with a few cheery handshakes, headed off out of town to find another shaded spot for the night.

Moose trotted calmly by my side as we left town. *"What did you stop for? I was enjoying that!"*

I reached down and scratched his head between his ears. "Because it's getting late, bud, and we need to find a camp spot."

His tongue lolling out of the side of his mouth, he looked up at me and grinned. *"Bloody spoilsport!"*

I laughed as I felt the last of the tension between us fall away. "I don't remember 'Hotel California' having a *howling* solo..."

He sneezed and gave his tail a sly flick. *"Well, if you can't appreciate some artistic licence..."*

I sniggered in spite of myself and got to my knees to give him a big bear hug.

"C'mon, pal – time to move."

Moose snorted and tugged at the turf with his claws before heading back out towards the path. I followed behind, listening to the cheer of the locals outside the pub fade as we trudged up the lanes and out of town.

The sun was getting lower as we peaked the headland and, after several weaves and winds of the road, came across an old quarry site surrounded by fields of harsh bracken, interspersed with magnificent arrays of wild colour. Flowers of every shade – blues and reds, violets and yellows – stretched out for miles and miles, amid pale scatterings of hot rubble and slag. Jagged cliffs and quarries held all of this in check to create a truly alien landscape, beautiful like none we'd seen since the stark landscape at Steart Marsh.

Once again, my mind wandered as Moose darted in and out of the bushes of thorny blossoms. Remnants of old foundations littered the place while the blasted quarry rock gave everything an ethereal aesthetic. I gazed across to a clearing that lay below us, shadowed into gloom by the surrounding peaks that circled the valley of these abandoned ruins. The earth seemed to thrum in the latent heat of the day as I imagined myself an advance scout on an away mission to some distant, hitherto unexplored moon. I stopped to take photos, as I didn't have a hope in hell's chance of capturing the essence of this eerie place.

The fading sun continued to play out a dance of shadows and light before we were both compelled to plod on – I was getting too knackered to care and Mooch looked on with unusual patience.

The next day, a little further along the path, we passed a mass of abandoned outbuildings next to a small airfield where we sheltered for a while just to get out of the sun for ten minutes or so. We guzzled water and munched down a snack each before heading back into the blazing sun and down into Portreath.

As soon as my feet hit pavement the pain in my feet returned with a vengeance.

The road to Portreath was a steep, winding decline into town past lines of grand houses set back from the pavement. Each slow step sent shots of pain up the heels of my feet and knees, as I strained and sweated under the weight of the pack and the effort of pushing myself on through the pain. I decided to try something new and broke into a fast-paced trot, hoping the speed would take away the sting as my boots pounded more lightly against the tarmac.

Now, as daft as it might sound, the bouncy jog down the hill did have less of an effect on my legs. For starters, it was considerably less painful on my knees. The pack bounced gently against my shoulders and settled me into a nice rhythm, which, in turn, eased the effect of my footfalls. It also meant that we got to the bottom a lot sooner – something Moose interpreted as a playful effort as he bounced along merrily behind. As we wound our way in from the bay, the gradient flattened. We found an open plaza featuring a grand building with the words 'The Portreath Arms Hotel' blazoned on the facia above rows of windows, and rested outside it for a few minutes. At the far end of the building, I pushed my way through the doors and into a cool, beautifully crafted taproom.

"Do you accept dogs?" I panted, wiping streams of sweat from my brow.

At the bar were a few customers and a barmaid, who warmly beckoned us both inside. I drew Moose across to the furthest reaches of the room, de-mobbed the pack and staggered back to the bar.

"Awww…" she said cooingly at Moose. "Would he like a drink?"

Moose threw me a pleading look.

"Err…yes, please. That's very kind."

I could barely see. I wiped the sweat from my forehead to take the fresh bowl of water from her hands. "Could I also have a lime and soda?"

"Pint or half?" she asked.

Gallon, I thought…

"A pint would be lovely."

"Ice?"

I just stood there and nodded dumbly before taking the glass, shuffling back to where I'd dropped the rucksack and collapsing into one of the chairs at the far end of the pub.

Moose instantly followed suit.

We sat there for an hour or so, slowly recovering from the day's trek, and I began wondering about our plans for where to stay. I glanced about, checked the bank balance and shrugged: this place *was* a hotel after all.

I went back to speak to the barmaid. "Do you have any rooms for the night?"

"I'll have to check – I'm new and rooms isn't something I know how to do." She paused and shouted the owner over, "Do we have any rooms?"

The owner looked at me, looked at Moose and glanced at the pack leant up against the wall next to our table with genuine concern on her face. "I'll look, but I'm sure we're fully booked."

I sighed – it was peak season after all. "Don't worry if you haven't."

"Nonsense – we'll get you sorted." She picked up a diary from next to the phone and began flicking through the pages. "If we can't, then we'll call around until we find you both somewhere."

A few minutes later, there was a tap on my shoulder…

Moose looked up at the owner, who stood there beaming. "You're in luck!"

I glanced back, somewhat confused.

"Debbie at the Menagerie has rooms!"

Once again, I shed a wee tear to the gods of good fortune and smiled. "I can't begin to thank you."

She waved away the praise before continuing, "… And if you come back tonight, there's a meal for you both – compliments of the house!"

I blinked, thanked them both and lumped my kit together to get across to the B&B where showers, comfort and a bed waited.

We received an equally warm welcome from Debbie the B&B owner. After walking for perhaps another quarter of a mile from the pub in the smouldering aftermath of the hot day, I stood at the door somewhat tentatively and asked the usual question about dogs.

"Of course, of course," she muttered dismissively, ushering us into her home.

Once inside, we were quickly shown to our room. It was a lovely twee set-up, complete with woven pillows adorned with bunny rabbits and considerate wall hangings filled with countryside motifs and yet more rabbits… I caught the hint of a theme here!

I used to have a huge house rabbit called Whisper, so I didn't mind the décor one bit. After I settled Mooch in the room, I followed Debbie into the dining room and we began chatting about the varied collection of animals that lived with her.

With each mention of one variety of critter or another came a unique story of how each had ended up living with Debbie in this wonderfully eclectic setting. Not only did Debbie share her home with wayward strangers such as myself, but also with cats, a dog, several rabbits, a bird…the list went on.

'Menagerie' indeed! I thought, smiling to myself.

Later that evening, I grimaced at my beet-red face in the mirror, showered and, once again, set about the task of patching my feet back into some semblance of shape. As the sun set, we limped back down to the pub for our late dinner.

What we'd encountered earlier that afternoon as we came in was a far cry from what we experienced when we walked through the door. The place was absolutely packed! Fortunately enough for us, the seating at the far end was still free.

I had a menu shoved into my hands while all the bar staff gathered around Moose to beset him with a flurry of hugs, cuddles and kisses. He lay there on his back, arched his neck and wiggled his toes while he winked at me as he was caressed into a contented snooze.

I paid little attention and savagely tucked into my meal.

The attention died off and I grabbed a cider to settle me in for the night. One of the wait-staff came over just after dark, leant across and gently told me that it might get even busier – tonight was open mic night!

I nearly fell off my chair – my little impromptu gig the day before had given me a taste for more! I looked over, determined to get a spot on the stage, and glibly asked the organiser if I could borrow his kit so I could play.

I threw Moose a warning glance. "Are you going to behave?"

"*Too tired to argue…*" he said, before flumping his head back on to the carpet.

That was my cue. As soon as my name was called, I limped up to the stage, tethered Moose to my waist and grabbed hold of what looked like a very expensive guitar. I began my set, somewhat distracted by the fact that Moose could tear me off the stool at any moment and send me, microphone and expensive guitar flying into the air if he so chose.

Thankfully, none of that happened and I handed back the guitar amid a round of applause and with immense relief. On our way out we were cornered by the owner and ordered to come back in the morning so we could exchange some details before we left town.

I staggered back to the Menagerie, filled with the warm glow of Rattler cider, rich applause and comfort in the fact that I didn't have to fork out for a £500 Takamine guitar. I collapsed into bed and was asleep in moments; Moose nestled into my shoulder and did the same.

We awoke to calls alerting us to the champions' breakfast waiting for us in the dining room the next morning. Moose and I strode in and sat opposite Debbie as we ate and chatted about all creatures great and small. The night before, I'd been cheeky enough to ask the favour of doing some laundry, which she'd placed neatly folded on the table next to us.

"I didn't realise you were doing a charity walk."

I shrugged, stuffing the last of the scrambled egg into my mouth. "How did you know?"

She nodded towards the pile of clothes. "It's written all over your T-shirts."

"Oh yeh." I laughed. "I'd forgotten about that."

"Well, your money's no good here." She smiled. "Consider last night as a gift from me."

Once again, the kindness of strangers left me lost for words. We hugged our goodbyes and headed back down the lane to the inn. At the bottom of the lane, we were hit by the stench that could come only from a working harbour.

"Someone really needs to jet-wash that dock." I gagged, seeing Moose's nose twitch wildly in the air.

"*S'lovely*." He beamed, tongue lolling out of his gob.

We agreed to disagree on that one. The smell was utterly dreadful and the morning sun wasn't about to make things any better. Outside the Portreath Inn, a chap was watering the hanging baskets.

He lowered the hose as he saw us approach. "She's waiting for you inside," he said, without missing a beat.

My jaw dropped slightly before I muttered a brief hello.

I walked into the pub to find the landlady sitting at the table. "Hello! Nice to have you back – I'm so glad you called back in."

"Morning," I offered, cheerfully.

We began chatting. It seemed that her mid-life crisis reflected my own, except that she had this grand pub to show for her efforts. Like me, she was a northerner settled down south, cutting her own path into the Cornish countryside as patron of the pub we were both sitting in. On my way out, she shoved a packed lunch into my hands and wished us well on our next phase of Kernow: our last southerly part of the journey.

As we headed around the stinky bay of Portreath, I made a mental note to return here one day. Like so many places we'd passed through, this one had captured another piece of my heart.

Moose looked back and sighed.

"C'mon, you daft bugger," I said, scratching the top of his head. "Onwards and upwards."

Moose turned and caught sight of an appealing piece of turf on the green, took a pee and followed on behind.

Chapter 12

Finding the Way

Portreath to Zennor

Another hot day awaited, and we stood contemplating the path ahead, gathering ourselves in preparation for the challenges to come.

"Güten Tag!"

I quickly spun around to see a family of four soldiering straight past, poles flailing as they manoeuvred their way around the winds in the path.

"Er…hello," I called after, unheard as they disappeared into the distance.

I looked down at Moose. "Kinda puts us to shame eh, buddy?"

He lifted his snout from out of the grass, staring blankly as he chewed at random strands that stuck out from beneath his jowls. "*Huh?*"

I shook my head slightly. "Never mind."

Grabbing a pole in each hand, I looked to where the German family had passed a few moments before and followed suit.

Before long, we were back up high on top of the headland; from there, the landscape opened up to expose a line of cliff and shoreline that would become today's travel. The flow of the land here was less severe than it had been the last few weeks and the contours of the path wound and undulated in steady curves and dips.

I could definitely get used to this – if I never encountered another bloody staircase again it would be too soon!

The ferns and brush grew higher on either side of the path and began obscuring the view out to sea. Before long, it became easy to imagine that we were walking on some inland trail as opposed to shadowing the lines of the coast. Dotted here and there to our right were car parks and the inevitable 'viewpoints', complete with benches and breathtaking views of stunning Cornish vistas. The sea glistened gently in the sunlight while the faint crashing of waves from far below hinted at just how high the clifftops were here. We stopped frequently at these spots, as did other fellow hikers.

Before long, we'd caught up with the German family (who actually turned out to be Austrian) and stopped for a better introduction. Moose, never one to pass up an opportunity for attention, immediately began circling the two kids.

Dad looked slightly panicked at first.

"Don't worry," I said, "he's good with kids."

Dad didn't look convinced – that is, until Moose flopped belly-up on the ground, tongue lolling out of his gob, and was inundated with a series of tickles, kisses and giggles from the boy and girl as he lay there soaking in all the belly rubs he could get.

He looked up at me and grinned. I'll give him his due: he definitely did have a way with kids.

Dad relaxed a bit and the conversation began to flow. I've always felt slightly ashamed of the linguistic proficiency shown by Europeans when it came to speaking English. Worse still was the fact that my mum is actually Austrian and yet here I was, conversing in English, trying like mad to think of a German phrase or two by way of return.

The young lad looked up. "Wie heißt dein Hund?"

A dim memory sparked. "Mein Hund ist...er..." my German faltered. "Moose?" I said questioningly, throwing a worried look at his mum.

She smiled and nodded while her little boy called out, "MOOSE!!!" More cuddles and kisses ensued and I glanced up at the couple with a shaky smile.

"Your German is good," the lady commented to me in English.

"Danke," I replied, giving her a wry smile, grateful for the kind compliment. Mein Deutsch ist Scheiße, I thought to myself, as I gathered Moose, picked up my kit and carried on down the path waving goodbye.

A mile or so down the path, we hit a tight curve that opened up to gaps in the tall gorse, giving stunning views of sharp drops and soaring cliffs.

PING

I looked at my phone – it was my dad.

> I've been watching the weather reports, really worried about the storms you're having down there.
> Stay Safe!

I looked up at the sun blazing away in the clear blue sky, wondering where my dad actually thought we both were.

> Don't worry – we're fine.

I pocketed my phone and carried on down to a huge clearing where coachloads of tourists were scrabbling up towards the path. I skilfully avoided them – as much as I liked company, I didn't feel like running off the whole spiel about coastal walking. I still had our stay at Portreath fresh in my mind and wanted to savour the experience as long as I could.

We found shelter beneath a huge tree and I unpacked the lunch lovingly prepared for us that morning.

Moose sat and stared as I tucked into the doorstop sandwich.

"*That looks tasty.*" He dribbled.

I shifted slightly to the side so as to shield my lunch from view. "Mmm. It is..."

He tilted his head and twitched up an accompanying eyebrow. "*I like sammiches!*"

I shifted my perch on the rock a few more degrees. "Yep. Me too," I said, with a mouth full of bread.

The Moose's head followed me around, his eyes bobbing slightly in rhythm to my chewing.

"Oh for God's sake!" I snapped, throwing the remaining sandwich at his maw.

SNAP!

Well, there goes lunch! I thought as Moose chewed gleefully before gulping the entire thing down whole.

"Happy?!" I asked.

He grunted, swallowed, and nodded. "*Any more?*"

I reached into the bag, drew out a bar of chocolate and slowly scoffed the entire thing as he looked on. "Not for doggies, there isn't."

He belched, gently turned and cracked my leg with his tail before sulking off. I rubbed away at the sting before getting up and following on after the bugger.

Ahead, the way lay clear but, glancing to my left, I could see roiling clouds far in the distance with the tell-tale mist of rain beneath. I thought back to my dad's text and checked the weather on my phone. I hadn't bothered with such mundane things as weather reports since I set off walking. I'd never trusted the damn things anyway. The app on my phone proudly announced an approaching storm that had hit the Americas earlier that week.

"So *that's* what Dad was on about," I said to Moose, who ignored me and carried on snuffling away in the heather.

Despite the heat, I couldn't help but gather an imaginary shroud around my shoulders as we picked up the pace towards St Ives. Thankfully, the sun shone proud and the clouds remained at an unalarming distance.

My mood was high and through whatever by-product of that, my brain fished an old riddle from the depths of my memory, which I began cheerily reciting as I walked along the path.

> Walking on the road to St Ives,
> I met a man with seven wives,
> Each wife had seven sacks…
> Seven sacks held seven cats,
> Each cat had seven kits!
> Kits, cats, sacks, wives…

I looked across at Moose. "… How many were on the road to St Ives?" I chirped.

He swished his tail and took a pee against a bush. "*I can only see one idiot on his way to St Ives!*"

I could hardly disagree.

"One idiot and his dog, on the way to St Ives." I shrugged, carrying on down the path, feeling somewhat foolish.

As we descended from the clifftops, the path plateaued and gave us a view of a lighthouse sitting merrily on a rock out to sea. I flumped to the floor and dug around the pack for a snack and drink of water. Moose stuck his head in his water bowl and started guzzling away for all he was worth. A group of ladies came down the path and, as soon as they were close enough, he jumped up and bounded across wearing his cutest smile.

The inevitable flurry of cuddles and kisses followed.

Today was quite the day for meeting continental holiday-makers, only this lot was from Switzerland. We exchanged stories while Moose vied for further attention by rolling around in the dust playing 'cute stupid doggy'. The ladies lapped up this new display of cutesy-ness, offering up more belly rubs for his trouble. After a while, we gathered up our things, said our farewells and headed down to the beach to continue traipsing the long stretch towards Gwithian.

"I'll give you this – you're a sodding charmer when you want to be."

Moose just swished his tail and loped off in front with a bloody great grin on his face.

Gwithian Beach was one of those deceptively long entities. It stretched out in front of us for miles, with the headland shimmering away in the distant heat. All told, it probably took us two or three hours to trudge across.

At a place called The Towans, a huge rock outcrop blocked off the beach, giving us no choice but to scale an immense soft bank of fluffy sand to get back up on the cliff tops. Sand's hard enough to walk on as it is, but this? This was work beyond toil! The weight of the pack meant that for every step I took forwards (or upwards, depending on your point of view), I slid back half the distance again in the sand.

After what felt like forever, I keeled over on the path at the top, gasping for air. Moose bounded about like a bloody kangaroo, eager to be back on the move.

Unbeknownst to me at the time, and in my eagerness to get to St Ives, I'd underestimated the route. This meant that we had a rather substantial estuary to get around. We headed into the first town along our route – Hayle – and then further on, to the bridge at Lelant. I hovered outside a big Asda and then accosted some bloke heading in, asking if he wouldn't mind picking me up some sausage rolls and a bottle of wine, a true meal of champions!

By now, it was getting darker and there was no way we'd make St Ives today. I followed the train line back up the opposite side of the estuary and made camp in the dunes just outside a sprawling golf course.

In the end, it didn't take all that long to get into St Ives the following morning. As we headed into town, the path turned into a meandering promenade of cobblestones and quaint little shops. Every second one sported the work of some local artist, each piece portraying one of the many beautiful scenes that could be found as we wandered about the town.

St Ives did not disappoint.

In the harbour, we found the obligatory Cornish pasty shop and tucked into our lunch beside the shade of one of the wharves. The sun rounded its peak and the heat intensified until, by mid-afternoon, the town, bustling with tourists and fishermen, sweltered. Dogs were also a common feature, so I decided to relocate somewhere out of temptations way. On the outskirts of town, we came across a playing field dotted with ageing World War II outposts. We lay in the shade and snoozed, as kids clamoured and shouted all around the place.

I glanced at my watch. "Time to get moving, bud – we still need to find a decent camp for the night."

Moose skipped to his feet.

On the way out of the park, I noticed a familiar South West Coast Path way-marker.

"Hang on…"

I walked closer, noticing another symbol etched into the wood beside the acorn.

St Michael's Way ⟵

My heart did a giddy little skip. "Oh my God... Moose, we're on the Camino de Santiago!"

He looked over and screwed up his face. *"Do they serve pasties there?"*

I threw him a filthy look. "No, you stupid sod, of course they don't sell pasties!"

"What, then?"

"It's the Way of St James." I grinned.

He shuffled his shoulders, snorted and dragged me back up the path, away from the sign and out of town. That night, we made camp in a sheltered terrace hidden in the terrain a few dozen metres below the coast path. As dinner was cooking away, I glanced out to several huge boulders poking their way out of the surf below and checked my maps.

"The Carracks," I muttered to myself, as I served up and settled in to watch the sun set beneath the waves.

The following morning brought rain – gentle and refreshing at first, but by lunchtime it was coming down in steady streams. I avoided walking in bad weather wherever I could now and decided early that we'd have a couple of rest days until it blew over. This spot was ideal; we had St Ives on our doorstep for supplies and this little nook was flat, comfortable and shaded out of the worst of the elements, with a stunning view out to sea. Moose lay with his head on my lap as the rain pitter-pattered on the outside of the tent.

He looked up with his big brown eyes. *"So, what were you prattling on about yesterday?"*

"Oh...interested now, are we?" I said, arching an eyebrow.

"Not really, but there's sod all else to talk about," he sniffed back.

Bloody dogs.

"Fine," I said, settling into a more comfortable position. "Do you remember when we first started talking about the walk?"

He picked his head up out of my lap. *"You mean the time you sold the couch?"*

169

I ignored that.

"Anyway," I continued, "at first, we weren't going to walk the British coast – we were going to go to France—"

"*What's France?*" he interrupted.

"It's a place," I threw out, keen to get back to the story.

I shifted a furry elbow that was digging into my leg before carrying on. "… In France, there's a path like the one we've been walking and it leads all the way across into Spain—"

Moose sneezed and looked up again with a slight grin on his face. "*What's Spain?*"

I rolled my eyes and ignored *that* comment. "Well *in* Spain, there's a town called Santiago de Compostela, which is the final resting place of St James the apostle."

I threw a cautionary look back at Moose as the quip began to form in his jowls. "*What's an apo—*"

I cut him off. "An apostle is a follower."

Moose picked up his head. "*Like me!!*"

I looked at the line of doggy-dribble staining my trouser leg and shook my head. "Nope, not like you at all," I said, starting to get cross with the constant interruptions. "Do you want to hear the story or not?"

He shifted his weight, placing his head on his paws, and looked up at me with big brown, innocent eyes. "*I'm all ears.*" He grinned.

"Where was I?" I said, scratching the stubble on my cheek with a finger. "Oh yes – St James."

I thought for a second and decided to take a doggy friendly approach to the tale.

"There's a bloke who people like to go and see," I started. "He lives very far away and people from all over the world go there to make pilgrimage…"

I faltered, expecting a comment about pilgrimages.

None came.

I looked down.

"*Carry on,*" he urged, a look of mockery glinting away in the corner of his eye.

I shrugged. "Well – we were going to go and see St James!"

Moose's face fell. "*Is that it?*" he asked, disappointment written all over his face.

"He was a very important person," I insisted.

Moose let his tongue loll out of the side of his mouth. "*Ah... I get it now.*" He grinned. "*Does he have a sofa?*"

I could tell that this conversation was going nowhere.

I shuffled Moose to one side and scrabbled out of the tent into the rain.

He poked his head out after me. "*Where are you going?*"

"For a pee," I called back.

"*But the story's not finished!*"

"I'll be back in a mo."

I scrabbled to the lee-side of the camp, found a quiet spot and stood there contemplating a new direction for the conversation as the rain, among other things, poured.

Trying to explain the finer points of religion and pilgrimage to a four-year-old mastiff cross is a lot trickier than you'd think. I began kicking myself for being drawn into this conversation in the first place. The more questions he asked, the more confusing and difficult the explanations became. Concepts like miracles he got straight away – I mean, why wouldn't he? I talked about the loaves and fishes and he instantly took to it (food did magically appear in his bowl every mealtime, after all). The more I talked about dedication and faith, the more confused he got.

By the time the story was finished, I came to believe that Moose was under the distinct impression that the Basilica at Santiago was home to a massive couch where St James would sit and lounge about all day, nibbling away at a multitude of snacks and treats brought from far and wide by random visitors, while every now and then bread and tuna popped into existence from thin air.

Towards the evening, I settled into making food for us both – a heady stew of meat and veg. We lay there that night with the constant patter of rain against the canvas as sporadic questions about fishes, clams and pillows interspersed the racket from outside.

We stayed at The Carracks for another day before heading off as the sun rose between the stormy clouds of the third morning. If ever we needed faith and dedication, then now would be the time. The road to Zennor would turn out to be one of the toughest we'd faced so far.

Our rocky and rainy journey to Zennor started early. We'd caught a brief respite from the weather, so I took the opportunity to gather up belongings and get going as quickly as we could. On the way back up to the path, we met a local who had a gaggle of dogs roaming free around her.

I held Moose in close.

"Oh – decided you're not living here, then," she sniped as Moose gave a low growl at one of her dogs who'd ventured in too close.

I ignored the sarcastic comment, stuck out my tongue and trudged on past. Fairly soon, the rain came in harder and the path disappeared to be replaced by a rough trail that would end abruptly and be replaced with huge boulder fields. By ten o'clock, the wind had picked up and begun tearing at us. I unlatched Moose as I literally crawled over rocks the size of cars in a desperate scramble to get back to something resembling a trail.

After clearing the last of these I stood, sopping wet and gasping from the exertion, my waterproofs and everything underneath sodden. The rain was in free-fall.

I mopped my brow and looked ahead through the storm hoping we'd encounter some sheltered place where we could rest up and regroup.

"*I bet it's not doing this in Spain*," shouted Moose over the din of wind and rain.

I looked down and felt a pang – the poor sod looked like a drenched rat. "Sorry, pal! Next possible place we find, we'll stop."

Like me, his waterproofs were saturated and he shivered from the biting wind against his wet fur.

He didn't look reassured.

"Promise!" I shouted over the storm.

We continued onwards, hugging the cliff lines as we wound our way slowly forwards. By lunchtime, the wind had begun to die down and the rain had settled into a thick blowy drizzle. My boots squelched with each step and every so often I'd stumble and fall into a heap in the mud. Eventually, we began to encounter kissing gates and, before long, a half-rotten way-marker with the word 'Zennor' written on it.

Here, the path took a sharp left and headed inland. Fairly soon, we were on a cobbled road and, there in the distance, stood the familiar outbuildings of civilisation.

Zennor was little more than a village with a pub, a shop and a church, surrounded by ancient houses, all nestled randomly into the topography – which, for the most part, remained rocky and steep. I looked down at me and then at Mooch. We were in an absolute state: both soaked to the skin and covered head to toe in mud.

On closer inspection, the pub was shut but to one side of the church sat a little village hall that had been converted into a café. I poked my head in at the door, asked about their dog policy, gratefully trudged inside and took a pew at the furthest corner I could find.

A waitress came over to take my order. I looked up and muttered an apology for dragging in half of the Cornish weather with us. She waved the apology away and took our order of tea and 'whatever they had that was warm'. I began peeling off layers of dripping clothes and towelling Moose down. He slumped next to one of the floor heaters and was soon snoring away. I hadn't even begun worrying about a place to camp for the night when in came three equally sodden bikers who asked about local camping spots. Money exchanged hands and they were quickly shown out towards the back of the café.

I rushed to my feet and made a similar enquiry, hardly believing my luck.

We chose a lovely shaded spot beneath a huge tree. The rain had let up by now, so I quickly set up camp and began hanging up all the wet stuff in the shower room to dry for the night. I had a wash, shaved and spent the remainder of the evening supping tea in the café.

Later that evening, we settled in our tent. From there, I could see the three bikers across the way, busy setting up their bivvies for the night. For those of you who have no idea what a bivvy is: they're super-lightweight tents that essentially comprise a small tarp that you peg and tie as best as you can. On a night like this, it wouldn't be my first – or even last – choice.

"Well, best of luck to 'em!" I muttered as I zipped up and settled into the sleeping bag with Moose. Five minutes later, I could hear the rain begin to pound at the tent and sent a sympathetic thought out to the three blokes huddled across from us.

Five minutes after that, Moose and I were soundly snoring away.

Chapter 13

Turning Point

Zennor to Land's End

Thankfully, the rain stopped in the early hours and Zennor found itself waking up to a little bit of sunshine. I went to check on my clothes in the shower room and found that most had dried off overnight – with the exception of my boots, which were still wet inside and out.

I groaned. That meant a day walking in my trainers; considering the terrain we were on, that was less than ideal.

The boys in the bivvies were surprisingly sprightly, considering they'd basically camped out in the open rain all night. I joined them for breakfast inside the café and we chatted about the road ahead. Because they were on mountain bikes, they expected themselves to be in Land's End before the end of the day. Moose and I would have no such luck, though; we might get there before the end of the week but that depended largely on the weather, the terrain and whether my feet could hold out.

On that subject, one of the lads reminded me of the old camping trick of wrapping one's feet in plastic bags to keep the water out. The way I figured it, the opposite must be true too. I could wear the trainers until they became impractical and then swap them for my wet boots with my feet wrapped in plastic.

The cyclists upped and left while Moose and I were still halfway through our breakfast. Moose was ever the optimist and I once again found his head nestled between my knees while he eyed up the last of the sausages on my plate. Other diners sat there lapping up the charade as he did his best 'starved doggy' impression. I was having none of it – I knew better by now! The little bugger darted from table to table mopping up all the scraps in the room.

What did I care? The big galoot ate better than I did most of the time, anyway.

On our way out, we were stopped by a woman who'd spent the night in one of the B&B rooms upstairs. Her window had overlooked the garden where we'd camped and she'd noticed the charity flag I'd draped over one of the benches that morning to get dry. Out of interest, she'd looked up the website and read about our story. Congratulating us both on our effort, she gave me a £20 note for the charities and another as a treat for me and the pooch next time we had a stop somewhere.

"Get yourself something nice for dinner," she said, wishing us well on our journey.

I was in awe of the kind offer and just stood there, dumbly nodding as she got into her car and drove off – I never even had the presence of mind to ask her name before she left.

Fifteen minutes later, we were back on the main coast path. I looked over my shoulder at Zennor. We'd had far more interesting things happen to us on our journey…but there was something about that place. Something I'll never quite forget.

Fortunately, the rain held off for most of the day, albeit with the odd smattering here and there. Out on the headland about a mile or two from

Zennor, I could see a point in the distance with the suspiciously familiar tell-tale of a lighthouse. I checked my maps – sure enough, there was a familiar symbol with the words 'Pendeen Watch' written next to it.

"That's it then," I said, looking down to Moose, "Pendeen Watch it is!"

We followed the trail, which had become disturbingly reminiscent of North Devon, mostly comprising steep rough-hewn stairs followed by sharp ascents that seemed to go on forever. What was most infuriating was the convex nature of the path in relation to the headlands. A far-off peak seemed so close but, as we walked around a bend, another huge valley would open up and shatter the illusion of distance.

We'd periodically rest so that I could swap trainers for boots-in-plastic…which had mixed results. It's fair to say that the bags kept the sogginess out of the boot – but they also kept the sweat from my feet in. In addition to changing footwear, I went through my entire contingent of dry socks.

As we cleared yet another hidden valley and I stared into the abyss of the next, I noticed the foundations of bygone settlements. We moved further south and these became more and more prominent until virtually every bend and curve in the path held some long-forgotten ruin overgrown with ivy and fern. Huge stone vents topped with steel cages became a constant feature, along with rusted red metal signs warning against straying from the path lest we fall down some hidden mineshaft, never to be seen again.

The path flattened out and coursed gracefully through the barren ferns as Pendeen Watch Lighthouse came into sight. To the left and right were huge stone houses left by the miners of Cornwall, roofless and windowless, staring out to sea. The land played one last trick and quickly fell away to reveal yet another valley, staircase and incline.

"*Not again*," Mooch grumbled.

"You can carry the pack if you'd like!" I said, sarcastically.

He clamped his mouth shut, shook his head and carried on down without further complaint.

An hour later, we were standing beside the huge bell crystal of Pendeen Watch Lighthouse. To be honest – and, as excited as I was to finally get there – I couldn't help but be a little underwhelmed by the sight of it. On the approach to many lighthouses, the only thing you'll see until you're right on top of them is the bell. Once you get close enough, though, you can bask in the magnificence of a huge column of concrete and brickwork, atop which sits the glistening beacon. Not so with Pendeen. There was no tower and no hulking great column; just the top bit burrowed into the earth like some giant, stubby screwdriver that had been shoved, shaft first, deep into the bedrock.

I glanced down at my wrist. It was too early to stop but getting late enough for me to start worrying about finding a spot for the night. We continued past the rugged bulk of Pendeen and carried on deep into the fern beyond to find somewhere more suitable. The landscape was becoming more and more barren, with sharp rock formations cutting deep contours all around the pathway. Here civilisation seemed to fall away, and, as the cloudy sky closed in and darkened the landscape, it felt much later in the evening than it actually was. Twisted ruins peeked above the bushes until I saw one and then another, and before long more than I could count.

Dotting the horizon were dozens of chimneys. At their base stood the undeniable, indomitable forms of Cornish engine houses. This was one of the things I'd been most looking forward to on this adventure – the deepest heart of Cornish history, a landscape made famous not only for sheep and grazing cattle but also for its miners.

As my footfalls crunched in the fragmented rocks, my heart did a giddy little flip. With nothing but foot power, determination and a touch of stupidity, we'd made it all the way from Portishead in Somerset. We'd finally crossed an invisible line from the new world and into the old, bringing us inevitably to Geevor Tin Mine.

The traditional entrance was inland, positioned between the towns of Pendeen and Trewellard. Moose and I, however, were arriving in style! We came in via the coast path, the most unconventional – and spectacular – way to get there. It was getting on for half past six but there were still a few straggling tourists meandering about the place wearing yellow hard hats, something I assumed was a gimmicky offering from the entrance via the gift shop.

I perched just outside of the main thoroughfares, hiding in the outbuildings while we waited patiently for tourists and staff alike to bugger off so we could keep the lion's share of Geevor to ourselves for the night. I'd learned my lesson at Tintagel Castle and now thought it was better to beg forgiveness than ask permission. Tonight, we'd be sleeping among the ghosts of Cornwall in this stunningly haunting, UNESCO World Heritage Site. The way I saw it, it's a 300-year-old mine, so a few five-inch pegs in its grass would hardly damage the décor.

That evening, the sun burned a fiery red as it lit up the clouds on its way down to the horizon; this was a night like no other we'd had since leaving Somerset. I thought back to our camp spots on Brean Fort and Steart Marsh…still, silent and surrounded by such ancient history that my soul was humbled by the privilege of being there. Even Moose seemed to adopt an air of calm, almost as if he could feel the presence of those long-forgotten folk, who wandered among these hallowed ruins – little more than memories, now.

Moose and I sat together in the fading light, just soaking in the atmosphere of this eerie place as it faded around us into the darkness of night.

I set the alarm for early the next morning so I could be out on the path before bands of tourists began crashing in on our camp or – worse yet – we got arrested for trespassing. Technically, wild camping in England is illegal. As much as that didn't usually bother me, this place was pretty important and us rocking up and pitching a tent without permission was bound to piss somebody off!

We were back on the headland before the sun rose. The steady sun of the previous day meant that we were mostly dry, albeit a tad smelly leftover from the drenching we'd had at Zennor. My contingent of socks had all dried out and I was in fine spirits ahead of this last southerly leg of Cornwall.

The land undulated with severe dips and up turns as it had yesterday – but, on the whole, the views were so extraordinary that I forgot the harshness of the path and just enjoyed the unique setting. My feet still ached, of course, and the pack felt like a dead elephant on my back but just being here in this breathtaking place seemed to make all that disappear. Even the coastal path way-markers began to assume a rich take of their own as they turned from decaying, half-rotten wooden stumps to beautifully etched stone posts, indomitably pointing the way to the end of the world.

I could hardly believe that Land's End was just a few miles away now. I looked over my shoulder into the imaginary distance we'd covered so far and grinned at Moose.

"Today's a big 'un!"

He looked up and, for the first time on the trip, reflected real understanding in his eyes. *"Last night was awesome – I loved it there."*

I was taken aback a bit. Without a smattering of insult, that one comment had made me finally feel that all this effort and upheaval was worthwhile.

"Are you OK?" I asked, a bit concerned.

His eyes softened as he grinned back at me, tongue off to one side glistening in the sunlight. *"This is the best walkies!"* he said, tail racing back and forth with gentle excitement.

Finally, I thought before tentatively asking, "You've forgiven me for the couch, then?"

He sauntered up, dragged his tongue slowly across my cheek and carried on walking up the path with a contented swish of his tail.

Minutes later, we walked out on to the stunning scene that was Cape Cornwall.

Over the last few days, I'd been checking Facebook and had seen that a former colleague of mine had been diagnosed with cancer. I hadn't spoken to the bloke since I left my job back in April so, on the headland at Cape Cornwall, as I stood beside a long stone storehouse complete with the usual panorama of sea, rocks and sunshine, I dialled up his number on my phone.

"Well, bloody hell," came the response. "Ghosts from the past!"

"Hiya," I said, smiling in spite of myself. "How's tricks?" It was so nice to hear a familiar voice after so long walking in the wild.

"I'm fine," he said. "I had a right bloody scare, though."

"I heard," I said, leaning in to get a better signal. "Are you on the mend yet?" I asked.

"Oh, I'm fine – just a small thing on my nose."

I smiled as Martyn continued in his deep Somerset drawl, "Back at work now, looking like I got punched in the face."

"Where you at?" I asked, realising once again that I'd forgotten what day it was.

"South of France!"

"Bloody expensive call, then..." I joked.

He laughed.

We chatted for a few more minutes before agreeing to meet up in Bath one day when all this madness was over.

I hung up the phone with a smile and looked over to Moose.

"*What you grinning for?*" he asked.

"Nothing," I said, picking up the pack and turning back towards the path.

Moose skipped ahead and ploughed headlong into the ferns and brush that lined the path. We encountered ruin after ruin as we followed an abundance of markers and stone signs pointing our way to the tip of the Cornish peninsula. Like the days before, our journey towards Land's End was not as simple as the landscape had on first glance led us to believe. There were bays within bays and, just as the sharp rocks cleared into scenes of flat beach, we still weren't quite as close as we expected ourselves to be.

After clearing a particularly precarious trek around an outcrop of immense jagged rock, I looked down at what I'd thought would be the final stretch of the day. We manoeuvred ourselves down from the cliffside and on to a huge expanse of sandy beach – the first we'd seen since leaving St Ives. I became giddy at the thought of reaching the town glittering away in the distance: surely *this* was the last stretch?

I looked down at my map and saw 'Sennen Cove' written in bold type across the beige smear of ink before the big black dot that signalled our ultimate turning point of the trip.

I looked at Moose and then gazed into the distance, rounded my shoulders and strode on!

Whitesand Bay was buzzing with activity. The day had become hotter again so I took the opportunity to take off my damp boots and socks to walk fresh-footed in the sand. Whenever I did this, I felt less a passer-by and more a holiday-maker, blending in with the rest of the folk around us. At the far end, the sand receded and a bold quay led the way to a plethora of shops, eateries and pubs. Outside one such establishment, I saw a littering of water bowls in the shadow of the tables.

"Doggy friendly!" I announced cheerily to Moose. We sauntered up, found the first convenient bench and slumped down beneath it. I ditched the pack and sat there, bent over, massaging Mooch's cheeks.

"We made it, bud – Land's End!"

He grinned back up at me.

"Can I get you anything?" came a voice from behind.

Startled, I bolted back upright and looked straight into the smiling face of a waitress holding a pad and pen in her hands.

"Could I have a menu, please?" I asked.

"Certainly." She looked down at Moose and suddenly her face fell into one of those 'coochy coo' expressions. "Aww! He's sooo cute!"

My eyes rolled.

Moose's lit up.

Hers melted.

"Please can I pet him?"

I looked down at Moose. "She wants to pet you, bud."

Without saying a word, he immediately rolled over on to his back and assumed his 'Belly Rub Position Number 1'!

I turned back to the waitress. "He's fine – go nuts."

Pen and pad were thrown to the table as she crouched and began raking wide scratches across the exposed belly. Moose responded by bringing out his secret weapon – the lolling tongue – and twitching his curled-up paws while he groaned contentedly beneath her fingernails.

Deciding to leave the two of them to their own amusement, I picked up a menu and started leafing through the choices. After a minute or so, I thought, *Enough's enough...*

"Ahem. Could I order a couple of cheeseburgers, please? No onions or garnish on one."

She straightened instantly and retrieved her pen and paper from the table. "Sure – anything to drink?"

"A pint of Rattler." I beamed. "We're celebrating!"

She looked intrigued. "Oh? What are you celebrating?"

I looked down at Moose, then over to the rucksack and then back at the waitress. "We've been walking for over a month and we've finally made it here to Land's End."

Her face dropped. "You're in Sennen Cove, love. Land's End's about a mile further around the bay."

I instantly blushed. *Shit!*

Moose burst into laughter beneath the bench.

"Oh, thanks for letting me know," I said, somewhat sheepishly.

Our food arrived shortly afterwards and I ate in subdued silence while Mooch laid into me for all he was worth. After finishing our meal, I paid at the bar and then loaded back up to carry on.

Moose looked over, barely hiding the stupid grin he had plastered across his face. *"And here's me thinking we were done for the day!"*

"Ha-ha, very funny."

He snorted and shuffled around in his panniers before dragging me back towards the path.

Thankfully, we didn't have that far to go.

As we left the café, the lay of the land opened up to expose Land's End in the not-so-distant…distance. Twenty minutes later, we and a mass of tourists hit the headland, all queuing around a white picket fence. Beyond the fence stood the unmistakable way-marker of Land's End.

I was giddy inside. What a photo that would make! Me and Moose, stood in front of that renowned symbol, forever proving that we'd made it this far. I boldly took my place in line expecting to be led to our well-earned spot beside the iconic white signpost, and the subsequent photograph that would forever seal our place in history. I wrapped Moose's leash tightly in my hand and boldly took a step through the gate.

"It's twenty quid, mate!" the bloke standing on the other side of the gate blurted at me.

"I'm sorry?" I asked, somewhat bemused.

He looked at me with a bored expression. "If you want to be photographed in front of the sign, it's twenty quid!"

My northern 'thrift' gene kicked in and twitched. "… To stand in front of *that* sign?"

The guy stood there and nodded. "Yup. Twenty quid but the photo's included," he urged, as if *that* would cinch the deal.

I grabbed Moose and wheeled around.

Moose looked at me in horror. *"Did he just try charging you a score for a bloody picture?"*

Damn, I'd taught my boy well!

"He did," I grumbled.

He snuffled and kicked up a paw full of dust. *"Well, I'd have told him to f—"*

"Be nice," I interrupted – there were children present, after all. "Let's try the sneaky approach, instead."

Moose grinned, sauntered up to the little white fence in front of the sign and sat ready with his photo face. I could see the guy on the other side silently seething.

"Big smiles, pal!"

Snap

Examining the picture on the screen, I said, "That'll do nicely."

I grabbed my pack and trotted off with Moose before we got told off.

If I'm honest, Land's End was a bit of a let-down.

It would seem that, at some point in the past, some planning officer had had the brilliant thought that the best thing for this iconic location would be to turn it into a cheesy theme park. Shops and attractions were bedecked with gaudy flashing lights and surrounded by fibreglass dinosaurs and cheap-looking diners (which, in reality, were anything but). The only thing that was missing were stalls selling gumballs and 'kiss me quick' hats.

We headed back to the cliff-head and sat outside one of the pubs, at once excited about reaching the landmark and disappointed by the unfortunate garb it had now been dressed in. I slowly drank a cup of tea while, all about, fellow adventurers milled around, either on their way to or arriving from John O' Groats.

This was the first place I'd visited where I didn't feel we were achieving something special – everyone here was doing something similar. In a strange way, it was nice to blend in for once.

As evening crept in, I decided to start making a move. The artificial promenades and walkways held no promise of a secure place to stay, so, after just a few short hours in Land's End, we finally decided to head back out on to the wilds of the coast path. As the sun set with this iconic location at our backs, we took our first significant turn on the compass of our grand adventure. Our steady south-westerly trek, unchanged since we'd left Portishead, was finally at an end. For the first time on this journey, we began heading due east – and back towards civilisation.

Chapter 14

The Longest Day

Land's End to Newlyn

We eventually found a place to camp on a narrow spit of grass beside the coast path a few miles outside town. It was a wonderfully clear night and so we spent most of it looking up at the brilliance of the night sky.

Here, where there was barely any light pollution, the heavens opened up to an incredible spectacle above our heads, stretching from horizon to horizon. It's just something you never get to see if you live anywhere near a city and I gazed on in absolute awe. Moose, snoring gently by my side, didn't seem too bothered by the heavenly light show.

The following morning, we were up early again, fed and back on our feet just after sunrise. I had it in my mind that today we'd take things slowly. With one big landmark under our belts, I wasn't in a hurry to get anywhere fast. The sun was up but not baking us as it had in previous weeks. The terrain was challenging but with enough easy stretches so as not to make the journey arduous. On the whole, I decided, today would be a good day.

There was also a stark contrast to yesterday: we encountered virtually no one this side of Land's End. I loved days like this: just time for me, Mr Moo and the path. Before long, we were back under shaded canopies, where pooch set about his little game of 'catch-a-fly'. He merrily skipped on ahead, his mouth snapping away at the air in front of him while I brought up the rear, lost in thought.

Portishead to Land's End – I could barely believe the achievement! But, all the while, I was thinking about the next.

"Crossing the Thames, I suppose…" I muttered to myself.

Moose stopped, turned around and cocked his head to one side. *"Did you say something?"*

I shook my head slightly, bringing my mind back into the now. "Oh…er, sorry, pal," I mumbled. "I was just thinking out loud."

Moose sneezed and went back to catching insects.

An hour later, we were in St Levan and back among crowds of people, where exactly, my map stated clearly, there shouldn't be any. Were it not for the hard evidence of the sea still glittering off to our right, I might have thought we'd taken a wrong turn somewhere. Villages like this were sparsely populated at the best of times and yet here we were, surrounded by dozens of people all crowded along narrow paths to form lines as though waiting for some magnificent parade.

I looked at my map and the penny dropped – the Minack Theatre! We'd rocked up just in time for the afternoon matinée.

People milled all around us in an excited buzz as stewards wearing hi-vis tabards corralled them into narrow lines along the approach to the theatre entrance.

Moose looked back at me, puzzled. *"What's so special about this place?"*

I thought back to our discussions about the Camino and phrased my response accordingly. "Well, it's an open-air amphitheatre," I began, instantly realising my slip.

"*What's an amphitheatre?*" he asked, innocently.

I groaned inwardly. "It's a place where people come to play ball," I gently lied.

He liked that.

In reality, the Minack Theatre is one of the oldest theatres in Britain. It's open-air and cut directly into the rock at the top of an ancient cliff edge. The stage's backdrop being a stunning panoramic view out on to the Atlantic Ocean.

"People travel from all over the world to come and watch plays here," I explained.

Now whether he was being polite or the air around this incredibly unique place somehow spoke to him, he didn't pursue the matter any further. "*Sounds great,*" he said, with a simple swish of his tail.

As tempting as it was to see if they had any last-minute tickets, Shakespeare's not really my thing – besides, I doubted Moose would sit still for over two hours of *thee*s, *thou*s and *forasmuches*, without so much a ball thrown throughout the entire proceeding. We weaved our way past the crowds and back out on to the slight path that cut down by the side of the theatre.

Reaching the top of the path, we looked down and saw...the staircase from hell.

"Errr...bud?" I called to Moose. "Looks like we've found the rest of the 'down' from the clifftop theatr— uh, ball-throwing arena."

He looked up at me with trepidation. "*...It's quite steep...*"

"Yeah," I replied, peering down in alarm at the path ahead. I clipped Moose's lead on to my belt.

We had to climb down the sheer face of the cliff below the Minack, on steps that could only be described as 'severe'. The problem *I* had was the dead elephant strapped to my back – and, to complicate things, I had an even more unpredictable animal now tied to my waist. To make matters *even* worse, there were crowds of people scrabbling their way up in order to make it to the play on time.

I stopped regularly, nearly fell twice, and kissed the sweet earth when we both got to the bottom in one piece.

Once we got to the beach, the path took an unexpected turn inland. The going got easier and quieter from there. Huge estates began to spring up, stealing away our view of the ocean. We meandered through woods and tailored gardens as the South West Coast Path did its best to hug the shoreline. Sand turned to rocky pebble beaches, something both Moose and I found challenging to walk over with any degree of steady footing. We passed another secluded lighthouse and, before long, found ourselves scaling sharp rocks again as the path disappeared on to the side of yet another cliff face.

By late afternoon, we'd got to the village of Lamorna, where all the shops and cafés were busy closing up for the day. I contemplated digging around for the map in the hope of finding some sweet spot to rest up but, instead, ended up chatting to one of the shopkeepers.

"Yer next place for a stop-off would have to be Mousehole," she said, pronouncing it '*Mao-zole*'. "But that's a tricky route," she added, stacking chairs neatly in the corner of a pagoda.

She looked up in time to see my face fall to the floor. "There *is* a bit of a short cut though…" she continued with a smile.

I thanked her for the advice as she began giving me directions, which I scribbled on the end of a receipt that some earlier patron had left screwed up on a nearby table.

We left both town and the coast path behind as we followed the diversion route inland and over the top of a small peninsula. Steel kissing gates became more frequent as the fields either side of us began filling up with assorted cattle and other farm animals. We hit the mainstay of the farm minutes later, and I gathered Moose in and told him to behave himself.

He didn't object.

We meandered through wide muddy thoroughfares, flanked either side with hulking pieces of farming machinery and open-faced barns. On our way past the last building, the signage directed across to a perpendicular path that led us into a field of planted maize. It was still light but, as we became surrounded by neat rows of the tall plants, an uneasy feeling rose – remnants, no doubt, from the dozens of cheesy horror movies about scarecrows and ghouls lying in wait to chase us down through the rows of corn. Thankfully, it didn't last long and we were soon heading across an open field where the tell-tale line of cliff edge and twinkling sea lay beyond.

Despite its unassumingly small 'blot' on the map, Mousehole was a very built-up town. I checked at all the local inns to find that they were all full – not a surprise, as this was still peak season. It was getting late now and night was beginning to close in. My feet were killing me. I was starting to seriously worry about where we'd stay for the night – we'd found ourselves firmly in deepest, darkest suburbia.

The road out of Mousehole was just that – a big, busy road with nowhere either side of it to squirrel ourselves away for the night. A panic was slowly beginning to build. As a rule, I never slept in or anywhere near big towns, and the next place we were headed for was about as big as it gets in this part of the world; Newlyn was nothing to be taken lightly. It sits at the bottom of Mount's Bay and is arguably one of Cornwall's largest and busiest working fishing ports. I trudged along the pavement, aching from head to foot, desperate for a small siding of grass to pitch up undisturbed.

Just before the town centre, the pavement split off into a side cycle track, complete with shaded verges and grass. I shrugged; this would have to do. I quickly threw up the tent and pegged my charity flag on the grass beside it. Hopefully, any passers-by would be put off from disturbing us by the words:

Charity Walk around Britain

As it got dark, I sat with Moose and contemplated our first day since leaving Land's End.

"So much for taking it easy today huh, bud?" I said, tussling his head lightly as he groaned and lay his head on my lap, falling fast asleep.

I checked our GPS for the day. We'd walked just over seventeen and a half miles and climbed an elevation just shy of 3,000 feet. I looked down at Moose, slightly nervous about the idea of getting some sleep.

Chapter 15

Angels of Fire and Snow

Newlyn to Rinsey

Despite my misgivings from the evening before, our little camp spot turned out to be ideal. That morning, we awoke to whispers outside the tent from people chatting excitedly about 'those adventurers camped by the side of the cycle track, walking the coast of Britain'.

Moose let out a low growl.

I heard a shuffling just beyond the canvas, followed by the words, "There's a bloody dog in there!"

A woman's voice laughed. "I wonder if that's Chris or Moose."

I unzipped the tent just far enough to stick my head out. "That would be Moose." I grinned.

A couple in their fifties took one look at me and involuntarily stepped back.

"Good morning!" I continued, trying to put them both at ease.

"Oh...good morning! We didn't mean to wake you."

"Nah..." I said, shaking the sleep out of my head. "I've been awake since dawn."

They looked relieved.

Moose shoved his head next to mine through the small gap in the tent flap, and gave the pair a suspicious stare. The gent took another involuntary step backwards – but the lady's eyes melted.

"Here it comes," I muttered under my breath.

"Aww, he's gorgeous!" she cried, crouching down and beaming straight into Moose's big brown eyes. He gave me a knowing wink, turned back to the woman and began swishing his tail elegantly from side to side.

"Hello, Moose," she cooed, akin to the way you'd talk to a four-year-old, as Moose's tail bashed repeatedly into my back. "Aren't you a handsome boy!"

I glared from out the corner of my eye and whispered in his ear as he squeezed cockily past me, "How come I never get comments like that?" He caught me on the end of my nose with the tip of his tail by way of reply.

"Is he friendly?" she asked, her bloke looking on with a mixture of interest and dread.

"Most of the time," I said, rubbing away indignantly at the sting.

Her fella was about to object when she cut in: "Come here, Moose!"

He needed no further encouragement; seconds later, he was on his back, legs akimbo, indulging in early-morning scratches and cuddles. I shook myself free from the tent and stood up. "As you can see – he's very terrifying."

The bloke seemed to relax, as I hauled myself to my feet and proffered my hand. "Chris," I said.

"Mike."

"Oh, and I'm Sue," the woman said, tearing one hand away from Moose long enough to give mine a quick shake.

We began chatting about our travels and what our plans were for the next few days. As for Mike and Sue, they happened to be visiting from Wiltshire – so, talking about the places we'd set off from and travelled through was a bit more engaging because of their familiarity with them all. After a few more minutes, we wrapped up the chat and wished each other well. They moved on back up the path towards the road to Mousehole. I quickly packed up and started down the cycle lane towards Newlyn. Here and there along the way were other tents that had sprung up overnight.

"So much for worrying about camping here," I muttered to Moose, who completely ignored me.

I looked at my phone, which was flashing red, warning of its near-empty battery. All my charging packs were dead, too – it'd been so long since we'd stayed anywhere besides the tent that I resigned myself to finding a friendly pub and charging my stuff up for a few hours.

The friendly pub turned out to be the Swordfish Inn, and the 'couple of hours' turned out to be most of the day.

As frustrating as it is sitting on your hands all day, it gave me time to listen to the conversations that drifted in and out of the pub. As I mentioned before, Newlyn was one of the last proper commercial fishing ports in Cornwall. The Swordfish Inn wasn't one of the touristy boozers that squatted in the centre of town; it was perched just along the harbour road across from the main quays. For a 'locals" pub, this place was immaculate – and it had one of those vibrant atmospheres where locals struck up conversations with strangers, as opposed to staring at them and whispering from behind full pint glasses.

For me, listening to the chat between the fishermen held particular interest. As an engineer, I'm used to going for a pint with the lads after a hard day to talk shop, and with the exception of the nature of the work, this place was no different. I sat there quietly flicking through Facebook on my phone, listening in to the conversation between two blokes sitting in front of the bar.

"You lot were in early today?" said the first.

"Bloody drive motor's gone again," replied the other, before taking a sip of beer. "I'll 'ave Frank next time I sees 'im."

"You managed to get a decent 'aul, then?"

"Nah – maybe enough to pay the lads, is all..."

... And so the chatter went.

People drifted in and out and, by four o'clock, all my stuff was charged up. I offered my thanks to the bar staff, pooch in hand, and set off on into Newlyn. A fine drizzle had begun to mist the town so I quickly threw waterproofs on us both before continuing up the streets into the town centre.

Up ahead, streams of coloured lights adorned every shopfront and arcade as Newlyn blurred into Penzance. For all the contrast between the two, they were so close that they might as well have been the same town. The commercial fishing feel of Newlyn had vanished to be replaced with the bustling vibe of a touristy seaside town. Stuffed effigies of privateers bedecked huge fibreglass pirate ships dotted all along the promenade. Out in the bay to my left stood the indomitable form of St Michael's Mount, perched starkly on a mass of rock half a mile or so out on the flat sandy beach, overlooking the bustle of these bipolar twin towns.

My experience of the folks I'd met so far took away any worry I had of camping here. Up past the train station there were even flats of land with signs boldly stating:

```
No Caravans, Campers
Or
Wild Camping
```

I looked around at the myriad tents and campers set up for the night, shrugged my shoulders, unslung my pack and pitched the tent just as the drizzle turned into a steady stream of rain for the night.

So much for signage.

*

Leaving Penzance behind the next morning, I was filled with a touch of regret. I looked longingly at St Michael's Mount, knowing how unfeasible it would be to attempt a visit with my rucksack and Moose in tow. I made a mental note to return here one day and explore in a manner more deserving of its grand stature. In the early-morning hours, we marched in fine drizzle through the damp, empty streets of Marazion and back up towards the coast path. As we hit the headland, I looked out on to Mount Bay and said farewell to St Michael's Mount, Penzance and Newlyn, before turning the corner to leave them behind.

I hadn't stopped long enough that morning to make breakfast for myself – I'd simply thrown Moose's bowl down to keep him occupied while I'd packed everything away. Come eleven o'clock, I was ravenous!

We'd come across a part of the trail that led us through luscious woodland, where I'd scavenged around for wood for my stove – all of which turned out to be still damp from the night before. Nevertheless, I sat and tried cooking up some breakfast. Instead of the delectable feast I'd imagined, however, I ended up creating a smouldering bellow of wood-smoke and wasting half of my water… I could feel myself getting annoyed!

Moose looked up. *"Are you OK?"*

I took a breath, gave him a smile and a nod, and threw the smouldering tinder into a nearby stream before deciding to walk on. We immediately hit a series of stiles and gates set out before us like some sort of eccentric assault course.

Now, I'm all for the logic of barriers when it comes to protecting cattle, but this was ridiculous! Every twenty metres or so we were met by another gate – and not the easy kind to get over, either. I unclipped Moose and left him to his own devices while I groaned over each one with the bloody pack bearing on my back, only for us to encounter another a few dozen yards down the track.

I looked over at Moose in dismay. "Seriously, pal – what the hell are all these gates for?"

He sniffed his indifference at my frustration and found a nice bush to pee against. I carried on with my tirade. "There's no bloody cattle around here!" I fumed, twisting wildly from side to side as if to emphasise the point.

Moose, who could clearly tell I was getting annoyed by the whole thing, smirked and waited patiently until I'd ranted myself out before calmly nudging my leg with his head. "*Can we crack on, now?*"

I couldn't help but laugh in spite of myself as I looked down the line of the path. The assault course seemed to carry on forever – stile, after stile, followed by bridge, followed by gate, followed by...yet more stiles! I shrugged and started walking with Moose close at my side, limbering up in preparation for the next struggle.

Eventually, the drizzle dried out and the sky cleared, allowing the sun to bear down on us once more...making me tetchy again. After months of scorching days, I'd begun to resent the burning heat of the sun on my face. We tromped around Cudden Point as the sun continued to soar and, by the time we'd reached Praa Sands, I was beet-red, dripping in sweat and angry at everything from the weight of the pack to the dull thud in my feet. As was typical at this time of year, a sign was tied to the rail proclaiming Moose was banned from the beach, also now giving him something to complain about:

"*I don't see why they're picking on me!*" he spat, kicking a pawful of sand at the notice.

"It's because you smell," I threw back haughtily.

He furrowed his eyebrows. "*Don't take your pissy mood out on me!*"

I could feel another argument coming on. It was *that* kind of day.

I looked beyond the sand and spied a lovely-looking eatery perched on top of the sea wall. It had a large seating area outside complete with umbrellas and, on closer inspection, water bowls for dogs.

"Let's go in here, mate," I said, hoping the place would be just the thing to pick us both up. "I think we've earned a breather."

Sulkily, Moose followed me in.

I slid the pack off my shoulders. It fell with a dull thud against the bar, grabbing the attention of the barman. "What can I getcha?" he asked.

I looked at the pump heads proudly peering over the top of the bar and spotted the Cornish cider. "Pint of Rattler," I smiled, "and a menu, please."

The young chap on the other side obliged without comment – we must've looked a right state! I grabbed the cold glass and moseyed around inside the tavern to find a place to sit and relax. Inside, it was spacious and cool; the huge flagstone floor was decked with tables, comfy chairs and sofas.

Never one to stand on ceremony, Moose wasn't waiting for an invite. Loping to the nearest couch, he hopped on to the leather and flumped into its cushions, exhausted. I hadn't the strength to argue. If we were chucked out, we were chucked out! I let out a long draught of air, put the pint to my lips and nearly downed the entire thing.

"Ahh, that's better," I groaned.

Moose twitched and responded with a loud snore.

I was sat there with my face buried in the menu when a waitress came over to us holding a notepad. She stopped without saying a word and looked at me. Then she looked at Moose, snoring away, and then back at me.

I looked up from the menu. "Um…sorry. Is this OK?" I said, throwing a sideways nod at the dog.

She looked as if she wanted to protest but then shrugged her shoulders. "Ah, he's fine," she announced, flipping over the paper and tapping it with the tip of her pencil. "What would you like?"

The thought of having to cook later was not a pleasant one and, glancing down at Moose, I tried to think of the last time he'd had anything other than dog food. "Burger and chips, twice please!"

She raised an eyebrow.

"One's for him," I clarified.

She sniggered and turned to leave.

"Oh…and another pint of Rattler, please!" I called after her. She nodded as she disappeared around the corner.

I lay my head back into the welcoming cloud of cushions…and awoke with a loud snort as the waitress put down the fresh platter of food and quietly ambled off.

I tapped Moose on the head.

"*What do you want?*" he grumbled. "*I'm tired!*"

"Fancy a burger?" I asked.

Instantly alert, he began twitching his nose at the steaming plates on the table. "*You're kidding!*" He slobbered. "*Are those for me?*"

"*One* of those is for you," I said, his eyes lighting up. "I think we've earned it today." I reached over and placed his portion on the floor beside the table.

I ate mine quickly, he ate his even quicker and, before long, we were both contentedly settled back into the cushions with full bellies. I took out my phone and started scanning social media. A band I knew from back home had just posted up a recording ready for their new album launch. I shuffled about in the pack to retrieve my headphones and settled in for a listen. Usually, I wouldn't use up battery charge on such frivolous things as music but, thankfully, I'd found a socket at the foot of the table and was charging up all my battery packs.

I sunk into the sofa and hit play.

Seb's meticulous guitar-work flooded my ears as the haunting melody began, before his wife, Nat, echoed out the first vocal harmonies of the song. Their band, Sinnober, had that annoying knack of being extremely talented. I laid my head back and was swept away by the immaculate nodes and tones of their music; a rare treat, this was just what the doctor ordered after my morning of unexpected gymnastics. What struck me most while I dozed was the contrast implied by the themes wrapped around this idea of '*Angels of Fire and Snow*'. As the song concluded, I immediately hit 'play' again, allowing it to iron out the worries of the day from my aching soul.

I awoke sometime later with Moose slobbering his tongue all over my face.

"Pfft – pack it in!" I groaned, opening my eyes as I tried to remember where the hell I was. I gazed blearily around at the bar – it was much later and a *lot* busier.

"Damn! Must've nodded off," I muttered, giving Moose a shake. "Sorry, pal," I said, reaching over and scratching him behind his ears, "I reckon it's time to go."

He wagged his tail in agreement and jumped off the couch. I gathered my things, stuffed them in the pack, bought a bottle of wine from behind the bar, and set off out of town. My headphones were still in my pocket and I decided to indulge once again.

The car park out back led on to a huge playing field where the coast path clipped towards the seaward side and up between a row of holiday homes. Before long, we were back in the wild, meandering over a rolling hill of fine grass that stretched on before us. As we peaked its crest, we were met by perhaps one of the most haunting sights I'd seen so far.

Now, whether it was the recent flood of music or my tired and slightly inebriated state, but the sight of a solitary engine house nestled in the valley beyond made my heart skip. It instantly brought forth sepia images depicting hard toil in the harshest of conditions, by a proud people tied to their land, committed to their labours, all for the love of the families they supported.

"Angels of fire and snow, indeed!" I muttered, before setting off down towards the haunting structure in the distance.

The sun was still high above but much of the heat was dissipating from the evening air. As we approached, I was captured by the untainted blue of the ocean, the calm stillness of the air and the eerie grace that seemed to infuse the picture-perfect setting. We made our way down along the side of the path and circled the structure, which sat on an even bed of earth about fifty yards from the edge of the hill's crest. Below, the land fell away in a series of terraces, each giving beautiful views of the beach far below as, beyond, the sea stretched out to the infinite.

I threw down my pack and approached the solitary titan to lay my hand flat against the brickwork. Looking up I saw a neat metal plaque fixed to the block, bearing the simple words:

```
WHEAL PROSPER
1860
```

"I think we've found our camp spot, mate," I said, a sense of serenity settling over me. He looked up and nodded in silent agreement.

We were far enough away from anywhere to risk being disturbed, and this magnificent structure hulked high above us with an ageless grace, offering protection. I couldn't believe this place was all ours for the night!

I quickly pitched the Banshee and pulled out some biscuits and snacks for us both. As the sun set slowly in the distance, we sat near the precipice of the cliff and watched as the disc flared into a fiery red before slowly dipping below the horizon. On one of the lower terraces, some other campers had arrived to enjoy the evening and magnificent views. Although they were too far away to be heard, I could see the vibrant excitement between them as they pitched tents, lit a fire and settled in to soak up the same view. As darkness came, the warmth in the air clung on.

High above, a blanket of stars began to peer out to reveal the splendour of the Milky Way, sprawling across the Cornish sky from horizon to horizon. I sipped my cup of wine while Mooch, wrapped in my sleeping bag, snuggled in close and rested his snoozing head on my lap.

I glanced over my shoulder. Deep in the gloom, I could see the imposing figure of Wheal Prosper looking on, with our little green tent nestled in the foot of its shadow. The weeks of solitude culminated that night into an overwhelming feeling of fulfilment and awe at finding ourselves in this special place, on that particular night, under that starry sky. I plugged my headphones into my ears once more. Angels of fire and snow carried my mind off into the heavens.

I can honestly say that the experience will stay with me forever, linked inexorably to that haunting soundtrack. Even now, that song takes me back to that quiet place just outside the village of Rinsey, to the special evening I spent there under the stars with my best friend.

I woke the next morning to the snuffling of a dog nose outside the tent. Moose's eyes flickered instantly open and let out a torrent of snarls that sent whoever it was on the other side of the canvas scurrying off in a panic.

"Will you turn it down a notch!" I moaned, sitting up with a dull throb hitting me behind my eyes. I looked down at the empty bottle of wine next to my pillow and turned to Moose. "Why did you let me drink so much?"

He fixed me with a hard stare, snorted in my face, trotted in a tight circle for a few turns, farted and flumped into a ball on the sleeping bag. Two seconds later he was snoring.

Meh! I thought to myself. Too hungover to care, I grabbed what sleeping bag I could, wrapped myself up and followed suit.

When I woke again later that morning, the tent was lit up by the morning sun and the heat inside was slowly becoming oppressive. I opened the zip to let in some air, crawled out on my hands and knees, and tried standing up. Another 'zap' of pain behind my eyeballs and I was back on my arse in the grass.

Moose popped his head out. "*Still delicate, are we?*" He sniggered.

I ignored that. "Do you want feeding or not?" I asked, watching his wagging tail hitting the inside of the tent as he stood there grinning at me.

"Bloody dogs," I muttered.

After breakfast, I packed everything away and sat for a few moments on the dry turf. I took one final walk around Wheal Prosper, standing proud in the morning sun. Today was going to be another hot one – I could already feel it. Yesterday's peevish mood had long since dissipated and the magic of last night had imbued me with a renewed sense of vigour and optimism. I made my way to the edge of the terraces and saw that last night's campers had long since gone. Looking back, I saw that His Majesty was sitting patiently next to the rucksack.

Time to move, I thought, as I marched back to the dog, picked up our stuff and found the coast path waiting for us – right where we'd left it.

Chapter 16

Things in the Mist

Rinsey to Lizard Point

Trewavas Head unveiled itself before us.

On the headland, I could see the chimneys of another two engine houses reaching up to touch the early-morning sky. The pounding in my head had simmered down to a dull throb and, by the time we approached these great monsters, it'd all but disappeared. Moose paid little attention to my suffering and busied away, nose first, through the roughage as I trailed along behind, fumbling for my sunglasses.

The dual mines of Trewavas were in a poorer state than their brother we'd just left behind at Rinsey. They were both perched precariously on the cliff edge, high above the crashing waves below. As we wound our way along the path beside the first one and then the other, the staggering engineering achievement of these structures took me aback as I contemplated the toil and pride of the people who had built them in the first place.

PING

Damn, I thought, dropping the pack to the floor so I could fish out my phone.

It was Donna, a friend of mine who I used to work with.

I'm down in Cornwall seeing my sister...
Fancy meeting up? 😈

It'd been ages since we'd last seen each other so I quickly texted back:

I'm near Porthleven... 😖
...Is that far?

PING

I'll just check...
...I can be there tomorrow.

I grabbed the map out of the bag. I'd be in Porthleven that afternoon, so there was no need to panic. I tapped out my reply on the screen:

...I'll be there soon – I'll hang on for you!

With that, I shoved my phone in my pocket, stowed the map and glanced ahead. Porthleven wasn't too far off – perhaps an hour or so? That'd give us a chance to scoot around town for a bit and then find somewhere local to camp until the morning.

Little did I know that the weekend was already here and that Porthleven was to host its regatta that entire weekend, starting tonight.

Timing or what!

Double bubble, I thought, as we walked into the cobbled town amid a bustle of preparation and excitement. By now, my feet were killing me again, stone cobbles being the worst possible surface to walk on. Every time I stood on an uneven edge, my instinct was to shift my weight off it, which consistently caused me to almost fall over. To an onlooker, I probably looked like an early afternoon drunk as I stumbled into town avoiding sharp edges and cracks between the paving stones.

As we came in beside the quay, there was a mass of people throwing up marquees and sound-checking for the band. My aches fell away to be replaced with the contagious excitement palpable in the air throughout town. On my way into the main harbour, I met with a local lass, who told me all about the weekend planned ahead. We joined forces for a while and chatted as we followed the line of the seafront where, eventually, we said our goodbyes and parted ways.

Towards the bottom of the quay, near the slipways, we encountered a crooked street that led out the other side of town and down to a car park overlooking a small bay at the far end. As in Penzance, campers filled the car park – and it was out towards the edge of this that we found our idyllic little camp spot for the night.

Moose looked on somewhat confused. *"Bit early for stopping, isn't it?"*

"Donna's meeting us tomorrow," I remarked as if that were all the explanation needed.

Nonetheless, Moose did an excited little shuffle; it would seem he remembered who she was. I smiled and began pulling kit out from the pack.

We retired early that night…part of me was still feeling the wine from the night before. I fell asleep excited at the prospect of witnessing another regatta and meeting up with an old friend.

We met up just after noon the following day, in one of the harbour-front, dog-friendly pubs.

"You've lost weight." She smirked, grabbing me into a big bear hug. "Urgh! And you smell, too!" she remarked, shoving me away again.

Moose circled her feet, tail wagging his keenness to get some cuddles of his very own.

"And how's the beautiful boy?" she cooed.

He looked at her with his tongue hanging out between a huge grin. *"Did you bring treats?"*

She laughed and knelt to a crouch, fishing out some meaty sticks from her pocket. Moose froze and sat back, tail swishing across the dusty floor as he obediently offered a paw.

"Good boy," she said, as he guzzled them both with a couple of swift chomps.

Looking up and laughing, Donna pronounced, "Well he's not changed." She stood and tilted her head towards the bar. "Are we eating?"

"I should bloody hope so," I replied.

We sat poring over menus and began chatting about all the things we'd missed. It was nice to hear about stuff going on at home. After weeks of talking about nothing but the 'Waggy Walk', it was nice to relax into a conversation about something else. Our food arrived quickly, Moose hardly believing his luck at the treat of two burgers on the trot! We finished up and began contemplating a walk back to our campsite. She followed Moose and me out of town to where the tent lay in the shallows of the car park above the bay.

She stared at the tent bewildered. "I can't believe you two fit into that."

I looked down. To be honest, I'd so gotten used to the thing that I'd forgotten how small it actually was. Vango had labelled this tent 'Two-Man' with a very generous mindset.

"Try it, if you want," I offered.

Donna clambered half into it and immediately began nudging her way back out again. "It smells worse than you two in there!" she said, wrinkling her nose.

I couldn't really argue; God only knows what toxic remnants were now imbued in the fabric. We sat out on the grass watching the sun set while we continued chatting. As the dimness of evening drew in, Donna got up, gave us both a hug and set off back to her car to begin the long drive back up to Bath.

I sat there watching as she disappeared up the path back into town and felt a pang of homesickness – the first I'd had since we'd set off back in June.

Early the next morning, we were back at the harbour. Teams of rowers hauled their gigs around the quay, slowly launching each one off the slipway. There was a distinct buzz of excitement about the day's events and throngs of spectators already lined every inch of sea wall waiting for the spectacle to begin. Settling into a nice spot with Moose to wait for the races to begin, I thought of Sian in Appledore all those weeks ago. As the late morning sun drifted across the sky, the boats hit the water and began dashing out across the bay. Just like in Appledore, I was captivated from the outset.

Sometime after noon, I picked up Moose and headed back to strike camp. Along the coast path on the way back up the cliff, we encountered a sign telling us that due to a damaged section of path we'd have to take a five-kilometre detour. I shuffled my shoulders under the pack.

"Sod that!" I said, confident that we could navigate our way around any damaged sections of path.

We clambered over the flimsy barrier and carried on down the original path. About a quarter of a mile along, I saw the problem. At some point in early spring, there must have been a lot of rain that had pretty much washed away a whole section of path – about 100 metres long. Peering up the steep incline of the hill, I saw walkers headed our way who'd obviously thought the same as me and had carried on, ignoring the detour. I sat and waited until they safely hit the path a few hundred yards ahead.

"Can we get through?" I shouted over to them.

One of them looked up. "Yep! There's a parallel trail just up there on the ridgeline," they said, one of them indicating the direction with his arm. "When you get past the headland you can drop back down to the original path again."

I nodded my thanks and ushered Moose on to lead the way.

"*Why do I get to go first?*" he asked, outraged.

"Let me ask you this," I said, tightening one of the straps on the pack, "if I fall off the cliff, will you pull me back up again?"

Moose almost snorted with laughter. "*No!*"

"Exactly!" I said, nudging him forwards with my knee.

True to the walking party's word, the path reasserted itself right back where they said it would. We crossed a wide, flat expanse of coarse sand interspersed with patches of grass and moss. To our left, the landscape swept inland to be cushioned beneath a huge forest in the distance. We inched our way across to the next line of cliffs in the distance, stopping here and there for a drink of water and to catch our breath.

Back on higher land, we traced our way past a small fishing cove, peaking once again to stunning views over the glittering ocean. The land up here was barren, flecked here and there with masses of the wild flowering brush that we'd seen when leaving Minehead. As the plateau levelled out, I saw a sprinkling of abandoned outbuildings in the distance, surrounded by a series of old wired masts that swayed gently in the late summer heat.

As we approached, I noticed a series of plaques standing testament to the marvels of what once had been the forefront of modern technology. Moose sniffed around the fences, cocking a leg here and there as if to claim a part of this heritage for his own. All around, a slight whistle of wind hummed as it clattered through the intricate tangle of pylons and wires.

Curious, I read the inscription on one of the signs:

TRANSMISSION OF TRANSATLANTIC RADIO SIGNALS, 1901

On December 12, 1901, a radio of the Morse code letter 'S' was broadcast from this site, using equipment built by John Ambrose Fleming. At signal hill in Newfoundland, Guglielmo Marconi, using a wire antenna kept aloft by a kite, confirmed the reception of the first transatlantic radio signals.

I looked up at the abandoned rusting structure as it swayed above. "Look at this, Mooch!"

Moose pulled his head away from yet another alluring fence post. "*Wot?*"

"This is where the first transatlantic broadcast was made!" I said excitedly. "Here!" My engineer genes were geeking out at the very prospect.

Moose wasn't so interested and shrugged. "*There was a lovely collie on heat that passed through here a few hours ago.*"

I rolled my eyes. "There's nothing *you* can do about that, anyway," I said, slyly.

As if remembering some forgotten trauma, he instantly dropped his tail and narrowed his eyes dangerously. "*Yeh...about that!*"

I held my hands out innocently. "Don't blame me! The dogs' home did *that* to you, not me."

He snorted loudly, turned around and casually kicked up tufts of grass into my face.

On our way past the structure, we encountered a faded stone monolith bequeathed to the efforts of these long-lost pioneers; yet another hidden gem buried deep in Cornwall's heart.

A strange sadness struck me as we walked beyond this long-forgotten place.

*

High on the headland above Mullion Cove, we pitched our tent for the night. It wasn't that late but the aching of my feet and Moose's sullen mood put me to thinking that it'd be better to stop now rather than risk a night filled with petty squabbling. Our usual routine ensued and, by morning, Moose had forgotten all about the undignified memories raised by yesterday's conversation.

We crossed on to the Lizard Peninsula just as the sun was coming up – not that we could see much of it through the early-morning mist. Following a shallow beach upwards, we soon found ourselves high up on the clifftops, where the eerie mist began to settle on the farmland, ferns and heather.

Dotted all around this wild and beautiful landscape were signs welcoming us to 'The Lizard'. Clouded by the settling fog, we walked across vast wild terraces flanked by severe cliff edges that faded into the ghost-like gloom. Far below, we could hear distant waves crashing – but up here on the path, an unnerving stillness began to close in, as all sound became muted by the sea mist which swirled around us.

We continued walking along a path that cut into the wild roughage. Up here, it was becoming easy to lose focus; my mind had begun to wander and it was playing tricks on me. A cold brace caught us as we walked inland away from the cliffs and, for the first time since setting off, the chill air began to seep a cold dampness deep into my bones.

The pity of this was that I'd been told the landscape and scenery on the approach to the Lizard was second to none. Today, though, we could barely see ten metres in any direction. Even the crunching of my footsteps became dull and muffled in the stark, damp air as we carefully crept forwards in the thickening mist. We were on an inner trail now and, periodically, the gaunt presence of a wooden way-marker would suddenly burst forth from the swirling fog, only to be swallowed back up just a few metres after we'd passed it. I could hear the stolid crunch of my boot on the stones of the path, muffled underfoot as we inched our way forwards. The sounds of the everyday world were becoming swallowed up by this foreboding damp; it honestly felt as though we were treading among the ghosts of the underworld. Flickers of faint light danced as wild, white swirls of twisted air writhed and eddied in the current and drifted all around us, playing tricks, like the beckoning finger of some skeletal ghoul drawing us in even closer towards some unforeseen doom.

In the distance ahead, I began hearing the dull clanging of a metal chain against a steel gate. As we edged our way closer, the huge hulking outline of a farmhouse suddenly swirled into view. It was made up of rough-hewn sandstone blocks that had faded and blackened over time here; without the sun to warm its exterior, it sat, the stuff of nightmares lost in a ghostly wasteland. The entire structure sat, stark and foreboding against the white mist, seemingly abandoned – were it not for a faint muddy glow of orange light cast out from one of the upper floor windows.

Moose nudged my leg. "*Sod that! I am* not *going any closer.*"

I was glad it wasn't just me – the thing looked absolutely ghastly! "No argument here," I whispered, ushering him onwards.

We quickly found a smaller off-shoot from the path to the one we were on and, minutes later, the haunted farmhouse was lost in the mist – save only for the dull clanging of the chain, which faded as we trudged onwards through the atmospheric soup.

I looked at my watch. We'd been up here less than two hours, although it felt considerably longer. It was desperately quiet and an acute loneliness began to take hold. It was only the companionship of Moose, walking close by my side, that kept the encroaching sense of solitude and dread at bay.

It soon became apparent that leaving the main path had been a mistake. The fine trail we were on suddenly stopped and was completely lost in the fields of ferns and bush in which we now found ourselves entangled. Without the benefit of being able to scan the landscape ahead for references, I stood desperately peering into the thick smog for some tell-tale sign or hidden path.

There were none – except for back the way we'd come.

"Shit…" I said, grabbing the edges of my coat around me in an effort to ward off the chill in the air.

Moose looked up, his ears lowered and tail shoved firmly between his legs. *"We're lost, aren't we?"* he whimpered.

"Don't worry," I said, trying to keep my voice calm, "we'll retrace our steps."

We turned and headed back up the small trail where off-shoot after off-shoot presented themselves among the tangled weed at our feet. I began following one dead end after another, taking random guesses as to direction, desperate to find the one back to the haunted farmhouse. I strained my ears, desperately listening for that distant clanging of the metal chain but, like us, it was lost somewhere in the fog.

Suddenly, to our left, a brace of quail erupted from the undergrowth, jarring our senses. Moose started and leapt after them, charging off in pursuit. I grabbed the leash to hold him back – but the clasp caught on a jagged edge in the brush and snapped off. Moose bounded away and was quickly swallowed up in swirls of thick mist.

I panicked.

"Mooch!" I called.

Nothing.

I peered hard into the blanket of murky white.

"Moose!" I twisted and turned, straining my eyes and ears.

"Moose – get back here – now!" A hole opened up in the pit of my stomach as I stood there limply holding the remnants of the lead. Mind racing and heart pounding, I called out his name again and again.

"Moose!" I screamed, lost in desperation and fear. I felt a light brush against my leg, let out a gasp, tripped over my feet and hurtled backwards into the gorse.

"What the hell are you screaming for?"

I turned sharply to find him calmly chewing on a few strands of grass a couple of feet away.

"You little shite-bag!" Instantly relieved, I dropped the pack, ran over and scooped him up in a huge bear hug.

"Alright – alright..." he complained as I squeezed him tight.

"Don't you ever do that to me again!" I yelled.

He saw the concern in my eyes, softened his stare and slowly drew his tongue the length of my face. *"Sorry, bud,"* he said, spitting out the grass and giving me another long lick against my cheek.

I repaired and reattached the lead and sat in the thorny grass trying to clear my head. We had to get down out of this fog before it drove me cuckoo. I took out my map and – for the first time on this journey – my compass.

"We'll do this the old-fashioned way," I said, mentally brushing off my orienteering skills. I traced our path as best I could and decided to take a bearing south, though it'd mean lots of cross-country walking.

Eventually, we hit the coast path perpendicular to our route at Kynance Cliff.

"Stay close and no bloody wandering off this time!" I muttered.

Moose wagged his tail in agreement.

We blindly followed the compass and, half an hour later, I heard the faint crashing of waves ahead. I breathed a sigh of relief as Moose panted his. Five minutes after that, we were standing back solidly on the security of the South West Coast Path.

I took one last look at the mist closing in behind us.

"Thank God *that's* over!"

As we made our way down to a wide staircase leading us into a valley, the mist began to clear and my senses reasserted themselves. Ahead, I could hear snippets of conversation and, as we turned a corner on the steps, the world opened up to reveal a well-placed café on an even terrace overlooking the ocean. We grabbed the nearest table, dumped our stuff beside it and went off to grab a cup of tea and two Cornish pasties. Moose wolfed his down in less than a dozen quick chomps, whereas I savoured every bite, slowly supping my tea as the surreal experience of the day drifted out of my mind.

My nerves were absolutely shot! Of all the experiences we'd had on this trip, that was the most surreal by far, trumped only in fear-factor by our clash with the winds on the approach to Crackington Haven.

We left the café, made our way to the sandy stretch at the bottom of the bay and began scaling the steps on the other side. The bustle of people here made it less daunting to be heading, once again, into the fog. Fortunately, the heat of the day was beginning to assert itself and was burning off the rich blanket of cloud, leaving just a faint white mist. Visibility was still close but nowhere near as bad as the thick pea-soup it had been earlier. It was as if a veil had been lifted, albeit only enough to give a thin strip of visibility across the headland. There were other walkers here, too, and seeing their bright blue and red waterproof jackets dotted along the path here and there removed the atmosphere of foreboding solitude.

There was something else here, too. Far in the distance, I became aware of a deep groaning sound that would periodically rumble in from somewhere ahead. At first, I thought it was the far-off mooing of cattle but this sound was grander somehow, and it punctuated the air at impeccably timed intervals. I was beginning to ache all over; the mist had brought with it a cold and damp that had seeped its way into my core. It was getting on towards late afternoon and the distant rumble had evolved into a low sombre howl, a warning to ships out to sea of the dangers in the foggy waters that lay below the ineffective lighthouse beacon at Lizard Point – the southernmost tip of mainland Britain.

On the grass outside another café, we sat and caught our breath. We'd caught the attention of a group of youngsters nearby and, before long, we were chatting about our respective journeys to get here. Unlike Moose and me, these guys had driven across from Plymouth. They treated me to a small bottle of cider as we all sat there together, staring at the mist out to sea while the moan of the foghorn periodically pierced the air. I became acutely aware of the shocking state I was in, making the silent decision to scout around the Lizard to try to secure lodgings for the night.

I tried my luck at a YHA on the off chance they'd have something, although I wasn't optimistic – every other time I'd tried, we'd been turned away.

I wasn't disappointed.

"Well, at least they're consistent," I muttered to Moose as we headed back out on to the coast path to try to find somewhere else to spend the night. On the far side of the lighthouse was a huge RNLI launch, where we sat for a few minutes contemplating our next move.

"Mind some company?" a voice came from behind.

Moose erupted and I turned to see a chap in his fifties, kitted out in waterproofs and rucksack, with the scraggly demeanour of another wild-camper.

"Sure," I said, bringing Moose to heel and making a space for him beside us on the wall. He took off his rucksack, slumped down and began shuffling around inside the pack.

"Do you have a cup?" he asked.

"Err – yeh…" I said, somewhat confused. I offered him my battered tin mug and he quickly pulled out a small bottle of whisky and poured out a generous measure.

"To walking in the fog!" he said, raising his cup in a toast.

I smirked and did the same. "To walking in the fog."

We chinked our cups together and drank.

Moose sniffed disapprovingly at the sharp vapour while we traded introductions. Steve had also tried for lodgings and, due to the absence of anything better, was also looking for a camp spot for the night. We left the station and crept down the steep incline of a valley to a flat grassed area tucked into the side of the brush.

"Ideal!" I announced.

Steve nodded in his agreement, slinging his pack to the floor while I paced the ground looking for a good spot to pitch our tent. We chatted as we ate supper, swapping our stories of the road. He, much the same as us, was prone to taking long periods off work and buggering off to explore the coastal trails of Britain.

He'd been on the road for three weeks; we'd been there for considerably longer.

It was now mid-August.

Chapter 17

Quarries and Ferries

Lizard Point to Maenporth

That night, I lay in the tent with Moose, trying to drift off to sleep with the constant howling of the foghorn in the distance. Steve's whisky helped, and before long I was drifting uneasily through nightmares of unknown terrors stalking Moose and me through the mists above the Lizard.

I awoke with a start early the next day and could hear Steve's snoring drifting in from his tent, which was pitched not far from mine. The booming of the foghorn in the distance still punctuated the air and I decided to rise early and set off, putting the haunting memories of this 'lost' peninsula behind us. I gave Steve's tent a farewell nod as we headed back on to the path, his faint snoring fading into the distance behind us as we followed the rising path, out of the valley.

Along the way that morning, we met walkers heading in the opposite direction who assured us that the path from the Lizard would be smooth sailing, but as things turned out, it wouldn't be as simple as that.

It was not as easy a path as we'd been led to believe, as each step became more and more difficult with every passing mile. On a positive note, the mist was far fainter than it had been the day before, meaning at very least, we could see out a good distance on to the headland.

I groaned inwardly; today our challenge would be the terrain.

Staircases, steep inclines, sharp downturns – by now, we knew how these went! The effect was much the same as it had been during past encounters with gradients like this. At Cadgwith, we encountered a stunning rock feature out to sea called 'The Devil's Frying Pan' – think 'mini-Durdle Door', and you're not far off. It was close enough to the vantage point on the cliff so as not to be obscured by the mist. In all honesty, I was too tired to fully appreciate it as I puffed and panted past with only a sideways glance.

Moose began complaining. *"Are we nearly there yet?"*

I stopped and threw him a look filled with daggers. "You have got to be kidding me!" I started, although in my exhausted state it probably came across more like irritated desperation than annoyance.

Eventually, the contours evened out and, at the far end of the head-land, I began to make out what appeared to be a cottage sat in solitude overlooking the ocean. It was still hard to tell at this range – the mist made everything seem like something else until you were stood right on top of it and this was no different. The 'cottage' was actually a little bird-viewing enclosure and, by that, I mean it had four walls, a roof, a door to let you in, and a large window looking out over a place called Black Head.

We muscled our way inside and I absently chucked the pack on to one of the benches lining the interior. Beneath the window was a table littered with various bits of literature about birds, famous people and the history of the area. Buried among all that was another, far more interesting book: the one with all the signatures!

In my opinion, visitor books are a modern-day interpretation of those etchings and scribbles you'd find adorning the walls of really historic buildings (and not just the kind you need a National Trust membership for, either).

The last time we'd encountered one was on the North Devon–Cornwall border at Ronald Duncan's lodge. I'm sure you'll have encountered them yourself – places where you see:

Deb & Trev
4-ever
'82

…etched into stone or scrawled into the wood in hard-cut biro or marker pen. Some would call it vandalism, but I always wonder if, in a hundred years, they'll call it something else like insight or history.

They tell stories of journeys, for which these pit-stops are just a small part. I love reading about what goes on when an individual has travelled so far, reaches a place and is driven to scribble down their immediate thoughts before moving on. I've done this myself, never giving any consideration to the idea that people would actually read the trite I'd written on the spur of the moment.

Well, today I had time – and lots of it, too!

My feet and back ached, so I dragged the chair across from the corner of the room, quickly made myself a cup of tea and, as Moose snored comfortably beneath the desk, I read through every single entry.

The last note had been written a couple of days ago, leaving a full third of a page yet to be filled. I fished a pen out of my bag and set about adding us both to the journal. I reckoned we were easily worth what was left. After five minutes of writing, I sat back, re-read the entry a couple of times and smiled.

"That'll do, Pig," I said to myself, smugly.

"Oii!" said Moose, raising his head off the bench. *"Who you calling pig?"*

"I wasn't…" I started. "It's from a…" I shook my head slightly. "Never mind." I sighed, keen to switch topic. "I thought you were sleeping, anyway?"

He poked his head from under the table and yawned.

"All your muttering woke me up." He grinned as he half-walked, half-stretched out into the room before giving himself a solid shake for good measure. *"Are we staying here tonight?"* he asked, excitedly.

I stood up, stretched and walked over to put the rucksack back on. Moose took the hint and shrugged. *"Guess not, then."*

After two days of walking in thick fog, my clothes were starting to get as damp as my spirits. Rain was something that could be avoided with a bit of luck, but mist…well, that just seeps into every pore, and there's no getting away from it. I was beginning to feel a chill settle deep into my bones. As the day progressed, I found myself feeling the miles, and the solitude, and the damp. Moose kept to himself as he trotted silently by my side.

Eventually, we came down from the plateau and into the picturesque village of Coverack. At the far end of the quay was a dog-friendly pub where we stopped off to get out of the damp and gather our senses. I asked at the bar if there was anywhere local to stay for the night – I could've killed for a hot shower. The chap on the other side took one look at us and, possibly through some altruistic intention for the pathetic, began calling local campsites to find us a space. A few minutes later, he came from around the bar to where we were sitting.

"Good news." He smiled. "Head back up the hill about a mile and they're waiting for you at a place called Little Trevothan."

A mile! I thought, barely able to stand. I gave a tired smile of thanks and asked for directions while I psyched myself up for the trek.

"Head out of the pub and up the lane," he began, "you'll hit a chicane in the road," his hands began flailing wildly, "…and the site's just there on your left, but not the first left – that's a field – the second left."

I thanked him as best I could for his efforts, once again grateful for my luck. Grabbing the kit, I led Moose back on to the hill and out of town.

"Best of luck, pal!" he called out, as the swinging bar door clattered shut behind us.

One mile's walk takes about twenty minutes or half an hour if the terrain's steep. That afternoon, it took me almost an hour. I was, in every conceivable way, absolutely done in by the time we got to the site. As we finally arrived, I staggered down the approach to the reception area, where we were met by one of the owners, Sue.

"Could I have two nights' stay, please?" I gasped, between breaths.

She looked at the shocking mess standing on the other side of the counter and shook her head in pity. "You've been on the road for a while, haven't you?"

I nodded weakly, "Since the end of June."

Her eyes widened. It was the 20th of August!

"When was the last time you stayed somewhere?" she asked, concern written all over her face.

I shook my head. "I honestly can't remember," I said. I fished out my wallet and offered to pay.

"Are you walking for charity?" she enquired, noticing the print on my filthy T-shirt.

I nodded and briefly told her about what we were doing.

"You put your money away, then!" she said firmly. "This is on us!"

Minutes later, we were led to a secluded spot where I pitched the tent, ate more dry food and immediately collapsed, fast asleep.

*

Just before dawn, I awoke with a start and crawled out of the tent. I stood there trying to make sense of my surroundings before realising where I was. As the delirium passed, I breathed a sigh of relief, crawled back into the sleeping bag next to Moose and drifted off again.

Later that morning sparked a turn of mood for me. I had the stark realisation that the attitude I'd adopted so far was completely untenable. It dawned on me that I could be, quite literally, walking myself to death. 'Exhausted' didn't even begin to describe how I was feeling.

As I crawled out on to the safe, flat ground of the campsite, I realised just what an awful condition I was in. Moose wasn't complaining – but, to be fair to him, he was a dog and his loyalty meant that he rarely would. He looked up at me simply with his big, brown, liquid eyes.

"Are we ready for the off, then?" he asked, somewhat timidly.

I nearly burst into tears as I crouched down, held his big head in my hands and caressed his ears. "Not today, pal." I sighed, giving him a gentle kiss on the tip of his nose. "We're having a couple of days off."

The look of relief on his face said it all and I realised that I really was pushing us both way too hard. I looked down at my T-shirt and noticed that it was the same one I'd changed into that night outside Land's End. I scratched my cheek and found the beginnings of a beard there.

"Time to sort this out," I asserted, climbing back into the tent, fumbling around to find my wash kit and something relatively clean that I could use as a towel. I counted back the weeks and realised that the Menagerie in Portreath was the last time we'd showered or washed clothes. Fourteen days – literally two weeks ago! Thankfully, a shower block and laundry room were close at hand and we were here for a full two days. I grinned in spite of myself at the very thought of hot running water. Oh, the paradise that awaited!

First things first: I desperately needed to find the laundrette and get some washing on the go. The good thing about carrying minimal clothing is that it all fits in as one load of the machine. As the thing whirred up and began its cycle, I trudged across the yard to sort out the rest of the mess.

"Wash time," I said to Moose, looking around eagerly for the shower block, which I eventually found at the far end of the compound. No sooner had I crawled in and spun the water dial than he had his nose under and was gobbing away at the spray spilling out of the showerhead.

"Will you pack that in," I moaned.

He ignored me and kept on snapping at the water.

"Oi!" I said, getting somewhat irritated.

He stopped, looked up at me, grinned and carried on.

Sod it, I thought, shoving his head to one side with my knee and standing under the stream of steamy water. As soon as I started adding shower gel to the mix Moose lost interest and sneezed a line of soapy water up my leg before backing out.

"Well, that'll serve you right!" I said smugly, massaging soapy suds into my hair.

He ignored me, collapsed to the tile floor and – rather disturbingly – continued staring at me while I finished showering. That done, I set about tidying up my face. I looked in the mirror at the scrawny, scruffy reflection staring back. My skin was still beet-red from all the sun, which had also bleached my hair a mousey blonde.

"Well, at least the grey's not showing through anymore." I shrugged.

I grabbed a new Bic razor and damn-near blunted the thing on just one shave. Then, I grabbed a set of scissors from my bag and trimmed my hair to try to bring a bit of order to the chaos. Wiping the condensation off the mirror, I stood back and took stock. On the whole, I thought I'd done a pretty good job.

I turned to Moose, spread wide my arms and grinned. "Whaddaya think?"

He looked at me with bored disinterest. *"You're still ugly."* He snorted.

"Charming," I muttered, dropping my arms to my sides and turning back to the mirror. "Time to get dressed and face the world," I said to my smiling reflection.

I looked back into the corner of the shower room at my filthy clothes rotting a hole through the tiled floor near the door. The only bad thing about carrying the bare minimum was that these rags were all I had to put back on until my washing was done. My skin crawled at the clammy touch and stink of fortnight-old clothes being dragged across my clean frame. I walked out of the shower block, leaving behind a torrid waft of two-week-old sweat mixed with lime-fresh shower gel, to the peevish giggle of my dog.

Two days later, we said our farewells to Sue and her husband, Mark, and marched out of Little Trevothan Camping and Caravan Park feeling thoroughly refreshed. Back in the bay at Coverack, we found the coast path and followed it up towards the other side of town. The flat terrain we were promised began to reveal itself, as we gently meandered around the bends and twists of the coastline where coarse grey beaches started separating the land from the sea.

Several miles beyond the town we encountered a huge abandoned quarry, which presented itself like some modern, garish ruin misplaced from a stark dystopian future. Unlike other secluded places we'd visited before, the ruins here were definitely twentieth century – hulking, grey and still, silently exuding an air of alien abandonment. We rested on one of the huge concrete outcroppings and had lunch as the sun made an appearance once again. I was determined not to push too hard today and was hoping to find a camp spot well before sundown.

At Porthallow, we found our spot – a lovely little campsite run by a farm just outside of town. As we sat to eat our evening meal in the café, I got chatting to a few of the other campers; we sat together and swapped stories of the road until late in the evening. In addition to the local conversation, I'd decided to make a few calls home to catch up with family and friends, each with some surprising results. We were getting close to the August bank holiday weekend and both my brother *and* my best friend wanted to come down to visit for a few days.

To be honest, the company would be nice. As great as this adventure was, I missed just sitting around and gassing about the everyday things in life. Considering how low I'd been just a few days before, I arranged to meet them both at the end of the month. I eagerly sprang out of the campsite the following morning spurred on by the excitement of meeting up with some familiar faces in the not-too-distant future.

Falmouth was now clearly in our sights and, as we twisted and turned along the path, its craggy edges began to smooth out as we descended on to a gentle slope, through meadows and luscious woodlands. At Nare Point, we came across a sea of bright yellow, swaying under the brilliant glare of afternoon sunlight. Before us, a field of sunflowers stretched high and far into the distance. Moose scurried off, lost among the towering, swaying stalks of the beautiful behemoths, as the sun held on to the last of its summer glow.

I walked around the last peak before heading into the tiny estuary of Helford Passage. As per usual, the gravel path became tarmac road as it dived through a rich treeline, down into the village and, finally, to the ferry crossing at the base of the river.

Moose stood there wagging his tail in excitement. *"Are we going on another boat?"*

I smiled – the last time we'd taken a ferry was at Padstow and he'd loved the experience then. "We are, pal," I said, delighted at the thrilled look on his little face.

He made a giddy little twirl as we waited on the edge of the slipway. As the ferry docked – and by 'ferry', I mean 'tiny little boat' – Moose had become even more excitable.

"Oi! Calm down, you!" I said as he stood, tail wagging ten to the dozen.

We boarded quickly and found our seats near the prow. The chap at the tiller swung the boat around and we began put-putting our way across the river. As we reached the halfway point, Moose, unable to contain his excitement any longer, stood and promptly flung himself overboard, nearly tipping the boat in the process.

"Whoa!" the ferryman cried out, shifting his position in an attempt to even out the lilt of the boat, which was rocking back and forth wildly. He glared at me with a mixture of annoyance and concern. "Will he be alright?"

Stunned, I could only muster a confused "dunno" as I frantically scanned the water near the massive splosh into which Moose had disappeared. Two seconds later, a flurry of jowls, paws and fur emerged as Moose madly doggy paddled next to the boat.

"You flamin' idiot!" I yelled.

He splashed alongside us with a stupid grin on his face as we made our way across to the landing on the other side where I stumbled out of the boat and muttered my apologies to the ferryman. He waved them away and laughed. "I'll be tellin' that story for a while, don't you worry!"

He spun the boat around and headed back across the river while Moose stood on the concrete, shaking the water out of his fur.

"What the hell was that all about?" I asked, hands on hips.

"*Wot?*" he asked, shaking more water out on to the jetty.

"Never mind *what*," I snapped, trying not to smile as I told him off. "Jumping in the river – that's what!"

"*Just cooling off,*" he said with a swagger.

"Well...*never* do that again!" I shouted, trying to hide a smirk.

Just as it had been on the other side, we found ourselves following a manicured pavement pinned to the side of a single-track road. It wound between trees until, eventually, it opened up to reveal a lovely little pub on the edge of a small marina – which, like most places around here, was dog-friendly. No doubt it was the kind of place with soft furnishings within and so, painfully aware of Moose's sopping state after his little swim, I decided to take a bench in the beer garden out by the river.

He'd dried off somewhat by now and, as we sat there enjoying the view, I decided to take things a little bit easier. Leaving my pack by the table, I moseyed back into the pub to grab myself a couple of pints of Rattler and some snacks. On my return, the group at the next bench noticed my pack and the charity flag draped across it (which I'd taken to leaving over the pack whenever I abandoned it, as a plea to any opportunists not to steal our stuff while we were gone).

They asked us what we were doing.

I began talking and before long had piqued the interest of the other people sitting at tables within earshot of mine. Waxing lyrical, I recounted the story of our journey so far, with its humble beginnings in Portishead – a town none there had heard of – to our trek down across Somerset, North Devon and, now, Cornwall.

By the time I'd finished, my audience had grown considerably and many were perched on the edge of their seats, or sitting on the edge of tables – first time that had ever happened! I elaborated on our adventures, leading up to Moose's 'dip' in the drink on our way here. Suddenly, a fresh pizza slid its way on to the table in front of us.

"Oh, sorry," I said, catching the attention of the waitress. "I didn't order that."

The woman turned and came back to stand by our table. "Compliments of the Shipwright's Arms!" She smiled, wiping her hands on her apron.

Moose stuck his head up from underneath the table, nose twitching furiously. "*I loves pizza!*"

I glanced down. "Hush – I know you do," I said. "That's very kind of you but I can pay," I offered, looking back at the woman.

"Pfft! Nonsense," she said. "It's our gift to you *and* this handsome chap!"

She bent over and started giving Moose's ears a good rub. "Aren't you a cutie!" She smiled.

Mooch threw on the puppy-eyes, rolled to his back and presented a proud chest, ready for a good scratch.

She obliged accordingly.

I took my chance and began scoffing pizza, much to Moose's bewilderment as he looked on, caught between food and affection. "It's either food or belly rubs, pal." I shrugged, stuffing more pizza into my mouth while he lay there mid-pamper.

He narrowed his eyes, either through envy or the gentle massaging he was getting under the table. *"You'd better save me some!"*

He knew better than to ask.

Once the plate was empty and I'd polished off my two pints of cider, we made our way out of town and around the headland to find home for the night. The approach to Mawnan took us through some thick, forested trails that led us beneath a canopy of trees towards several terraced tiers of soft, loamy undergrowth perfect for camping. I took us a fair way from the path and settled in for the night. Tomorrow, we'd be approaching the outskirts of Falmouth – where, the day after, we'd be meeting up with friends and family. I was practically giddy with excitement. I could almost forgive Moose's impulsiveness at jumping off the ferry earlier that day, such were the high spirits I felt when drifting off to sleep that night.

I blinked…and we were up again, faced with another glorious day of walking. As we headed out from the path, I could see the vast harbour of Falmouth glittering away in the distance, sun blazing on from above. The coast path struck a steady course along cliff lines until we reached the beach at Maenporth. To my astonishment, the beach looked green – the first like this that we'd encountered on our trip. But, far from the glittering sands of crushed emeralds I romantically envisioned as I walked to it from the cliff line, I found out later that the hue was attributable to the algae clinging to the grains due to infrequent high tides. It was still a spectacle, nonetheless.

As we walked along the promenade, we were met by a family of tourists who insisted on buying me a cup of coffee at the café sitting at the far end of the bay. It was still early and, not being much of a coffee drinker, I opted for a glass of orange juice instead. We sat on the benches outside where I chatted to the adults while the kids indulged Moose with belly rubs and ear tickles. Nattering away, I could hear excited giggles from the children and a contented groaning from the dog as they played together in the sand.

Suddenly, my phone rang; it was my brother.

I held the phone to one side. "Would you excuse me for a minute?" They nodded as I wandered off the side of the bench and picked up the call.

"Hi?" I asked.

"Hi," came my brother's voice down the phone.

"You OK?"

"Yeh, fine," he continued. "Where are you camping? We'll be setting off early in the morning."

I hadn't even thought about that. "Err… I found a site just outside Falmouth?"

"Well it'd better not be a bloody swamp in the middle of nowhere," he ranted. "I want a proper campsite."

I gulped. "Nah, it looks lovely on the website," I lied.

"Good. Text me the address and we'll see you tomorrow." The line abruptly went dead.

I looked down at Moose, who'd untangled himself from the kids. "No pressure there, then!" I shrugged.

I went back to where the others were sitting, said my farewells and wandered around until I found decent internet signal. Well, enough to google some local campsites for the weekend, anyway. Thankfully,

I found one at a place called Pennance Farm that lay about two miles inland, back the way we'd walked. I called the owners and booked three spaces before setting off down the roadway, eventually making it to camp just before 6pm.

The owner was a tall gangly bloke with long lank hair and a demeanour that just screamed 'hippy'. As I explained about the late arrival of the other guests, he stuffed into my hand a tattered A4 piece of paper with a map of the site printed on one side and some vague instructions as to what camping spots lay where on the other. I meandered through the site and found a neat snug of free spaces and, as much as I could, spread my kit across all three pitches to indicate that they were taken. I took out my phone and sent a text to my brother and Greg, letting them know where we were.

After pitching our tent, I made our supper and settled in with Moose for the night. I sat there eating my dinner with that giddy feeling all kids get the night before Christmas – I couldn't wait until the morning. It felt like a lifetime since I'd last seen them and as I settled down to sleep, I turned, gave Mooch a quick peck on the head, and smiled myself to sleep.

Chapter 18

Family

Maenporth

The next morning, we were sitting on the grass enjoying breakfast when my brother and his wife roared on to the campsite. The big galoot piled out of his truck and immediately grabbed me in a massive bear hug that lifted me clear off the ground.

I gasped.

"You stink, you scrawny sod!" he boomed, crushing me in his massive arms.

"I love you too, mate," I retorted, hardly able to breathe, "but you're breaking my ribs!" I gasped, writhing in his grasp as he chuckled into my ear.

I eventually managed to wriggle an arm free to give him a good dig in the ribs. "Let me go, you daft arse!" He relaxed his grip and air whooshed back into my lungs as I landed firmly back on my feet...before falling arse-first back on to the grass.

I looked over to the truck, and the suspiciously empty passenger seat. "Where's..."

"Doris?" he interrupted. "She's paying at reception."

In all the excitement, I'd forgotten about Moose. Not one to be left out, he chose that moment to run over and launch himself at Dave, nearly knocking him off his feet. "Well you've not changed, ya daft bugger!" He laughed, grabbing Moose in a friendly headlock. Moo went in for a slobbery kiss but was firmly pushed away by a meaty hand. "You can forget any of that an' all," he said, pulling his face out of harm's way. Dave wasn't one for doggy kisses, choosing instead to give him a good scratch behind the ear.

Down the path, I could see my sister-in-law, Julie, puffing her way up to where we were camped. Dave turned as she approached. "All paid up, Doris?"

She just rolled her eyes, ignoring the quip. "How've you been?" she asked me, sidestepping her husband and planting a gentle kiss on my cheek.

"Fine," I said, "and all the better for seeing you two!"

Dave tromped to the back of the truck, lowered the tailgate and began pulling masses of camping kit out on to the grass. He paused while holding a particularly large bundle in his arms. "New tent." He winked.

"Bloody expensive one, too…" Julie muttered under her breath.

I dragged Moose to one side and left them to the business of setting up. After ten minutes or so it became apparent that the new tent resembled something more akin to an inflatable house. It was massive – one of those modern things with wide inflatable supports as opposed to flimsy, fiddly poles.

Dave, finished with the exterior, took a step back and proudly beamed at his handiwork. "Not bad, eh?" He looked around. "Where's yours, Tarzan?"

I *hated* that nickname – a leftover from when I had long hair in my twenties, and something Dave had never let up about since.

"It's over there." I nodded, pointing to our squat little two-man Banshee.

He sniggered, turned and began unloading a king-size blow-up mattress along with a hoard of quilts, cushions and pillows. "You wanna get yourself one of these," he teased.

I began thinking about what it would take to lump that lot around the coast path and shuddered. "I think I'll stick to what I have."

I looked at Moose who was sat drooling away with envy. "Forget it!" I said, nipping any ideas of opulence in the bud.

"*But...*" he started.

I turned and cut off any further discussion, grabbing my bowl up from the grass to slump beside our little Vango tent, and carried on eating my cereal. Moose grumbled but, begrudgingly, followed.

We both sat there finishing our breakfasts to the random soundtrack of expletives interspersed frequently with the word 'Doris', from inside the blow-up palace. It still bewildered me, as I listened to them both making camp, that such a mismatched pair held on to a fierce love for one another under the constant veneer of bickering and name-calling. I sat back and smiled at the exchanges between them. God, I'd missed them both! It was a pity my nephews couldn't be there, too.

PING

It was Greg.

Getting into Falmouth station for 20 past 11.

I looked at my watch. "Crap!" It was nearly eleven. "Oi," I shouted in the direction of the homemakers. "Time we were off."

Dave stuck his head out from the tent flap. "When's he land?"

"Twenty minutes!"

"Damn!" he muttered. "We're off to pick up Greg, Doris."

After marching straight out of the tent and slamming closed the tailgate on the way past, he jumped into the driver's seat of his truck. "Coming?" he asked as if *I* were the one faffing around. I grabbed Moose,

235

dived into the back seat and, seconds later, we were speeding out of the campsite in the direction of Falmouth train station.

Thanks to Dave's efficient concept of time and over-exuberant use of the accelerator pedal, we got there just as the train was pulling up. I flung open the door, clipped on Moose and found a nearby bench below the platform to wait. As the doors to the train shunted open with a series of beeps, I saw Greg exit the train amid a flow of other tourists. Eyes front, he obliviously wandered past us both and then down on to the ramp leading to the car park below. I smiled and got up from the seat to follow behind, deliberately letting Moose's lead off the catch so he could push ahead. He weaved in and out of the mass of strangers and leapt up on to Greg from behind as soon as he caught the familiar scent. Entangled in a flurry of paws and squeaks as the full weight of Mooch hit him from behind, Greg fell forwards in surprise.

It's fair to say that Greg is possibly Moose's favourite 'hooman' (with the exception of yours truly, of course).

They hit the floor and rolled in a blur of kisses, cooing and slobber, much to the annoyance of those left trying to depart the platform. Both carried on with each other regardless, like the long-lost friends they were.

"Mr Moose!"

Kisses…

"Great to see you."

Tail-wags and more kisses.

"Have you two finished?" I asked, feeling distinctly third-wheel-esque.

Greg looked up, struggling to get a thirty-five-pound dog off his lap, and laughed. "Hiya, mate, good to see you."

Moose noticed the shift in attention and responded by dragging the entire length of his tongue across Greg's cheek. Dave, who'd been watching from the comfort of his truck, boomed out, "Are you lot coming or what?"

We quickly loaded up. Moose and Greg carried on in the back seat and, pretty soon, we were all speeding back through the streets of Falmouth.

Back at the campsite, greetings were exchanged as tents were put up. Despite the early hour, we were soon sitting on camping chairs, drinking cider and catching up in the sun.

Dave and Greg had always got along and, as the afternoon drifted into evening, so too did the conversation. The humour and one-liners exchanged by the two were only enhanced by the rapid consumption of bottle after bottle, befitting any weekend camping trip. Credit to my brother: when he went camping, he bloody well prepared for the event! A bottle of Scotch appeared at some point and a barbeque was lit, where a healthy portion of the local farm shop stock was soon sizzling away on the grill.

Moose sat obediently while all this was going on, understanding full well the spoils that were to follow if he strategically placed himself at the dining table. His understanding of the advantages of meeting up with people after long periods of time primarily revolved around the generosity of scraps pushed to him by sleight of hand from various members of the party. By the time the sun had set, he'd probably eaten more than any of us.

He came up to me and optimistically wagged his tail. "*Is it dinner time yet?*"

I gave him a sneaky glance. "You've just *had* dinner, mate."

His eyes softened, eyebrows twitched, and ears lowered. "*But I'm wasting away,*" he pleaded.

I could still see the remnants of burger grease and ketchup around his nose. "Don't kid a kidder," I said, turning my chair away slightly.

He sneezed at me in a huff, walked over to Greg and repeated the same pleading pantomime.

Sausages were duly awarded for the effort.

*

Throughout the evening's chat, I was inadvertently reminded that it was Saturday – something I'd completely overlooked up to that point. Not only that, but it was also August bank holiday weekend, meaning that Dave and Julie would be staying on the campsite until Monday morning and, for lack of anything better to do, Greg and I decided to do the same. Greg was to be with me for a while longer and had agreed to walk some of the coastal path with Moose and me. God help the poor lad; I honestly don't think he realised just what he was letting himself in for.

The clamour of other parties around the campsite began to simmer down to those few stalwarts who would inevitably carry on until the early hours. Ours was one such party – with the exception of Julie, who'd decided enough was enough and had gone to bed.

Three blokes, a dog, copious amounts of alcohol, and a roaring fire can only ever promise one thing: a messy night! The jokes got ruder, the laughter louder and our awareness of our surroundings became less and less acute. Sometime during the proceedings, we all heard a huff from inside the tent. "It's three o'clock, for God's sake!" Julie shouted.

"Don't worry, Doris," slurred Dave. "We'll keep it down."

There were sounds of fumbling and unzipping, and a bleary-eyed Dave looked up straight into the harsh stare of his fuming wife. "Don't you bloody 'Doris' me!" she retorted, angrily snatching the whisky bottle from his hand and holding it up to the light.

I could see the pathetic remnants swilling away in the bottom of the bottle, leant into my brother and grinned. "A million Scots'd be proud of you, lad, good effort!"

Julie glared at me.

I clamped my mouth shut and kept the remainder of my opinions to myself.

"Bed – the lot of you!" she barked, abruptly turning on her heel and disappearing back into the canvas.

"But my bottle," Dave started…

"Now!"

I looked at my brother, winked, fell out of my chair and crawled all the way back to my tent to collapse in a tangled mess with Moose. As we lay there, I could hear the distant rumbling of apologies from my brother before I drifted off into oblivion.

I awoke several hours later to the unforgiving glare of the morning sun lighting up the inside of the tent like a beacon. Moose groaned, rolled to one side and kicked me in the ribs for good measure before letting out a series of loud snores. I tried for the zip and unceremoniously tumbled out on to the grass, almost garrotting myself on the guy lines of Greg's tent. As the world swam back into view, I tried sitting up.

"Morning!" came a cheery voice.

I blinked and slowly turned my head. Greg was sitting on one of the chairs, bright-eyed and bushy-tailed, with a book nestled in his lap.

"Is it?" I groaned.

He laughed. "Feeling a bit delicate, bud?"

I tried shaking away the cobwebs only to be hit by an intense and beautifully crafted hangover pounding on the back of my eyeballs. I rose – slowly – and grabbed on to one of the chairs to sit beside my friend. I contemplated the previous night's choices.

Nodding over to the huge tent, I asked, "Any movement?"

"Julie's up," he said, taking a sip from his cup of tea. "She's just nipped over to the shop to get some supplies for breakfast."

"… And Dave?"

Greg held a long finger against his lips. From inside the inflatable pavilion, I could hear faint snoring coming from what I assumed was my brother.

I smiled and pinched my nose in an effort to try to settle the turmoil erupting in my head.

239

"Good night last night," Greg chirped.

I couldn't help but agree. "Indeed it was."

"Rough?" he asked.

"You have no idea."

Several hours and two painkillers later, I was beginning to feel more like my usual self. We'd all decided that a long walk through the surrounding forests would be just the thing to reignite our enthusiasm and blow away the cobwebs. Moose was in his element as he darted between the trees, snapping at bugs and butterflies as he skipped along.

"Don't go too far," I yelled. He dutifully ignored me and disappeared headlong into the brush.

I sidled up beside my brother. "How you feeling?"

His face was still tinged with a murky tone of green. "It's just a good job we decided to call it a night when we did." He groaned.

Julie's face was a picture!

On our way back up the hill, we encountered a little holiday village. Nestled among all the chalets was a modern-looking bar/restaurant with a large outdoor seating area. Breakfast was becoming a long-distant memory, so we looked at one of the outdoor menu boards and decided to grab a bite to eat. Moose collapsed heavily on to the decking boards, rolled over and promptly fell asleep. I handed the reins over to Greg and went inside to order drinks and enquire about food.

It was a freeing experience – and something I'd not been able to do in months – just the simple action of walking into an establishment without having to go through the usual rigmarole: asking "… *Are you doggy friendly?*" and then having to worry about causing a ruckus if there was another pooch hiding in a dark corner somewhere.

I came back with a tray and duly handed out four pints of Rattler cider. My brother looked at me like I'd just given him a vial of poison. "Don't be such a soft arse." I grinned. "That'll put hairs on your chest!"

As the food arrived, Dave took the plunge and opted for another pint. By the end of his second, a nice rosy glow was returning to his cheeks. As per usual, Moose deftly wound his way under the table to grab scraps, rewarding each offering with a gentle grunt of approval and a kiss on the fingertips from a soggy doggy tongue. We finished up and made our way back through the estate to the campsite, where another night of chat, cider and laughs commenced.

The following morning saw another early start for us all as we began dismantling our camps. Once loaded, Dave and Julie unleashed a flurry of hugs, kisses and promises to catch up and do this again someday soon. As they sped out of the campsite, I felt that pang in the pit of my stomach. "'Parting is such sweet sorrow'," I muttered to myself as I stood in their wake, watching them turn on to the road and disappear from view.

I looked back at Greg, who was by now sporting his own rucksack, and reached down to give Moose the usual scratch behind his ears. I sighed and nodded in the direction of the coastline. "Are we off, then, or what?"

Chapter 19

Greg

Maenporth to Pentewan

There was very little by way of coastal path as we walked towards the bustling port town of Falmouth. Once we'd cleared the crags that held the remnants of World War II battlements, the bay revealed itself from beyond the thorny hedgerows, in a spectacular view over the immense harbour.

From our vantage point on the road, we saw huge industrial operations taking place in the dry docks surrounding the town on a scale that I'd never seen before. The 'boats' there were not worthy of such understatement: these were *ships*, massive and hulking, patiently waiting in the shimmering waters of this grand port to be repaired and upgraded.

Greg had made it clear before coming down to meet us both that he wouldn't be trifling with the nonsense notion of wild camping. For him, this was a holiday and it was one he bloody well intended to enjoy. I, for one, didn't mind at all. After the experiences Moose and I'd had coming around the Cornish peninsula and the isolation we'd found ourselves in at the Lizard, I embraced the opportunity to spend the week in relative luxury. I'd not discussed this with Moose but I knew he wouldn't mind either; I was just saving up the surprises for later.

The three of us bustled into one of the cafés at Discovery Quay to meet someone who'd heard about our walk on Facebook. We found ourselves a seat on one of the less rickety tables and were halfway through cappuccinos when she arrived.

"Hello, Moose!"

I looked down at his wagging tail and to the woman waving at us, wondering why it was that he always managed to get the first greeting in. He leapt out from under the table, knocking our drinks everywhere, and greeted the stranger with his usual warm demeanour, leaving Greg and me to mop up the mess. After tail-wagging and kisses subdued, she sat and chatted with us for ten minutes, mainly about our adventures so far and our time in Falmouth. Eager to be moving, we said our goodbyes and pressed on to the St Mawes ferry crossing where we'd been contacted in advance by the operators with the offer of free passage.

Facebook is a marvellous tool when it wants to be and, as much as I'd like to think it was down to my charm as an individual, I grudgingly conceded that it was probably Moose inadvertently pulling his weight with his internet appeal. As we mounted the slipway and got on to the boat, he was particularly interested in some of the more distinctive features on deck and began barking at them.

I abruptly cut him off. "Pack it in!" I grunted, casting awkward glances as I blushed at the other tourists.

I looked over to Greg for help but he just sat there sniggering away to himself; such would be the support I could expect from him for the next week!

I glared back at Moose.

"*But...*" he began.

"But nothing," I cut him off. "C'mere and sit down."

Moose, not knowing who to defer to, scowled at me and my sniggering companion, before settling down at my feet for the remainder of the crossing.

One thing that really struck me about this particular crossing was how the huge steel ships rose majestically out of the waters, dwarfing us throughout our passage. We crossed the bay and these towering monsters just sat there, bobbing gently in the water as we glided by, boggling the mind as to how something so impossibly huge and heavy could gently float beside their smaller wooden counterparts. I felt like one of those wary sailors in a classic epic movie, rowing tentatively between colossal stone Titans fearing that they might spring to life at any moment and strike us down.

Eventually, and after a quick ferry change, we reached the isolated port at the village of St Mawes. After disembarking and standing on the shoreline, we found ourselves looking at a myriad of different way-markers, contemplating our best way forwards. After several minutes, I inclined my head. "C'mon," I decided quickly, "it's this way."

I looked over to Greg, who was lost in his phone. "I'm not sure, bud," he started, pointing towards another path, "I think it might be down there."

My jaw dropped. "Are you looking at maps?" I asked, somewhat insulted.

"Well, yeah..." He feigned, somewhat innocently.

"Trust me, pal, I've made it this far without them," I said, grabbing him by the sleeve and shoving him roughly towards the most convenient way-marker. "It's definitely this way!"

Greg looked down pleadingly at Moose who shrugged. "*Don't look at me*," he said. "*He's a grumpy arse when it comes to directions.*"

Greg sighed and put away his phone, following along behind while I strode off, brimming with confidence. Five minutes later, the path abruptly ended at a locked gate with the word 'PRIVATE' written all over it. I could hear the sound of canine sniggering behind me as I turned.

"*This is usually the part where he throws a hissy fit,*" Moose said slyly to Greg, who was also busy trying to hide a grin.

"Where to now, mate?" Greg cheerily enquired.

I stood there flushing as Moose collapsed on the floor in a heap of laughter.

It was going to be a very, very long week!

With a nifty little detour in the bag, we eventually made it to the lighthouse at St Anthony's Head, where the path led outwards along the cliff lines until we found our little haven for the evening. As previously stated, Greg was not one for wild camping; he had dutifully booked us all a nice little spot at a place on the headland just outside of town. As luck would have it, it was fish 'n' chip night, so we quickly pitched up before marching off to grab our share of the sumptuous British feast. With the hot parcels of paper under our arms, we wandered to the foot of the hill to find ourselves a nice perch overlooking the sea to watch the sun set. As ever, Moose was less concerned with what was happening on the horizon and more transfixed by the steaming portions of food Greg and I held in our laps.

We stayed there for perhaps an hour, feasting away while the sun disappeared in a spectacular fiery red glow. Feeling the evening chill begin to bite, we wandered back to our tents and we were surprised to find the entire place bustling. I reminded myself that this was still summer break and that parents were probably eager to squeeze in one last weekend before the kids were back in school. As sites go, this one was quite well-established; all along the main walkways, the orange glow of bollard lighting lit the place up. Children ran around in the open spaces and played football in the twilight as we weaved our way between various camps, each still alive with the chatter of adults hunched over barbeques and fire pits.

We stopped off at the camp shop and decided to hire a brazier for the evening, along with purchasing a jumbo-size bag of marshmallows.

As I set about getting the thing going, I couldn't help but feel the change in pace from months of isolated hiking to what I could now only describe as glamping! As the kindling took light, another weary walker drifted in and was ushered to a spot a few metres away from where we were pitched up. I'll give the owners their due – they didn't half know how to milk the space for every inch it was worth!

It'd been dark for an hour or so and I could see the new camper eyeing up the warmth generated by our modest little fire. Moose pricked his ears and wandered across to say hello.

"Hi," I greeted the stranger, nodding my head at the approaching dog, "I promise he won't eat you."

She smiled, reached out and gave him a tentative scratch on his head. "He's lovely," she admired, gently massaging his ear.

"You're more than welcome to share the fire with us," Greg piped up, scooching around the fire pit to make space.

"If you both don't mind." She beamed. Before long, she was sitting with Mooch's head in her lap, their faces lit by the flickering fire.

"You'll have to forgive the dog," I began, "he's a glutton for attention."

She waved away the apology. "He's fine," she said, looking down at his sleeping face – from her angle, not quite able to see the line of dribble soaking into her boot. Moose picked his head up slightly, licked his chops and winked at me before dozing off.

We began swapping stories and it turned out that Anna had started walking two weeks earlier and was trying to make it to Plymouth before her holiday ended. My mind raced at the prospect; that was a mere five days away – the way our pack was moving, we'd be lucky if we got there before the end of September! As the fire burned down and the last of the wood was spent, we all yawned each other a goodnight and sauntered off to our respective tents.

*

When I woke up the following morning and got up to stretch my legs, I looked over to Anna's tent only to find a blank patch of flattened grass. "Early bird gets the worm," I muttered to myself, no longer in any doubt that she'd get to where she needed to by week's end. I limped over to Greg's tent and rustled the canvas. "Oi, lazy-arse, rise and shine!"

Nothing.

I tried again but this time unleashed my secret weapon. Much to his annoyance, I woke Moose up, ushered him out from under our sleeping bag and got him worked up nicely so that, when I opened the zip into Greg's tent, he burst in, tail a-wagging. A second later, his head reappeared wearing a blank expression. *He's not there.*

Well, *that* took the fun out of things! I looked back at Moose. "Where is he, then?"

He sneezed and stretched his way back out of the tent. *"How the hell would I know?"* he snapped. *"I was happily asleep until you woke me up."*

He gave himself a good long shake from head to tail and turned to yawn in my face. *"When's breakfast?"* he asked petulantly.

I heard a rustling from behind. "In about twenty minutes, Moosey-boy."

I turned to see Greg striding across the grass with armfuls of bread, eggs, tomatoes and sausages. I grinned. Moose nearly fainted with excitement.

"Cheers, bud," I said, grabbing some of the packets from him before gathering my things to get the stove going. As it all began sizzling away, Moo was torn between dozing beneath the gracious strokes and belly rubs of Greg's fingers and the urge to stick his nose against the edge of the pan where breakfast was cooking away. Torn between his two favourite things, he resisted the latter with admirable fierceness. I flashed him a knowing grin and stuck out my tongue. He threw me an evil look, rolled from his shoulder on to his back and settled for cuddles before breakfast.

247

*

Once we were fed and watered, packed and ready, we headed back to the edge of the Cornish coast, where the path lay glittering in the morning sunlight. For me, this was an exultant experience: here I was, not only carrying out my deepest desire to walk the nation's coastline with my dog, but with my best mate here with me – now *that* was real affirmation. After the first few miles, though, it became apparent that Greg didn't share my philosophy. He groaned under the weight of his pack and complained endlessly about his feet and the rolling terrain. I looked on in sympathy, keenly remembering my reflection in the mirror at the hotel in Weston-super-Mare and the lines of bruises that had crisscrossed my torso. It was only now, seeing Greg endure the trials of walking, that I realised how far I'd come and how resilient my body now was to the challenges of the path. Moose looked up at me with pleading eyes, glancing back periodically at the heaving mess that was my best friend huffing and grunting up the hills behind us.

I decided enough was enough. "Tea break!" I yelled back down the path from a sheltered lea I'd found in one of the shallower inclines. Greg lifted his head and nodded vaguely as he inched on behind. I reached into my pack and dug out my stove and got some water on the boil. By the time he'd reached our little rest spot, my little silver pan was bubbling away. I looked up and immediately felt a pang of pity – he was drenched in sweat and thoroughly exhausted from the climb. He smiled weakly before unceremoniously collapsing next to an outcropping of rock in an attempt to avoid the sun, which had begun to burn through the clouds.

"How the hell you do this every day is beyond me!" he said through gasps.

I handed him a cup of hot tea. "Drink up, bud," I said. "It'll make you feel better."

He took the cup and began sipping the comforting warm liquid. "I sincerely doubt that," he panted, struggling to separate himself from his pack. After a few minutes, the redness washed away from his face and his breathing steadied.

"Good?" I asked.

He threw me a look brimming with the joy of tea redemption and nodded beneath the rim of his half-empty cup. "It's amazing what a nice cuppa can do."

Later that afternoon, we decided to divert from the coast path and head inland to another site Greg had found online. As he lay in the sun to one side of our little pitch, I stretched out, grappled my boots off and massaged my feet. The pain that had followed me since Devon was slowly getting worse but, thankfully, the combined power of a weekend's rest with my brother and the slower walking pace of the last few days had eased things somewhat. I settled into my usual routine of rolling my feet barefoot on the grass until the ache in both heels gently subsided.

"You still having trouble?" Greg asked.

I shook myself out of a daze and looked down at my toes. "I'm fine, mate," I said, trying to sound bright and reassuring.

He didn't look convinced. "You need to get that sorted."

I privately agreed with this but outwardly shrugged it off. "I'm OK, bud, it's just the usual aches."

"You're still carrying too much weight." He snorted and, thinking better than to press the issue, got to his feet and sauntered off to the shop to get something sorted for that evening's dinner.

Over the next few days, we continued to inch our way along the southern coast of Cornwall, heading up towards the next major town: St Austell. The lag between Greg and I got more frequent; his patience also becoming as worn as the soles of his feet. By the time we reached the historic fishing port of Mevagissey, he decided he'd had enough and threw his pack down by the harbour wall to collapse in a heap on the cobblestones. "I'm broken, pal!" he breathed, looking thoroughly fed up.

I looked across at Moose, who was busy chewing grass along the corner of a green. "Oi, Mooch – fancy a break?" The chewing stopped instantly as he lifted his head to see what the fuss was about.

"*What was that?*" he asked, random strands of green still hanging from his jowls.

I couldn't help but smile. "I said: do you fancy stopping here for a few nights?"

His eyes melted.

I looked at Greg, red-faced and panting, and then back to Moose's stupid grin and realised, for what felt like the hundredth time, that I'd been pushing us all way too hard. "Well that decides it, bud," I said, turning back to face Greg. "Fancy calling it quits for a few days?"

I don't know how he managed to do it, but no sooner were those words out of my mouth than we were being ushered into our own room in a hotel in the centre of town. He stood there at reception making the booking as I edged in with my enormous pack, trying desperately not to knock half the wall art on to the floor on my way past.

"How the hell did you get prime rooms in the middle of peak season?" I asked, peering in awe at the family suite as I closed the door behind us.

Greg launched his pack on to the bed by the window. "Dibs," he called absently, before falling face-first on to the mattress.

I shrugged, dumped my pack by the side of the other double bed and looked down at Moose. "Sorry, lad," I said, shrugging. "Looks like you've copped for the single."

He snorted at me and, in a single bound, leapt over the foot of the bed and landed with a snore on the pillows. Greg rolled over and looked across at me. "What were you saying about rooms?" he muttered.

I shook my head almost indifferently. "Oh, nothing. I'm just surprised you got a suite in peak season, is all."

He looked at me through a furrowed brow. "Peak season's over, buddy," he replied through a stifled yawn.

I looked down at the date in the corner of my watch face and realised, with a certain amount of shock, that it was indeed now September.

Summer was practically over.

Mevagissey became our base for the next two days – and what sheer bliss it was, too!

No pack.

No walking.

No godawful foot-ache.

Warm showers, clean clothes, good food and even better company!

I'd actually forgotten what it was like to have another person around who I trusted enough to share Moose responsibilities. The first thing I did was to leave them both up in the room while I explored town on my own. At first, it was odd; I'd walk into stores and automatically begin the '*Are you dog-friendly...?*' circus only to realise that I could come and go as I pleased.

It was an incredibly liberating experience. As I walked from shop to shop, looking for nothing in particular (although a new pair of boots would've been nice), I began to realise how much a part of each other we'd become, Moose and me. It'd been less than an hour but I was already keenly missing his presence by my side. As I walked back onto the quay I looked up as a faint speckling of rain hit my face. I smiled to myself. "You've ruined me, you little sod," I muttered under my breath as I turned on my heels and headed back to the inn.

That evening, we all went out together and explored our way around the quay, taking our pick of the many restaurants that were now practically empty by comparison to the week before. Mevagissey's a great place for dogs and Mooch was welcomed in practically every establishment we tried. The meal that night was a far cry from our usual cardboard – and both Moose and I relished every bite.

As with most anticipated but unexpected things, our time in Mevagissey went by much too quickly. As much as I would've wanted to stay longer, we were aware that Greg's time with us was also finite; we wanted to get a lot more coast done before he headed back off home. Back on the road, we twisted our way along narrow pavements until they disappeared into a tall and rough verge on the edge of town. We clung to the sides of the road, single file, practically throwing ourselves into the bushes every time a car or a van went speeding past.

"Where's this bloody path?" Greg shouted as we nearly got sideswiped by a campervan.

"Dunno," I yelled over the din of the traffic. "Up ahead somewhere." Moose was tugging on the lead, eager to be back on a path away from traffic. "Oi! Slow down," I shouted as he strode down the line of the hedge.

"*You tell that to the traffic,*" he barked over his shoulder, barely even glancing back.

We followed the road around a sharp bend and there, not a dozen yards ahead, was a solitary way-marker with the familiar acorn symbol. Moose bolted for it, pulling the lead right out of my hand as he bounded clear off the road to sit waiting on the path beyond. Greg and I huffed and puffed our way after him. We careered through a kissing gate to an open stretch of grass, where we all plonked ourselves down to catch our breath. I looked up to find the pair of them glaring at me expectantly.

"What?" I asked, somewhat defensively.

Mooch piped up first. "*Where to now, cap'n?*" he asked, with a flippant flick of his tail.

I looked across at Greg, who was trying to hide a grin. "You see what I have to put up with?" I said, fishing around in my bag for my map.

No sooner had I unfolded the first half than the wind grabbed the rest and threatened to tear it from my hands.

"Where are we going, anyway?" Greg asked, mopping his brow.

"Some place called Pentewan," I muttered absently while trying to wrest some control back from the weather by sitting on the map. I smiled up at him as my grubby fingers traced their way over the lines. "We're virtually there!" I said, folding up the map.

Moo chipped in, "*That sounds familiar...*"

I ignored that and threw a thumb towards the bushes. "Don't you need to go pee or something?" I asked flippantly. He snorted, turned tail and wandered off to sniff at the nearby fence posts.

Things were easier now we weren't spending half our energy dodging traffic. The weather had been slowly threatening to turn and, while the rain hadn't quite kicked in, the sun no longer had the unbearable impact it had had over the last couple of months. We rounded the trail and descended the valley to Pentewan. The views were spectacular if slightly marred by the sprawling mass of caravan sites that swallowed up the beaches to our right. We bypassed these and ended up in a wooded area on the far side and followed a stream to the campsite, where we were booked for the remainder of Greg's stay: our final two-night stopover.

Moose took one look at the stream's water babbling by in the sun and bolted for it, nearly pulling me in along with him. I fell flat on my face, the weight of the pack crushing the air from my lungs with a great 'whooooosh' as I slid along behind Moose on my belly. Watching me get dragged halfway down the bank, Greg creased in laughter while Moose barked and leapt for the water.

I lay there on my front, trying to breathe under the weight of the pack still strapped to my back, as I fumbled desperately to unclip the hasps under my chest while letting go of Moose's lead. Once I'd grappled them open, I rolled everything to one side and lay flat on my back, fighting for air.

I turned my head towards Greg and narrowed my eyes. "What are you laughing at?"

He clamped his mouth shut under my glowering stare.

"*He's laughing at the idiot in the dirt,*" came the joyous reply from my stupid dog, who continued to prance around in the river.

I sat up slowly and began patting the dust off my face and clothes, reaching over to grab my pack – only to find a handful of air. I looked around in confusion and eventually laid eyes on it merrily bouncing down the grass verge to join Moose in the river with a resounding *splosh*.

"Noo!" I yelled, forgetting about my recent 'trip' and wading hip-deep into the river to retrieve my pack before it, and everything in it, got soaked through. Moose bore down on me with a smirk, splashing water all over me.

"*Game time!*" he sniggered, resuming his tirade of water-splashing.

I swore and waded back towards the shore, pack over my head, and heaved it across to Greg who was waiting on the bank. Tromping through the weeds and reeds, I pulled myself back up through the mud until I was once again on my back and panting for breath beneath the open sky. To my left, I saw Greg come running over. "You OK, buddy?"

I gasped and turned to my right to find Moose's soggy head not two inches from my face. "*We have got to do that again.*" He grinned gleefully.

He turned in a giddy circle and shook what remained of the river in his fur all over my face.

Like Mevagissey, we found the campsite we'd booked sparsely populated. While this was bad for the site owners, it turned out to be great for us. We had the lion's share of prime camping spots that, not a week before, would've been taken up by holiday-makers and families aplenty. We made our way over to the VIP spots, where I left Greg and Mooch to set up camp as I trudged off to find the shower block.

Once I got back, I began stripping out my pack – which, fortunately, had managed to escape its little swim in the river largely unscathed. By now, Greg had pitched up and was settled in a large seating area under a spacious pagoda. He shouted over, holding aloft a can of cider and shaking it gently in a knowing fashion. I shrugged and got up to join him for a bevvy. It was nice spending so much time with him again, although I was becoming conscious of how little time we had left. He'd be gone the day after tomorrow and it would be just me and Moose back on the road again.

That evening, we talked long into the night planning our final day together with all the optimism the occasion called for.

The next morning, Greg ran up to me like a giddy schoolgirl. "Aw, mate, guess what's nearby?" He beamed, practically hopping in his excitement.

I dreaded to think. "Breakfast…?" I asked, hopefully.

He brushed off the suggestion with a flicker of annoyance. "No, you pillock…for today?"

I shook my head trying to shift the fog, negligently wondering what Moose was up to. "Dunno," I floundered, "but I'm guessing it's not breakfast, then."

He shook his head.

"What, then?" I asked, getting slightly irritated by his early-morning exuberance.

I swear he did a giddy little jig. "The Lost Gard—" he started.

"Hang on," I interrupted, "where's Moose?"

"Well, he's…" Greg's sentence trailed off as I began fumbling for a pan to boil some water. "Are you listening to me?" he asked.

I glanced up. "Sure," I said, throwing a tea bag into my cup. "You were saying."

He furrowed his brow. "Well, it's The Lost Gardens of—"

"Hang on," I said, trying to shake away the cobwebs. "Where *is* Mooch?" I asked again, looking around.

Greg threw a thumb over his shoulder. "He's over there."

I looked beyond and spotted a group of shaking bushes near the hedge line, a sure indication that Moose was busy with his morning ablutions.

Greg was getting impatient.

"Err, gardens sound nice," I said enthusiastically, throwing him a crooked smile while I searched for the milk.

"We talked about them last night," he huffed.

I could barely remember. "Did we?"

"Yes," he snapped. "The Lost Gardens of Heligan!"

I decided not to argue and resigned to uphold the commitments made by my former, drunken self. "Sounds great." I yawned. "When are we off?"

"Well, you said last night we'd head off early and get breakfast at one of the cafés there."

"Did I?!" I must have been really drunk to agree to an early departure. "And how far away are these gardens?" I asked.

He shrugged. "A couple of miles."

Damn, I thought, scuppered by my sloshed self.

I finished making tea, gathered the dog and succumbed to my best friend's enthusiasm. Half an hour later, we left the campsite and took a country path that led us inland. As we headed away from the river, a magnificent woodland opened up before us. Mooch was in fine form, racing out across the flat, wide loam and off into the distance.

"Will he be alright?" Greg asked.

I shrugged my shoulders. "He'll be fine," I said.

We carried on talking as we passed through the wide woodland boulevards, Moose darting in and out between the trees. Along the line of the woods, we eventually came to a clearance that gave views to a magnificent wide valley. I stared out over the glorious green, the Heligan gardens shining out in the centre of it all.

This place was seriously impressive.

The gardens sat on the edge of the once-grander Tremayne estate, which had been sold off piece by piece through the twentieth century. The manor house had since been divided up and converted into a series of flats and maisonettes while the remaining land had largely been forgotten. Time had worked its magic to slowly reclaim the formerly meticulously manicured estate back into Cornish wilderness, and the beautiful gardens became lost from living memory. At some time in the late 1980s, some local investment and media attention began unravelling the story of Heligan and, since then, the gardens, outbuildings and woodland walkways have been painstakingly recovered in a project that still works tirelessly to this day. The treasures hidden beneath the brush have kept spurring on the restoration team to aspire to even greater discoveries.

Today, the site sits like a jewel among the many treasures Cornwall has to offer and stands testament to the diligence and commitment of the teams of people who tend this wonderful place. Vast organic sculptures litter the grounds amid myriad period buildings, greenhouses, botanic scenescapes and Victorian-style cafés.

Even Moose seemed moderately impressed.

It was a rare thing for us to have the luxury of being able to stop off somewhere like this and look around – and it would have been impossible if it were just me, Moose and the rucksack. We took our time and followed the various trails to explore the tropical garden that sat at the centre of the grounds. As the afternoon progressed and the weather began to turn, we realised that we still had half an hour's walk back to the campsite. We took stock and said farewell to this incredible place as we headed off back through the woods, vowing to return again one day.

*

We spent the remainder of the evening huddled beneath the huge pagoda, drinking wine and talking about the events of the week and the spectacle of Heligan. The rain gently pattered overhead. It began to dawn on me that my time with my best mate was coming to a close; I felt that odd butterfly sensation in the pit of my stomach at the thought of continuing our journey without him.

That night, I lay there wrapped up in sleeping bag-and-dog and thought back on the week that had been. This resurgence of ordinary life touched a part of me that forced me to recognise how far apart from civilisation we'd been over the summer. Like during those early days of the walk, an uncertainty gnawed at me: what would the coming weeks bring as we walked the final miles of our exit of Cornwall and return to Devon? It was only now that I once again took stock of the vast distances we'd travelled, and that Cornwall would stand as our first county completed on Waggy Walk. I couldn't help but smile at that thought as I drifted off to sleep amid a tangle of feet, punctuated every now and then with a wheeze, snore or sneeze from His Majesty.

The rain had petered out overnight, giving way to a bright Sunday morning. Greg was already up, and almost as though sensing his imminent departure, Moose bolted out of the tent and careered into him while he was busy folding up a jumper.

Greg landed on his back with the slobbering dog on top. "Mornin', ya daft bugger." He laughed.

Moose blessed him with an early-morning face-clean. I could hear Greg's spluttering as I stood up and stretched, wondering about breakfast.

"Do you want me to cook?" I asked, turning to the pair playing in the grass. "Or shall we get something in Pentewan?"

"Let's buy something," Greg replied, pushing Moose to one side. "I can't be arsed with cooking."

I shrugged. "No argument from me," I said, throwing down some scraps and a healthy portion of Butcher's tinned dog food. Mooch untangled himself from Greg and began wolfing down the lot.

"What time's your train?" I asked.

"Not till one but I have to get a taxi up to St Austell."

I looked at my watch. "We'd better get moving, then."

"Suppose so, pal." He sighed.

Moose looked up from his bowl, dogfood smeared over half his snout. "*Wot?*" he asked, paying attention to the conversation for the first time.

We both turned and answered in unison, "Never mind!"

He sneezed and went back to lapping up the last morsels stuck to the bowl and his nose while we dropped the tents and finished packing up.

"Are we ready?" I asked, preparing to swing my rucksack over my shoulders.

"That depends," replied Greg, nodding slightly to the massive pack in my hands. "Do you need me to take anything back with me?"

The question caught me off guard and, as I dropped the pack down to the ground, I did a quick recce and decided on impulse to offload the guitar. "Would you mind?" I asked, handing him the strap.

He smiled and reached out. "Bloody hell," he said as its weight dropped his arm. "And you've been carrying this since you started?!"

I laughed and nodded as I turned to Moose, who gave a reassuring tail-wag.

We walked back along the path next to the stream until we reached the Ship Inn at Pentewan beach. After we'd ordered a light meal it wasn't long before Greg's taxi was waiting and, not wanting to cause a fuss or confuse Moose, we agreed a swift departure. I stood by the pub entrance as he simply winked at me and threw himself, the guitar and his pack in the back before closing the door and speeding off down towards the main road.

Moose looked up, somewhat confused by the sudden departure. His brows furrowed in concern. *"He's coming back, right?"*

He could see in my eyes that he wasn't.

I reached down, scratched his ears and turned in the other direction. Moose looked over his shoulder one last time at the trail of dust left by the car speeding off into the distance, and lowered his tail, knowing as well as I did that we were now firmly back on our own.

Chapter 20

The Ache Sets in

Pentewan to Looe

September still held on to the warmth of summer and, as we left Pentewan, the coastal path once more opened up to reveal stunning views. The morning welcomed us with bright skies and very little wind – but, despite carrying a considerably lighter load, I couldn't help but feel a heaviness as we walked. The warmth of a week filled with friends had begun to melt away like the countless miles of coastline that had faded into the distance behind us.

I'd already decided against wild camping that night, confident that when we reached Charlestown there'd be accommodation up for grabs. I wasn't disappointed.

By mid-afternoon, we were both sat outside a café and I was enjoying a nice cuppa while Moose snoozed under the bench by my feet.

PING

Just got back into Aldershot.

I smiled and texted back.

> We're chilling in Charlestown 😎

PING

> Wow – so soon?

...

> Yeh – I'm not dragging a pensioner around today.

You can probably guess the reply I got to that.

We settled into our room early that evening. Unlike the more relaxed stops we'd had with Greg and the others, this one comprised our usual routine of washing clothes and planning ahead. As I strung out a line of hand-washed socks and underwear I wilted at the thought of the poor cleaner who'd have to come in after and the air quality we'd leave in our wake. My pack was still damp from its soaking in the river a few days before and, while I'd done my best to scrub ten-day-old socks in hot water and shower gel, I wasn't convinced of the quality of the overall result – especially after perching them on a radiator in a stuffy room for twelve hours. I shrugged off the thought and settled on to the bed beside Moose for the night, still feeling the absence of human company. Keeping busy, I took out my map and began to plot out the coming week.

"We're not far off Plymouth, pal," I started.

Snoring.

"...which means the end of Cornwall," I continued, with feigned interest.

More snoring.

I lifted my head and looked down at the heaving lump curled up at the foot of the bed.

"Are you listening to me?"

His eyebrow fluttered slightly so he could peel an eyelid back just enough to show the white of an eyeball. "Obviously not!" I shrugged, shaking my head slightly before going back to reading the map.

In the morning, I gathered my laundry from the various radiators, chucked a few coins into a bowl on the bedside cabinet for the cleaner, and shuffled out of the room before we could be accosted for the dim stench we'd left behind. Charlestown is a grand place with handsome old buildings, collections of quaint shops and one of those rare harbours that still has tall ships anchored along the bay. It's a Cornish village that cherishes these iconic images of the past; with a slight squint of the eye, you can almost see the wooden waggons rattling past and hear the cry of daytime traders calling out from behind their stalls. 'Picturesque' doesn't even begin to touch on it. If you've never been, I suggest you go there and see for yourselves – you won't be disappointed!

I was still getting used to the idea that summer holidays were now over and most of the tourists had gone home, and I was struck by how empty the place seemed. It had the air of some forgotten ghost town as Moose and I wandered through its near-abandoned streets. We were soon back on the clifftops, where the coastal path was almost absorbed by the fine terraces of golf course leading into Par. Dotted across the grounds here and there was the odd late-season golfer – no doubt taking full advantage of the empty fairways. In the distance, I could hear the sea and the far-off distant cry of seagulls, punctuated with the whine of golf carts racing past with their finely adorned occupants.

Then, abruptly, the path and beach ended. We were suddenly barred from continuing by an immense steel fence, adorned with my favourite phrase:

```
┌─────────────────────────────────────┐
│              KEEP OUT!               │
│                                      │
│     Trespassers will be prosecuted   │
└─────────────────────────────────────┘
```

Ah. It was going to be one of *those* kinds of days.

Retracing our steps, we found the way-marker hidden behind some overgrown bushes and duly followed the faded arrow's directions to eventually find ourselves stood on a roadside somewhere in Cornish suburbia. I looked at the map and understood the reason for the diversion – a ruddy great industrial estate! I decided against following any further signage, keeping instead to the roadside until we got around the estate and back on to the beach at the eastern end of Par Sands. The hours of pavement-pounding had taken their toll on my feet; I sat on the edge of the beach, took off my socks and boots, and began rummaging my toes around in the warm sand.

"Come far?" I heard a voice say from behind.

Spinning around, I saw a couple of fellow backpackers settling down on the bench next to me. "Bristol," I offered, not having the heart to go through the rigmarole of describing to them where Portishead was.

The chap threw his bag in the sand. "Bloody hell," he said, taken aback. "Not in one go, I hope?"

"Yup." I nodded, starting to massage my left heel with one hand. "Seemed like a good idea at the time."

Moose looked up. "*You're telling me.*"

I ignored *that* and turned back to face the couple. "Where are you headed?" I asked.

"End destination's Plymouth but probably as far as Looe today."

I grimaced at the thought – that was miles away. The woman sat on a nearby rock and began pouring tea out of a flask. "And you?" she asked.

I shrugged, switching my feet over. "Maybe Fowey if we're lucky."

Her forehead creased. "Where?"

"Fowey?" I said again, somewhat less certain…

"Oh." She smiled. "You mean 'Foy'."

I pulled out my map and pointed at it with a grubby finger.

The chap nodded. "It's pronounced 'Foy' not 'Fa-wee'."

"It's a good job you told me." I laughed. "I keep getting told off by locals for mispronouncing things."

"It's easily done 'round here." The woman laughed, sitting back and taking a sip of tea.

We spent the next few minutes trading stories about life on the coastal path. Unlike my ridiculous quest, they were on holiday for a week exploring the local haunts. They offered me some tea and even had digestive biscuits, which Moose eagerly took. I decided to re-don footwear and carry on, leaving the pair to tuck into their sandwiches.

Soon after, we were both pacing along the beach at Par, wondering where the bloody hell the coastal path had hidden itself this time. I hated getting lost, especially with the pack bearing down on my shoulders and my feet on fire, so it wasn't long before I began pacing and cursing.

Moose looked on in amusement. *"Do you know where we're going?"*

I ignored His-flippant-Majesty and carried on trudging through the sand.

"… Because I can lead, if you want," he carried on calmly before gnawing at an itch on his right wrist.

"You're not helping!" I moaned.

He laughed back at me. *"I'm doing better than you are."*

I sniffed at the comment and stormed off towards the base of the cliffs.

"Aw, is poor baba in a huff?" he called after me.

"Keep this up and you're on straw for dinner!"

Silence.

As we crested a series of sand dunes, I held my hand up to shield my eyes from the sun. There in the distance was the tell-tale silhouette of a way-marker. I smiled back down at Moose, who'd been sulking at me. "See?" I said smugly. "Told you I wasn't lost."

He just rolled his eyes at me, cocked his leg against the first convenient post and claimed it for his own.

Stating to the tea-drinking couple on the beach that we'd get to Fowey that day had been optimistic, but we did end up getting as far as Polkerris, which falls only a few miles short. We'd spent most of the afternoon back in mountaineering territory and, by the time we got there, despite periodic breaks to take my boots off and give my feet a bit of a massage, my feet were absolutely shot.

By early evening, I sorely missed human company (almost as much as I missed the prospect of a comfy bed). The ache of the road had settled back in and my ten days of luxurious living were now beginning to bite back. I began cursing Greg and our week living the high-life, making a mental note that once we'd camped and settled in, I'd send him a snotty text at my earliest convenience. Once we were pitched up, I grabbed my phone as if to mentally emphasise the point – only to find a message sitting there waiting on the screen.

Hi – Dunno if you remember us but it's Phil and Kinnon.

I blinked and grinned.

Of course I remember you – How are you both?

...

We're on holiday later this week – Where are you?

266

I looked at the map.

Fowey – although I've been told it's pronounced 'Foy'.

...

We know that, you silly arse! – We live here 😒

My fingers began tapping away at the screen...

Sorry...must be the sunstroke!

...

WTF – You have sunstroke?!

I chuckled.

Kidding!

...

Well, it sounds like you need company! Fancy a meet-up?

...

Sure – where?

...

Looe?

...

Is that Looe...or Lo-wey?

...

You cheeky bugger... ☺
    ...Phil says he's gonna crack you around the ear for that
one... Dinner's on us.

I settled back into my pillow with a smile and gave Moose a scratch behind the ears before dozing off for the night.

We woke in the early hours to a torrent of rain and wind tearing at the tent. I'd been drifting in and out of sleep for a few hours and the sudden opening up of the heavens brought me round with a start. It took me back to my early years, doing my Duke of Edinburgh Award. I'd made it to silver, which wasn't a bad effort for a 'can't-be-arsed' fourteen-year-old. I remember, during one camp on a rainy night just like this, being snug in my sleeping bag just listening to the pelting rain tearing away at the fabric of the tent while I was all snug and warm. I fell in love with the experience then and it's something that's been with me ever since. I can assure you, there's no better feeling in the world! Eventually, Moose's snoring enticed me to follow suit and the next time I opened my eyes, the dim glare of morning was shining through the flysheet. The rain had stopped sometime during the night.

As much as I wanted to explore Fowey, I now felt I was on a schedule, so we ended up just marching through. The constant pain in my feet was a huge drain on my enthusiasm; I found myself pacing through the major towns, just to get to a secure resting spot beyond so I could ease my feet.

You'd be surprised at the looks you get when you hunker down in the middle of the high street, take off your shoes and socks and start giving your toes a good ol' rub while Mrs Miggins is on her way out of Tesco.

One thing that *did* catch my eye as we were walking through was an immense cruise ship hulking in the harbour. I'd hardly have thought it possible because Fowey really isn't that big a town, but this huge white monstrosity just sat there in the water blotting out half the landscape. I wish we'd stayed longer to take in the spectacle but the ever-present throb in the heels of my feet kept me marching out of town and up to the headland to find a place to rest. I'd already decided that, once we met up with Kinnon and Phil in Looe, I'd take the opportunity to re-evaluate my footwear and try to nip into a shoe shop to buy some gel soles – and maybe even try yet another pair of boots.

Thankfully, the headlands above Fowey didn't disappoint and we found a flat pitch in the grass along the cliff tops fairly quickly. I pitched the tent somewhere with a great vantage point of the harbour mouth and let Moose run off for a while. As the sun was setting, I perched myself on a comfortable rock and, bare feet swinging in the wind, watched the ships as, one by one, they sailed out of the harbour.

And then something incredible happened.

A ship – *the* ship from earlier – peeked its prow out from behind the inlet and proudly sailed out of Fowey, just as the sun tipped the horizon and turned the sky a vivid red. I sat there in awe watching as this magnificent liner inched its way across the water to eventually disappear beyond the horizon, just as the sun did. It was a sublime view – and, tucked away up here, we'd had a completely unique vantage point. Once more, I was humbled by my sudden change in fortune; it was these unexpected moments on this trip that gave it life and made little things like the constant throb of my feet pale into insignificance.

While we were sitting there by the edge of our camp, an old boy with walking poles came traipsing up the hill from town just as I decided to get supper on the go. Noticing our camp, he took the opportunity to catch his breath and stop for a chat. He had a calm and steady demeanour which gave me pause to stop and listen as I stirred the boiling water in the pan.

He turned out to be one of the most genuine, lonely souls I've ever met on my travels. I never use the word 'old' lightly but this chap was definitely getting on, and as he leant his gaunt frame heavily against his two rotting walking poles, he told me about how he still regularly walked these trails, a feat he gleefully attributed to his sprightly physique. I thought back to my experience getting up here from Fowey – a climb not to be taken lightly! I took out dried noodle packs and fish and chucked them in the pan, while this endearing chap regaled me with tales of the times and tides of the village he'd lived in since childhood. At one point, he lifted a walking pole in the direction of a farmstead, silhouetted against the fading sky.

"That there's my house," he blurted, waving a pole wildly over his shoulder. "Been in the family for generations."

I started to interject with a question but his eyes became lost as he leant on both poles, settling in for a good chat.

"Well, me father was wounded in the war," he continued, "an' me gran'pa was lost in the great one."

I listened as he went on to tell me stories about his family and life out here on the Cornish coast.

At one point, I shook my tin cup at him. "Fancy a cuppa?"

He shook his head slightly. "No, lad." He shrugged. "Must be off, and it'll take me a good while to get back home." He leant in and gave me a sly wink. "Pins not too good these days and it's getting dark."

I couldn't help but agree; I wouldn't want to be wandering around these paths at night. He reached out, shook my hand and began his slow shuffle down the coastal path. As I watched his silhouette dwindle into the distance, I wondered about life here on the edge of the world and whether I'd find myself living out my days meandering up and down coastal trails.

I have to admit, the thought had a certain kind of appeal.

The next day we followed suit.

The ups and downs of the trail made the going quite tricky and just how the old fella had found his way home the night before was beyond me. As we meandered around twists and turns, I half expected to see him sat there catching his breath on a rock.

That day, we set and stuck to a steady pace. Due to the time of year, we were out here in the wilderness all on our own. Thinking back, it would be one of the last, spectacular walks we'd have in Cornwall and, boy, it did not disappoint! Wide valleys, steep inclines and a beautiful secluded cove hidden from the world. It was the sort of place that fed the imagination with thoughts of pirate ships and lost treasure and, as Moose ran freely, diving headlong in and out of the ferns, I plodded along behind and let my mind wander. It was nice to finally find our stride again, although I vowed to carry out yet another kit-cull and address the footwear issue when we met up with Phil and Kinnon at Looe.

The weather was on the turn now; autumn was setting in. The next day was a long slog through fine drizzle. I'd stopped off at a shop the night before and managed to cobble together a bit of a fry-up, beans included. I thought back to that awful night in Bossington and shrugged; there'd be plenty of time for Moose to clear his system before it was time for bed. I shook out the ash from my stove and bounced it lightly in one hand, truly beginning to appreciate the unnecessary weight it represented. "Time to change tack and move to gas," I muttered to myself.

Moose didn't complain about our breakfast and, as usual, was sitting inches from my plate, bean-juice still glistening on the end of his nose, for all the world looking at me like an animal starved. I inched around slightly, shielding my plate while I selfishly polished off the rest of my own portion before he could get his snout in. No sooner had I swallowed the last mouthful than he barged past me to go find some poor tree on which to take out his disappointment.

Walking into Looe was a long trek back into civilisation. We left the path's rough trail as it transitioned from woodland to eventually spit us out on the main thoroughfare into town. To the right of the pavement were lawn terraces interspersed with benches facing out to sea. This beautiful town was furnished with the wrought-iron style of Victorian England, and as we walked on by, huge townhouses began to spring up along high verandas all across the left-hand side of the road. The pavement-pounding had done my feet in, so I limped to the closest bench, unsaddled the pack and sat down.

I looked over at Moose, who was beginning to lag behind. "Fancy a rest, bud?"

Giving a silent tail-wag of approval, he shook himself off lightly before plonking himself beside me with a grunt. We sat there looking out at a breathtaking view of the bay, watching the bustle of ships come and go.

"Pretty part of the world, eh?" I said, giving him a light nudge with my elbow.

He didn't seem to be too taken with it. "*When are we meeting Phil?*" he grumbled from between his jowls.

I took out my phone hoping for a message. Nothing yet.

"Dunno, pal."

He sighed and settled his head on to the grass for a snooze.

Once sensation had returned to my toes, I nudged the snoring mass at my feet and we carried on back down the road into town. At the far end of the inlet, I could see a bridge about half a mile from where we were. I shuddered at the thought of having to trek all that way but eventually shrugged off the concern. "No point complaining about it."

"*There's every point in complaining about it,*" Moose muttered under his breath.

"What was that?" I asked.

He snorted and barged past me to take the lead.

As we got to the harbour wall, it seemed as though people were appearing out of thin air. We drew closer to the bridge and a chap in a beanie hat started making a beeline for us. He stopped a few yards in front of us and furrowed his brow menacingly. I drew Moose in close, expecting trouble.

"Can I help you?"

"You silly sod!" the man replied, reaching up and tearing the beanie off his head – it was Phil. "Didn't recognise me there, did ya?" He smiled.

I blinked. Moose had already sprinted the gap between us, at the first sound of Phil's voice.

I shook my head slightly. "Sorry! Long day."

He reached down and began fussing with the dog.

"Where's Kinnon?" I asked, looking around.

He looked up. "Back at the campsite."

"Campsite?"

"Yup. Just up on the hill." He stood and balanced the hat back on to his head. "We've booked two nights for us all."

I looked up towards the opposite end of the harbour and the incline up towards the ridgeline beyond. He noticed the look of dread that crossed my face. "You OK?"

"Fine," I said dismissing the thought. "I'm having some feet problems, is all."

He laughed. "I'll take it easy on you, then."

I followed Phil through the bustling streets of Looe, where we meandered through the busy high street and past several rather appealing shoe shops and even a camping shop. My heart did a little skip; I experienced a spark of hope regarding not just footwear but the hope of finding a lighter stove as well. On the edge of town, we wandered through a converted holiday village, which, to me, looked more like a converted internment camp. A series of squat, grey billeted blocks sat in a circle, looking more 'Village of the Damned' than 'Holiday Village'. I shuddered and quickly caught up to Phil, who'd begun to ascend the stairwell leading up to the cliff tops above town.

"When did you arrive?" I asked, panting behind.

"Last night," he said, without breaking his stride.

"Nice site, then?"

"Smashing," he said, turning through a gate and out on to a wide grass pitch. "We've got a great view out to sea from up here."

We crossed over to a country lane that took us on to a slim dirt track winding its way into a huge and extremely well-established campsite. As was now the case everywhere in this post-high-season Cornwall, we had our pick of plots – although Phil did gently remind me that it would get busier tomorrow, when the weekend ushered its way in. We made our way across the grass pitches and, as I weaved between glossy white motorhomes, I could see the familiar outline of their VW campervan. Kinnon was sitting on a chair just outside. As we approached, I let Moose off the lead and he bolted straight into her arms.

"Moosey-boy!"

He practically knocked her out of the chair before she had the chance to get to her feet.

"You've not changed, then!" She laughed as he assaulted her with a barrage of slobbery kisses, tail-wags and squeaking. Phil sidled past, hopped into the van and returned a few seconds later with a couple of cold beers. I threw the pack off, reached down to untie laces and loosen my boots, and graciously accepted the offering.

"It's bloody lovely to see you both again!" I said, holding Kinnon in a warm hug.

"Same," she said with a smile. "You're both looking well."

I laughed, reached up and absently scratched at the beard on my cheek. "Nice of you to say," I said, barely able to remember the last time I'd even had a shower, "but I'll sit downwind for the time being."

As stories of our summer escapades filled the air, Phil cooked a healthy dinner in the camper. Before the alcohol had had too much of an effect, I grabbed the tent and quickly pitched up on the soft, springy grass. Moose, who was expecting some sort of banquet, snorted when tins of dogfood appeared from the pack.

"*Oi!*" he snorted angrily. "*Where's my treat?*"

I couldn't argue; it was hardly fair that I sat there with a full meal while the only thing for him was Pedigree Chum. "Sausages for breakfast, bud," I said, reaching down to scratch his ear. "Promise!"

He grunted before devouring the contents of his bowl.

I looked back up to our hosts. "See what I have to put up with..."

Kinnon smiled, rose from her chair and returned minutes later with a plate full of cooked ham.

Moose grinned. "*I'm staying with these two,*" he said, sauntering off to sit by Kinnon for the rest of the night.

Chapter 21

Where the Heart Is

Looe to Plymouth

I woke suddenly to a flurry of activity from outside the tent – including the faint smell of bacon wafting in. A frantic Moose torpedoed around above me, trying his best to tear his way through the tent to reach the source. I grabbed hold of his backside and planted him firmly on the sleeping bag, bum-first.

"Pack it in!"

A stray tail caught me square in the face as he writhed under my hold, worming his way free again. *"But, but, but... FOOOOD!!"* he cried. I dived for the zipper and he nosed his way under and shot to freedom.

"Sorry!" I shouted to the chef outside.

I could hear sounds from beyond the canvas indicating that Moose had begun to make a nuisance of himself. Struggling to pull on my trousers and a top, I eventually managed to poke my head out of the tent flap. "Is he being a pest?" I asked Kinnon, who was busy at the sizzling grill.

She took a sideways glance at Moose, sitting not two feet away, obediently waiting with tail swishing furiously in the grass. "Not at all," she said, sneaking a cooled-off sliver of bacon into his waiting maw.

Phil appeared from the back of the van with coffee. "Morning," he said, offering the cup down to me.

I took hold of the steaming mug and took a sip before clumsily clambering out of the tent. I stood and stretched. "Sleep well?" I yawned.

Kinnon smiled. "We did – but then, we have heating."

I glanced back at our squat little tent glistening with dew. "I suppose that does help..."

I was handed a bacon sandwich.

"More to the point, how did you sleep?"

I rolled my shoulders, cup in one hand, sarnie in the other and tried to shake the sleepy fog from my head. "Fine, thanks."

Kinnon didn't look convinced.

Moose glided by, licking his chops. "*Snausages!*" he smarmed.

"I'd have never guessed!" I replied as I glanced at Phil, who was guiltily trying to hide a treasure trove of pre-cooked snacks and treats. Donning my trainers, I decided to leave my boots rotting away in the corner of the tent.

I raised an eyebrow. "A-hem...shall we make tracks?"

He stuffed the neat package of food into the top of his day-sack and slung it over his shoulder. "What do you have in mind?"

"We've got coast to walk!" I said, clipping Moose's lead on. "Do you fancy joining us?"

Phil nodded gleefully and I couldn't argue with the smile or the enthusiasm. I turned and began pulling on my rucksack.

"Oh, you can leave that here."

I looked at Kinnon, somewhat confused.

"Well I'm not walking all that bloody way." She shuddered. "Leave your stuff here and I'll pick you three up when you're done."

"Are you sure?"

She nodded and smiled. "I'm going to explore the town and have a relaxing afternoon."

I shrugged my shoulders, dropped the pack and nodded to Phil to get going.

The thought of walking a day without the pack was incredibly appealing – I'd never done that before. Phil smiled as he kissed his wife goodbye before leading Moose and me out of the campsite and back towards the coastal path.

I could not get used to this lighter-than-air feeling at all! For starters, my feet didn't hurt. Secondly, as I followed Phil down the country lane, I began to get that nagging feeling that I'd forgotten something.

I looked down at Moose, who shot me a sidelong glance. *"Hey, don't complain about it, bud!"*

I wasn't going to. I picked up my stride and edged alongside Phil to let him know how freeing an experience this was.

We followed the country road to the top of a hill…and past a monkey sanctuary, of all things.

Pretty soon we were striding across fields lined with huge, round hay bales and, as we made our way past the tell-tale signs of an impending cliff edge, the coastal path presented itself, cutting its way along the perimeter. The day was still slightly overcast but hints of a warmer afternoon were beginning to show themselves. As we followed the trail under a canopy of overhanging wiry branches, we stuck to the contours of the path, which wound its way up and down a series of cliff edges.

Phil's pace was somewhat more exuberant than mine. Moose and I fell back frequently as he marched on ahead, leading the pack.

"Oi – wait up!" I called out at one point, his marching pace speeding him off over the horizon.

Phil stopped and glanced back at the flagging duo in the distance; I was determined not to hurry.

"What are you rushing for?" I asked as he stood there waiting for us to catch up, impatiently flexing his legs.

"We've got a long way to go!" he chirped.

I, for one, did not care. The joy of walking without the burden of a pack on my back was something I was going to relish every moment of that blissful day; who cared about the destination? I began relaxing into this walk, stopping frequently to take out my phone and take pictures – something I usually only managed as an afterthought. Eventually, we hit a sharp decline that led us down to a beach. We sat for a while and sipped water while munching down the sandwiches Kinnon had lovingly prepared earlier that day.

Moose slumped down by Phil's feet and blurted out something that'd been on my mind since we'd started walking that morning. *"You're a bit keen, aren't you?"*

Phil looked up somewhat fazed and turned to me. "Did you say something?"

I coughed slightly and wiped some sandwich from my lips. "Oh, nothing, just enjoying my lunch, is all." I threw Moose a look of caution.

Phil's eyebrows furrowed slightly as he let the comment drop, although I could tell he wasn't convinced.

"So, where do you fancy getting to today?" he asked, taking off the beanie and wiping his brow with a hanky.

I shrugged my shoulders. "It doesn't matter; we'll end up wherever."

Moose's ears pricked up and he nudged my leg. *"But we're going back to the campsite, right?"*

Phil turned as if answering me. "Yeah, we've got something nice planned for dinner."

I chuckled.

His forehead creased. "What are you laughing at?"

I put my hand on his shoulder and shook my head. "Nothing. Sounds good to me, mate."

He smiled before grabbing his pack and steeling himself for the off. "C'mon, dawg," he ushered to Moose. I felt pooch's nose by my hand as he rose and set off down the beach after our enthusiastic new walking buddy.

Before long, we were walking in the shadow of towering cliffs. Mooch ran ahead with Phil as they both paced the sand into the distance. I couldn't help but relax, taking in all the sights and surroundings that lay before me. This new-found unburdened walking gave me a deep sense of freedom; I had a whole different perspective on the walk. I felt the sand beneath my feet, I enjoyed the sight of Moose exploring the shoreline, and I once again had another person to share the whole experience with.

It was low tide, which, on this beach, meant miles and miles of sand. The water had brushed away all the turmoil from the day before and so the only footsteps that were trodden into this vast plain of virgin sands were ours alone. I looked ahead at the line of prints, one of worn boots and one of doggy paws, trailing forwards to the distant figures larking in our peacefully empty surroundings.

What a difference a few weeks made! I thought back to not a fortnight ago when this place would've been bursting with tourists. To experience this now, in isolation, was something that struck me instantly as being a privileged occurrence. I smiled to myself and picked up my pace so I could join them and partake in the fun they were having.

"Where've you been?" Phil asked as he leant back and launched the ball towards the rocks.

Moose vaulted after the spinning projectile, snatched it up with a deft grab of his jaws and bounded over towards me, spitting out the slobbery blue globe at my feet.

I looked down at the glistening mess as he waved his tail at me expectantly. "What do I want that for?" I said coolly.

His expression fell as he scowled, plonking his bottom in the sand. "*You're no fun.*"

I playfully stuck my tongue out at him and turned to Phil, who was walking towards us both. He caught Moose's expression and looked back at me. "You guys OK?"

I looked at Moose, who got up and wandered off, busying himself with one of the rock pools. "We're fine," I said, smiling in spite of myself. "How about you?"

He reached down and ran his hand across his thigh. "My leg's hurting a bit."

I held out my silver walking pole – the one I'd had with me since the beginning of the trip. "Here," I offered, "take this; it'll help."

He took hold of the grip and tested the weight. "You sure?"

I'd taken both with me and needed neither without the pack. The land had been pretty flat so far, anyway. I nodded. "Yup."

About an hour later, we stopped for water and a breather beside a low drystone wall and debated where we thought we'd end up for the day. The steady pace we'd taken all morning suited me fine; I wasn't eager to push too far. I checked the Ordnance Survey maps on my phone – a luxury I allowed myself on the basis that I had company – and we agreed on Portwrinkle or Crafthole, whichever was more convenient to get to by road in the campervan. Phil held up his phone and began pacing the beach, searching for enough signal to text Kinnon. I stowed my canteen and carried on down the beach after him. Moose quickly got the idea and brought up the rear.

After a while, the sand gave way to stones. They were small at first but, as we walked, we very quickly found ourselves in the middle of a huge boulder field where rocks the size of VW Beetles were strewn across the beach from breaker to cliff. I began scanning the gaps between them, wondering if there was a way through or whether we'd have to turn tail and backtrack a few miles. I conferred with Phil for five minutes before we both decided that we'd try to push our way through, hoping that there was more sandy, flat beach waiting beyond. No sooner had I climbed the first one than Moose bounded ahead, vaulting stone after stone as if playing a game of giant hopscotch. These huge rocks kept increasing in size, with most affording a flat platform big enough to stand on. With care and attention, it was easy to slowly plod forwards – although the height of the things meant that one wrong slip could've easily caused a nasty injury.

As if on cue, I heard a commotion off to my left. I turned just in time to see Phil disappear in a clatter between two huge stones.

"Shit!" I cried, bounding over as quickly as I could. "Phil!" I shouted between jumps. "Are you OK?"

"Fine," came a muffled reply. I saw a hand plant itself on top of the stone – he began dragging himself back out of the crevice.

I reached down and grabbed his hand. "Seriously, pal – are you OK?"

He looked back at me as he clambered to his feet, more embarrassed than anything else. "I'm fine," he said, tentatively testing bones and joints, "just slipped on the bloody rock."

He stood and shook himself off as I looked onwards to the never-ending field of rock before us. "Right!" I said decisively. "We're turning back."

"But—" he began.

I quickly cut him off: "Nah, this is getting risky and there's no point." I inclined my head back towards the sand. "We head back and take the road."

He begrudgingly nodded his agreement and began to inch his way back towards the beach, leaving me to retrieve my walking pole. After fishing it out of the hole, I held it up and twisted it in my hand – the lower section was now sporting a distinct bend.

"Damn," I muttered, following after the two figures already dwindling in the distance.

Once back to the sand, I found Phil stretching out his arms and legs.

"Any damage?" I asked.

He rolled up his trouser leg to reveal a small cut on his calf muscle. "It'll be fine," he reassured me. "Sorry about your pole…"

I held it up. "Admittedly, it needs a bit of TLC. Nothing that's not fixable."

He grimaced. "Sorry…"

I waved away the apology. "Not as sorry as I'd be if I had to explain to your wife how I'd lost you in a hole."

He chuckled. "That'd be a conversation to listen in to."

I shuddered as I caught an image of Kinnon, hands on her hips and red-faced while I tried to explain misplacing her husband to her. "… I'd rather not have to if it's all the same to you."

We reached the small village of Portwrinkle a few hours later. As we descended the coast path into town we passed through fields of free-roaming goats.

"Will he be alright with this?"

"Who, Moose?"

Phil nodded.

"Yup. He's pretty good with farm animals; it's just other dogs he gets excited about."

He wasn't convinced until we turned a sharp bend and Mooch sauntered straight past a small heard without even turning his head.

I glanced over at Phil, who stood there stunned.

"Well, I'd have never believed it if I hadn't just witnessed it!"

I beamed, glowing with pride. "That's ma boy!"

We left the headland and the path behind and began making our way up through the narrow streets skirting the village. Most of the roads down to the bay were adorned with arrays of signs forbidding the use of motor vehicles. There was no way Kinnon would get the van down here – we continued trekking upwards, instead, and headed into the village of Crafthole for our rendezvous.

Our first thought was to nip into the local pub and wait for our taxi to arrive – but, as we headed around the corner, we noticed that it had, unfortunately, burned to the ground. Phil looked at me, swiped off the beanie and scratched his head. "Well there goes *that* idea, then."

I shrugged and nodded further down the road to a small corner shop. "Fancy an ice cream instead?" He grinned in approval and, five minutes later, we were sitting on a bench nibbling on chocolate cones and looking out over the fields, waiting for Kinnon and the van.

It wasn't too long until her arrival was heralded by the screeching halt of smoking tyre rubber. We quickly filed in and, soon, were all safely speeding our way back to Looe in the camper. As I sat there in the back, I remembered the first trip we'd taken from Crackington Haven to Launceston and Phil's keen driving style. It would seem that Kinnon matched her partner even in this respect and, as much as I'd have doubted it from her mild disposition, she gave his driving a run for its money.

We ploughed straight along roads that hugged the coastline. Looking on through the window, it was somewhat surreal seeing all the places we'd walked through that day. What was even more surprising was that, not half an hour later, we were back on the road leading to the campsite.

Kinnon hummed to herself as she sped right past.

"Oo, a mystery tour," Phil chirped.

She grinned and shook her head. "Nope! Somebody wanted a camping shop?"

A lightbulb erupted in my skull. "Well remembered!"

It dawned on me that I'd not really thought about my feet for most of the day, such was the difference not having to carry around that bloody huge bag all day. I looked down at my boots and wiggled my toes, hidden by the leather upper. Thinking about the pain made it return suddenly and I was instantly grateful to her for remembering to do this for me.

Once in town, however, optimism very quickly turned to frustration. There were several shops to choose from and I picked up a compact gas stove easily enough. The challenge, however, lay in finding better footwear. The boots available to me in Looe were either so stiff they might just as well have been made of lead or were absolutely perfect but out of stock in my size. In the end, I decided to stick with what I had and settled with trying out a pair of gel soles instead.

Back at the site, while Phil busied himself at the cooker, I sat on the grass chatting to Kinnon about our day. The story of our little encounter with the goats was met with some disbelief, while Phil's 'little incident' elicited peals of laughter. I trimmed down the edges of my new boot liners with a set of scissors. Phil piped up with exaggerated details of the entire affair.

I held up one of the floppy blue soles to the light to show off my handiwork. "Whaddaya think?"

"Very nice." Kinnon smiled. "Here's hoping."

I slid the things into my boots and squashed them into place with crossed fingers. "You're telling me," I muttered to myself.

We spent the remainder of the evening talking about our respective plans for the future. For us two, it was the challenges we'd face as nights got darker and the winter cold would inevitably start to creep in. As for Kinnon and Phil, they had ideas aplenty, the most interesting of which was to have a go at beekeeping and honey farming. I couldn't wait to taste the outcome of that little venture and, based on the glistening sheen of moisture along Moose's lips, neither could he.

The sun had set by now and the winds were beginning to pick up: we were all starting to get chilly. The realisation came that tomorrow would be a big day for Moose and me – our final one in Cornwall. I wished the other two a good night, grabbed the pooch and settled into the tent for an early night.

As I lay there drifting off with my dog wrapped up close, I could hear a silence settle over the campsite. I faded slowly into slumber.

The following morning, we stirred early and no sooner had I finished striking camp than it seemed we were bouncing back down country lanes to Crafthole in the camper. Once there, kit was unloaded, hugs and kisses were showered on to Moose, and I stood in front of this very special couple making promises to catch up again one day. I sat on a low wall and changed into my boots as their white VW sped off into the distance.

"It's just you and me again, pal." I smiled at Moose.

He walked across and gave me a nudge on my cheek with his nose. *"I'm really gonna miss those two."*

I reached up and scratched his ears. "Me too, bud." I sighed. "Me too."

I stood and tested the modified insoles by bouncing slightly on the balls of my feet. It was too early to tell but I knew I'd find out if they'd worked before the end of the day. I strapped the pack across my shoulders and tightened the straps. Clipping on the dog, I reached out and went to grab my walking poles...

"Damn!"

I looked around until the realisation hit me that I'd stupidly left them both in the back of the campervan! It was probably miles away by now. I was supremely annoyed at myself – I would *really* miss those.

I huffed as we made our way out of town along a trail that followed the road into Plymouth. Encountering our first stairway, I immediately felt the absence of the support I got from having a walking stick in each hand. I grunted my way unsteadily up each riser, kicking myself for my stupidity and absent-mindedness.

The path I was on gave way to fields but thankfully no cattle. The area close to the coast here was cordoned off; MOD signs boldly dotted the entire perimeter, warning walkers to avoid unexploded ordinance. I duly obliged, not wanting to add to my woes – standing on a mine wasn't high on my list of things to do that day. Fairly soon, we were in fields by the side of the road where, up ahead, a small camper sat idling in a layby.

I looked down at Moose somewhat dubiously. "That couldn't be," I absently muttered as we rounded another kissing gate. We got closer and I saw the suspiciously familiar silhouette of a man in a beanie leaning on the passenger door... Phil was brandishing what appeared to be two walkers' poles.

"These were nearly halfway to Devon, you dozy sod!" he shouted over to me.

Moose ran over and practically knocked him off his feet.

"When did you realise?" I asked, grinning at Phil. "I was really missing these!"

"We decided to stop off for a sandwich, and they clattered around in the back when we pulled into the car park!"

I took both poles and immediately felt whole again. "I definitely owe you two a pint the next time I see you."

Phil got back into the van as Kinnon leant over. "We'll hold you to that," she shouted as they pulled out into the road and sped off back the way we'd just walked.

Moose gave his tail a knowing wag. I looked off in the opposite direction to where the van had just disappeared, and to the rolling hillsides of Plymouth.

We spent the remainder of the morning walking alongside the B3247, narrowly avoiding the infrequent turn-offs which led back to the coastline and the armies of cows now populating every field we passed. The memories of being corralled by the bovine army on the River Parrett still haunted me. I was keen to avoid a similar experience at all costs. There was a part of me inside that begrudged their presence – they were stealing the final few miles of Cornish coast away from us! Instead, I concentrated on closing the distance to the approach to Plymouth, so that we'd have time to find a place with dog-friendly vacancies or perhaps even enough daylight to clear the city entirely.

Before leaving Phil and Kinnon at Crafthole, I'd balanced my phone atop a fence to snap one last photo of us all together so I could post it on Facebook. After that, I could feel my phone continually buzzing in my pocket as the app kept notifying me of the comments left on it. Later, as we sat on a bench just outside Millbrook to catch our breath, I idly began flicking through the messages – one of which was from my old manager.

Dave

Looks like you're going to be in Plymouth soon...
Fancy some fish & chips?

Bloody right I did!

I replied with speed and we arranged a meet-up once Moose and I had made it to the Cremyll ferry at around six that evening.

I looked at my watch. "C'mon, pal – we need to get a shift on!"

He looked up and frowned. "*Wot for?*" came the curt reply.

"Fish 'n' chips?" I said enticingly.

He practically dragged me off the seat.

The farmland faded as the neat gardens of suburbia sprang up in the wake of the city. At the top of one rise, the land fell away to reveal the magnificence of Torpoint Bay, which lay before us in all its glory. I took a moment to take it all in before I began fiddling with my phone to try to find the right path down to Cremyll, and on to the crossing that would take us to Plymouth. We opted for a path near an overgrown hedge and, fairly soon after, were in sight of the ferry landing.

Conveniently close by was a grand pub which hugged the shoreline, at which we decided to stop, grab a quick pint, and wait for Dave and the ferry. Moose and I sat on one of the benches overlooking the bay. I took out my phone, sent him a text and began compiling some photos into a video to publish on my Facebook journal.

Finally able to relax and take in the view, my wandering mind began reflecting on our time in Cornwall and I was hit with a barrage of memories. From the little wooden sign welcoming us to the county all those weeks ago, to the boulders at Zennor, from finding 'The Way of St James', to hitting Land's End and Penzance...it all came flooding back with a torrent of emotions.

Images of cows, Cornish mines and long sandy beaches mingled with the sound of seagulls, crashing waves and the echoing bang of that eery chain lost in the mists of the Lizard. I thought about our first day in Portishead all those months before, and the sense of great adventure that fuelled us on throughout those early weeks on the path. I sat and looked out to Cremyll Bay, taking in the evening sun as it glistened off the sparkling water, and wondered at the transformation within – and the now-familiar feeling of all those places left behind. Throughout all of our experiences in Somerset, North Devon and Cornwall, I'd spent so much of my time concentrating on the forward march that I'd rarely taken the time to reflect back on them.

Somewhere out there on the shimmering water stood the invisible boundary line that, once crossed, would see our time in Cornwall complete. It was to be our first big tick on the map; the first county we'd walked through in its entirety. At that moment, I felt unbelievably proud and yet deeply saddened by that thought as I realised we'd soon be looking at the Cornish coastline – this place that had shaped us, taught us and cared for us so well, from the outside in.

I realised that Kernow – almost a country of its very own, with its diverse culture and rich history – had adopted Moose and me in some way. As we'd travelled through its heart, it'd imbued us with an echo of its character while it secretly stole away pieces of our hearts to keep for its own. This unique place we'd called home for the last six weeks would soon become a memory: one that would stay with me forever. I lifted my glass to my lips and took a deep draught, reaching down to gently scratch Moose's head as he snoozed by my feet. Looking out to the distant reaches of the water, I watched as the small ferry bobbed into sight, inexorably creeping its way towards the launch and to where we were both sitting.

And then it happened: in that very moment, a sense of completion filled me and I couldn't help but smile wistfully. My soul laid bare, I once again raised my glass and nodded a silent assent, as though saying goodbye to an old friend.

Chapter 22

Epilogue

Whew!

Well how about that…we made it, sort of!

I'm guessing that you're either giddy with anticipation for the next instalment or trying to figure out how much you can flog this thing for on eBay so you can cut your losses. Whichever it is, I'd like to thank you for not only buying this book in the first place, but also making it all the way to the end. You might be interested to know that at the time of writing, Moose and I had managed to walk another couple of thousand miles or so, stopping for a bit of a breather when we eventually reached the Anglo/Scottish border at Berwick-upon-Tweed on the east coast.

In addition to taking the time to scribble down this lot, I've also been planning the continuation of our walk around Britain, which will take us up into the beautiful wilds of Scotland. The Covid-19 thing hasn't helped, but I need to consider myself lucky – for me it was little more than an inconvenience, but I know that for some others, it's been truly devastating.

Regarding the continuation of this story: I can assure you there's definitely more to come. Book two will pick up from where we left off, waiting for Dave and the Cremyll ferry at Plymouth. Just in case you were worrying, I can tell you Moose did indeed get a good helping of fish and chips when we got into Plymouth town. I think it's important not to withhold important details like this for the sort of durations it takes to get another book done.

After a short stop for dinner, our story then takes us across the south coast into South Devon, Dorset, Hampshire, Sussex, and – finally – the shores of the Thames, at Gravesend in Kent. The challenges we face differ from those we've encountered so far. As we complete the South West Coast Path, our concerns for things like terrain and blazing sunshine shift to those consistent with the onset of winter, and, also, what to do when your tent finally gives up the ghost! Along the way we meet other coastal walkers who are also trying to get around the UK, albeit going in the wrong direction (I mean, who goes clockwise around anything!?).

Oh – and I finally get the awful ache in my feet sorted for good.

If you'd like more Waggy Walk stuff, then check out our website and various social media channels, all of which can be reached by logging on to:

www.chrisandmoose.co.uk

Information regarding the charities, and how you can help, is also listed there.

I've also added a couple of annexes. One on our kit – and another on some great places.

Until next time, happy travels!

Chris & Moose

Annex I

Kit

It's worth pointing out that my opinion on my kit is just that – my opinion. Appraisals on whether or not something was 'bad' could've just been down to the fact it wasn't suited to me, and not that it didn't work well (as was the case with the BioLite stove – a brilliant invention that unfortunately just so happens to weigh almost a kilo).

As with most things in life, *my* preferences play to what *I* like. Don't blame me if you go out, order everything on the 'good list' and then start having trouble with it later. I can tell you now, some of the other coast walkers wouldn't touch half of the stuff I've listed here with a ten-foot barge pole!

To be truthful, that is the best advice I can give you when it comes to gear – try lots of things and settle for what suits you! You'll inevitably end up finding your own favourites. There were some bits I bought that were a complete waste of money, and others that absolutely saved my skin, so much so I now never go anywhere outdoors without them.

This list is by no means definitive. As you can probably tell there are some glaring omissions like underwear, anti-chafing gel, and soap, the details of which, I'll spare you from.

And then there's also the most obvious and important piece of kit of all – tea.

The Good,	The Bad,	...and The Just Plain Awful
Pains Wessex Personal Distress Flares	BioLite CampStove 2	Berghaus Ridgeway 65+15 Rucksack
Buck 'Bones' Knife 870	Quechua Self-Inflate Mattress	Trespass Waterproof Jacket
RADAR Key	Tesco Combat Trousers	Asda Solar Powerchargers
Silva Expedition Compass	Quechua Pillow Inner	My Blue 'Dad' Shorts
Emergency Whistle	Scarpa Go Up Boots	
Quechua 10l Water Bottles	British Army Poncho	
Vango Banshee Pro200 Tent	Washburn Travel Guitar	
Coleman Pathfinder Sleeping Bag	5" Fibreglass Flagpole	
Quechua Pillow Outer		
O/S Tour Maps & Tide Times		
Asics Trainers		
Bridgedale Socks		
Trespass Waterproof Over-Trousers		
Rab Gaiters		

The Good,		
Coleman Xtreme Camping Gas		
Coleman FyreLite Stove		
St John Ambulance Universal 1st Aid Kit (minus the bulky handle)		
iPhone X		
Squash XL Battery Packs		
Endura Snoods		
Halfords Cycling Sunglasses		
Trespass 'Crook' Walking Pole		
National Trust Walking Pole		

Annex 2

Great Places

It's no secret that as a society we generally don't appreciate what's on our own doorstep. Coming from a guy who knows this island we call Britain reasonably well, I can hand-on-heart state that there is such under-appreciated beauty here that it boggles the mind as to why we're not all out exploring it. One thing that continually struck me was that a staggeringly high proportion of the thousands of people I met on my travels were visitors from abroad. Staycations are all the vogue at the moment, and long may they reign in my opinion!

As such, I've listed for you (in no particular order) all my favourite places.

Brean Down and fort Brean Somerset TA8 2RS	**Steart Marshes Nature Reserve** Steart Drove Bridgwater Somerset TA5 2PU
Watermouth Valley Camping Park Watermouth Cove (A399) Berrynarbor EX39 9SJ	**Exmoor National Park** Exmoor North Devon
Appledore & the Taw Torridge Estuary North Devon	**The Angels Wings** Clovelly Court Park North Devon SS 3074525953
Hawker's Hut Morwenstow North Devon SS 199152	**Crackington Haven** Bude EX23 0JG
Boscastle & Tintagel Cornwall	**The Stargazy Inn** 1 The Terrace Port Isaac Cornwall PL29 3SG
The Portreath Arms Hotel Portreath Cornwall	**The Menagerie B&B** Portreath Cornwall
Geevor Tin Mine The Tin Coast Cornwall	**The Minack Theatre**

Lizard Point and Black Head Cornwall	**Wheal Prosper** Rinsey Cornwall
Little Trevothan Camping and Caravan Park Cornwall	**The Paris Hotel** Coverack Cornwall
The Kenidjack Valley Cape Cornwall Cornwall	**The South West Coast Path** Minehead to Poole

Lightning Source UK Ltd.
Milton Keynes UK
UKHW010625020321
379643UK00001B/67